SCREENING RELIGIONS IN ITALY

Contemporary Italian Cinema and Television in the Post-Secular Public Sphere

SCREENING RELIGIONS IN ITALY

CLODAGH J. BROOK

Contemporary Italian Cinema and Television in the Post-Secular Public Sphere

UNIVERSITY OF TORONTO PRESS
Toronto Buffalo London

© University of Toronto Press 2019
Toronto Buffalo London
utorontopress.com
Printed in Canada

ISBN 978-1-4875-0347-5

Toronto Italian Studies

Library and Archives Canada Cataloguing in Publication

Title: Screening religions in Italy : contemporary Italian cinema and television
   fiction in the post-secular public sphere / Clodagh J. Brook.
Names: Brook, Clodagh J., author.
Series: Toronto Italian studies.
Description: Series statement: Toronto Italian studies | Includes bibliographical
   references and index.
Identifiers: Canadiana 20190170948 | ISBN 9781487503475 (hardcover)
Subjects: LCSH: Motion pictures – Italy. | LCSH: Television programs – Italy. |
   LCSH: Religion in motion pictures.
Classification: LCC PN1993.5.I88 B76 2019 | DDC 791.430945–dc23

University of Toronto Press acknowledges the financial assistance to its publishing
program of the Canada Council for the Arts and the Ontario Arts Council, an agency
of the Government of Ontario.

**Canada Council
for the Arts**   **Conseil des Arts
du Canada**

ONTARIO ARTS COUNCIL
CONSEIL DES ARTS DE L'ONTARIO

an Ontario government agency
un organisme du gouvernement de l'Ontario

Funded by the   Financé par le
Government   gouvernement
of Canada   du Canada

MIX
Paper from
responsible sources
FSC® C016245

This book is dedicated to the memory of my father

Contents

Acknowledgments

First and foremost, my thanks go to the Biblioteca "Luigi Chiarini" and the Cineteca Nazionale, at the Scuola Nazionale di Cinema (SNC) in Rome. Their resources were invaluable for this research. I am also grateful to the other libraries at which the research for this book was conducted, especially the Biblioteca nazionale in Rome, La Sapienza University in Rome, Roma Tre University, the Università Cattolica del Sacro Cuore in Milan, the Pontificia Università Gregoriana, and the Cineteca di Bologna. The librarians (especially Zbig Gas) at the University of Birmingham deserve special mention.

I wish to express my gratitude to the University of Birmingham for awarding me research leave to complete the first draft of this book, and to Trinity College, Dublin, for allowing me the time and mental space to bring the book to completion. My warmest thanks go to everyone at the Department of Italian Studies in Birmingham and at my new department at Trinity for their encouragement and interest.

Finally, I take this opportunity to remember all those who have been close to me throughout this project. My father deserves special mention here: the many, often provocative, discussions we had on religion and politics over the years stirred, and kept alive, my curiosity about the role and place of religion in contemporary society. Cath for everything, my mother, my sister Shirley and brother Neill, Patrick, and my friends in Italy, Ireland, and the UK have all been patient, supportive, and wise.

A small part of the material in this volume appeared earlier in the following publications: "Post-Secular Identity in Contemporary Italian Cinema: Nostalgia for Catholic Values and the Suppression of History," *Modern Italy* 22.2 (2017); "Dissenso, potere e Chiesa cattolica nell'Italia contemporanea: un *impegno* anti-cattolico?," in W.H. Hope, S. Serra, and L. d'Arcangeli, *Un nuovo cinema politico italiano?* (Troubador, 2014); Clodagh Brook, "The Spectacle of the Unseen: Marco Bellocchio and Lure of the Catholic Church," *Italian Studies: Cultural Studies* 68.3 (2013): 399–410.

SCREENING RELIGIONS IN ITALY

Contemporary Italian Cinema and Television
in the Post-Secular Public Sphere

Introduction: Italy, Secularization, and the Post-Secular

The End of Religion in Italian Cinema?

There is perhaps no more shocking and iconic ending anywhere in the Italian cinema of the third millennium than Nanni Moretti's closing scene to *Habemus Papam* (2011). In St Peter's Square in Rome a sea of people waits expectantly for their new pope to appear. Flags wave, cardinals smile, all raise their eyes to the Vatican balcony. In a scene that was to anticipate Pope Benedict XVI's standing down a few years later, the newly elected pope (Michel Piccoli) appears and announces that he cannot lead the church. As he turns around and recedes from sight behind the thick red-velvet curtains, there is a palpable sense of collapse: the cheering fades, a dramatic vocal soundtrack slides down descending scales, the flags in the crowd below are lowered, bishops crumple visibly, their shoulders sagging and their heads buried in their hands. An intense disorientation overcomes them: no longer are all eyes on the pope. The grief-stricken crowds and religious leaders no longer know where to look. The final shot of the papal balcony shows all of the bishops and cardinals facing in different directions, a perfect visual expression of their rudderless bewilderment, their lack of unity and purpose. Motifs of descent, collapse, and disorientation dominate the mise en scène, the cinematography, and the soundtrack.

In this finale, director Nanni Moretti, long the barometer for the concerns of a significant segment of Italians, provides an apocalyptic image of Italy's main religion in the new millennium. In a single scene, he captures so many of the dominant features of religion in Italy today: the vast spectacle and power of the international Catholic faith, whose global beacon shines from the centre of the Italian peninsula; the anomaly that in Italy, a Western post-secular nation, religion still holds a significant public position; the formation of individual identity in a country dominated by a single faith; the fragility of institutional religion in post-secular society; the religious fervour among crowds of believers, despite secularization; the disorientation of humanity when deprived of a collective, shared system of belief. Moreover, if one deconstructs the scene, what emerges from the shadows is the silenced face of other faiths in Italy. What is the place of these faiths in a society that is increasingly multi-religious? Moretti's image of religious apocalypse – of collapse, disorientation, descent – sends strange ripples across the sea of the contemporary Italian film industry. It both resonates with what is happening there and does not.

What emerges from Moretti's film is a complex and dissonant vision of religion in Italian society: religion is part antagonist, part protagonist; it is out of step with secularizing Italy yet deeply embedded in it; it is part of Italian identity but uneasily so; it is magnificently cinematographic yet has been contested by many in Italy's predominantly left-wing cinema industry. *Habemus Papam*, made by a self-confessed atheist, signals both the depth of attachment to religion in Italy and the vulnerability of institutional religion in the contemporary world. The film presents what Catherine Wheatley (2014, 24) describes as a "confused and confusing" approach to Christianity, one that neither attacks nor supports it. She describes this as an identifying feature of contemporary post-secular European approaches to religion in cinema.

Moving beyond film content, the second point that *Habemus Papam* so perfectly illustrates is that, in Italy at least, religion sells. There is still a market for it, and audiences still want to watch it. A film bearing a Latin title and narrating the perturbations of an imaginary octogenarian pope was the most viewed film in Italy on the day of its release (Pinchiorri 2011). This fact is indicative of the key role that filmic constructions of religion continue to play in Italy long after filmmakers famous for their dramatic portrayals of it – Pier Paolo Pasolini, Roberto Rossellini, Federico Fellini – have disappeared. An evening stroll in any of Italy's large, twenty-first-century urban centres, in fact, takes one to arthouse cinemas screening questioning or anticlerical dramas, such as Marco Bellocchio's *L'ora di religione* (My Mother's Smile, 2002), Alice Rohrwacher's *Corpo celeste* (Heavenly Body, 2011), and Giorgio Diritti's *Un giorno devi andare* (There Will Come a Day, 2013). In a suburban multiplex, one might catch up with Harvey Keitel in his role in the Americanized thriller *Il mercante di pietre* (The Stone Merchant, Renzo Martinelli, 2006), in which radical Islam is a mortal threat to Italian masculinity. At an oratorio in a rural parish, one might stumble across screenings of films intended not just to entertain but to encourage the audience to reflect on moral and social issues. Switching on a television, one might catch one of Lux Vide's many Catholic-oriented fictions, such as the TV film eulogizing Pope Pius XII's work during the Holocaust, *Sotto il cielo di Roma* (Pius XII: Under the Roman Sky, 2010). Alternatively, one might choose an episode from the long-running detective series *Don Matteo* (2000–), featuring a priest in the title role, or from Paolo Sorrentino's recent TV drama, *The Young Pope* (2016). In watching these, one joins record audiences of more than ten million Italians who, since the 1990s, have been sitting down after dinner to watch religious-oriented prime-time fiction. Before bedtime, *Telegiornale* provides the opportunity to catch up on news that often mentions the Vatican. One might hear, for example, that a prominent comic film director and actor, Roberto Benigni, had enthusiastically presented Pope Francis's new book and excitedly predicted a return to Christianity (Giovanetti 2016). The broad diffusion of religion on the big screens of urban and rural centres as well as on the country's small screen signals that Italy is a key religious market. It is, in fact, the second religious market, after America, among large Western countries in terms of "dynamics, intensity, and quantity" (Diotallevi 2002, 138). To cite Jacques Derrida, "to think religion is to think Roman" (1996, 4).

However, if religion is deeply embedded in Italian cinema and television – and Italy, in this regard, is widely cited by sociologists, philosophers, and historians as a particularly fascinating and unique case (Diotallevi 2002; Pollard 2008) – this fact has received little attention in Italian film studies. Critical interest in religion and cinema has been rekindled in the United States in recent years, its flames fanning out from what has been described by some theorists as a "religious turn" (De Groot and Morgan 2014) and by others as a "post-secular turn" (Braidotti et al. 2014), but that interest is only rarely explored by scholars of cinema. The focus of recent critical studies of religion in filmmaking has instead been directed towards American thriller-blockbusters such as *The Da Vinci Code* (2006) and *Angels and Demons* (2009), which present speculative attacks on the Vatican, or towards controversial hagiopics such as Mel Gibson's *The Passion of the Christ* (2004) and Martin Scorsese's *The Last Temptation of Christ* (1988). There is also plenty of research being done on the representation of religious motifs and messages more broadly, but these are still typically centred on American filmmaking.[1] More recently, interest in Islam and in the national cinemas of predominantly Islamic countries has also been increasing (see, for example, Dönmez-Collin 2004; Pak-Shiraz 2011; Ahmad 2015),

---

1   Two sets of approaches are easily identifiable in American film and religion criticism. The first, which strongly dominates the field, focuses on representations of religion and religious messages in filmmaking. Discussions of religious figures, themes, motifs, and scriptures indeed represent most material written in the field. This approach is found in the work of, for example, Christopher Deacy (2001), Richard Aloysius Blake (2000), Craig Detweiler (2008), and Amir Hussain (2010). Closely related to this is work that is also largely representational in approach, exploring spirituality in film (Sontag 1964; Schrader 1972; Fraser 1998; Brent Plate 2008; Di Donato 2010; Campani 2010) or presenting theological readings of film (Johnston 2007; Deacy and Williams Ortiz 2008). A second key approach, while decidedly less developed, is nonetheless significant. This second approach is centred on the policy around, and distribution of, religion in cinema. This incorporates debates that range from analyses of Vatican teachings, policies, and missives on cinema and media (Siniscalchi 2001; Convents and Van Beeck 2009; Williams Ortiz 2003; Malone 2009) to the mediatization of religious messages (*Culture and Religion*, vol. 12) and discussions of censorship and institutional power in cinema history (Biltereyst and Treveri Gennari 2015; Treveri Gennari 2011; Quicke 2010).

having been lent impetus by the global threat presented by radical Islamic terrorist groups. By contrast, research on European religion in filmmaking is in its infancy. Some significant recent research has been published about Europe (Girlanda and Tagliabue 1988; Bradatan and Ungureanu 2015; Biltereyst and Treveri Gennari 2015); however, the field thus far is too small to balance the tide of critical works produced in the United States claiming to discuss religion and cinema in general terms, but often inadvertently using Hollywood's construction of religion as a global prototype.

That European critics discuss religion in film much less often than their American counterparts is the result of two key factors. First, the secularization myth is very strongly rooted in Europe (I will return to this later in this introduction). Consequently, European film critics have typically read religion as an unimportant "residue" (Williams 1973), so that discussions of religion in cinema are often sidelined at conferences and in publications. The second factor is that the academic field of religious studies is much better articulated in the United States than it is in Europe, and it is this field that has been contributing vocally to ongoing critical discussions of religion in film. The critic James Elkins (2004) suggests that outside departments of religious studies and theology, religion is perceived as the "undo[ing of] the project of modernism ... which is predicated on a series of rejections and refusals" (ix). Consequently, much of the work on religion and film is coming from the United States, and specifically from religious studies departments, whose work typically proposes particular research questions and whose findings are often overlooked by film scholars and cultural theorists.

Nonetheless, some research has been done on Italian cinema and religion. Wide-ranging volumes on religion in cinema tend to have an international scope – for example, those by John Lyden (2010), Sergio Botta and Emanuela Prinzivalli (2010), and Pamela Grace (2009) cite some Italian films. However, these citations are often brief or refer only to the most obvious and canonical candidates from postwar Italian cinema, such as certain films by Roberto Rossellini and Pier Paolo Pasolini. Contemporary Italian cinema is rarely mentioned. As the focus of these volumes remains firmly on English-language movies, their analysis of films from outside the Anglo-American context lacks the depth and the sociocultural contextualization these films deserve. Within the field of Anglo-American film studies dedicated specifically to Italy, two volumes stand out: Daniela Treveri Gennari's *Post-War Italian Cinema: American Intervention, Vatican Interests* (2009), and William Bruce Johnson's *Miracles and Sacrilege: Roberto Rossellini, the Church, and Film Censorship in Hollywood* (2008). These are the only two monographs to be published in English in the last twenty years that deal specifically with religion in Italian filmmaking. Both focus on the institutional relationship between the Church and censorship, and neither one treats contemporary Italian cinema. In English-language Italian film studies, socio-political approaches dominate and the debate on religion has been sidelined. This means that to date very little has been written in English on religion in contemporary Italian cinema. There is still no English-language, book-length study that deals with religion in contemporary Italian film, or indeed that deals at all with religion and film in Italy beyond the 1960s.

In Italy, some books have been published that document Italian religious cinema practices and policies, such as Giuseppe Chinnici's *Cinema, Chiesa e Movimento Cattolico Italiano* (2003), which traces the history of Catholic censorship, production, and distribution, although it focuses only on the period before the 1970s. Dario Viganò's *Cinema e chiesa* (2002) has a broader scope and details the Church's policies towards and responses to cinema, not just in Italy but internationally. Then there are several books written in Italian with promising titles, such as *Cinema e religione* (Cortellazzo and Quaglia 2008) and *The Hidden God: Cinema e spiritualità* (Bandy and Monda 2004) – these however are illustrated books, often produced in the context of film festivals, rather than academic discussions of the issues their titles convey. Though published in Italy, these books do not necessarily have much to say about Italian filmmaking, as their focus is broad and international. The books written and edited by Dario Viganò are among the few to deal with contemporary Italian film and religion in cinema and on television. *Il prete di celluloide: Nove sguardi d'autore* (2010) classifies and briefly discusses on-screen portrayals of priests in Western cinema, including some examples from Italy, and includes an appendix transcribing interviews on the subject of religion with Italian directors such as Pupi Avati and Carlo Verdone. Of all the volumes published in Italy thus far, it is Dario Viganò and Eugeni Ruggero's third edited volume, *Attraverso lo schermo: Cinema e cultura cattolica in Italia: Dagli anni Settanta ai nostri giorni* (2006), that goes furthest in providing an analysis of Italy's Catholic cinema culture between the end of the Second Vatican Council (1965) and the start of the new millenium. This is the period that attracts the least attention among critics, who prefer to deal in the pre-Vatican II relations between Church and cinema, a period when Church intervention in filmmaking was dramatic and comparatively well-documented. A couple of chapters in this volume proved interesting for my own study. Gianfranco Bettetini's chapter, "Chiesa cattolica e cinema: Dal Sessantotto a oggi," like some of the books mentioned above, explores the Catholic Church's policies on cinema, but unlike most of those, Bettetini takes his analysis up to 2005. Paola Abbiezzi and Giorgio Simonelli's chapter "Agiografia e costruzione della memoria nazionale nella fiction televisiva" (2006) assesses hagiopics on television, focusing on their productive context and on genre classification. Alberto Bourlot's "Filmare la Bibbia: la produzione cinematografica e televisiva (dal 1968 ad oggi)" (2006) provides an overview and classification of religious-themed films. More recently, Andrea Minuz and Guido Vitiello's edited volume *La Shoah nel cinema italiano* (2013) is dedicated to one of Italy's most important minority religions and includes a chapter by Claudio Gaetani on the Shoah in contemporary films. However, once again the volume's focus is primarily on socio-political issues rather than issues of faith and religious practice.

From this brief analysis, it will be clear that most of the major work already done on religion in Italian cinema focuses almost exclusively on the period before the Second Vatican Council in 1965, and even then it typically explores either the Catholic Church's media policy or representations of religious messages on film. These analyses have little to say about post-secular Italy, about the place of the established Church in Italy's public sphere, or about the engagement of Italian cinema with other faiths. Overall, then, the subject matter of this book – religion, cinema, and the post-secular public sphere – has not yet been the subject of any sustained academic discussion with regard to Italy.

Why Religion (Still) Matters: Secularization and the Post-Secular Frame

Religion has been a potent and at times even formidable force in society. It has "shaped the cultures, institutions, and maps of European states" (Barker 2009, 2). It has been instrumental in the creation of contemporary socio-political Europe. It has been held responsible for some of the darkest moments in recent history, from the Holocaust to *jihad*. Yet it has also been described as the crea- tor of a powerful heritage of architectural and artistic works, from monasteries and cathedrals to the Vatican treasures, from paintings, sculptures, and frescos to the rich imagery and narratives on which writers and poets have drawn for centuries, and from which filmmakers to the present day still draw. In *White: Essays on Race and Culture* (1997, 15), Richard Dyer defines its contribution to European society in the following terms:

> The European feeling for self and the world has been shaped by Christianity ... If Christianity as observance and belief has been in decline over the past half-century, its ways of thinking and feeling are nonetheless still constitutive of both European culture and consciousness ... Many of the fundamentals of all levels of Western culture – the forms of parenting, especially motherhood, and sex, the value of suffering, guilt, the shock of post-enlightenment materialism – come to us from Christianity, whether or not we know the Bible story.

Dyer's analysis of the importance of religion in the construction of the European sociocultural heart is, of course, perceptive. Nonetheless, his use of the word "decline" hints at teleological assumptions and is indicative of a cur- rent of thinking about religion known as the "secularization thesis."

The secularization thesis refers to a group of theories that argue that religion and modernity are fundamentally incompatible; thus when countries modernize, religion inevitably declines. Religion then plays a progressively less important part in society, becoming, in Raymond Williams's words, "a residual cultural element" (1973). This thesis is not new. Rodney Stark (1999) tells us that the fall of religions had been predicted as early as 1710. However, in late-nineteenth-century Europe, its proponents were particularly vocal. They numbered among them some of Europe's most powerful and seminal thinkers, including Sigmund Freud, for whom religion was a neurosis in search of a cure, and Karl Marx, who construed it as an instrument of political repression. Freud and Marx predicted that religion would decline as improvements in psychic development and in society, respectively, were achieved. They thus unequivocally yoked religion to illness (whether of the individual or society) and secularism to health. By the end of the nineteenth century, all leading social scientists, from Émile Durkheim to Georg Simmel and then Max Weber, were speaking of secularization as inevitable.

As described by the proponents of secularization, the demise of religion is linear and irreversible. The roots of that demise are found in the broad social changes that have accompanied the rise of modernity. The renowned sociologist Steve Bruce (1999), one of the theory's modern defenders, identifies three key factors that advance secularization. The first of these is rationalization. In a word, the Enlightenment, with its emphasis on rationality and science, made it more difficult to conceive of a world inhabited by miracles and spirits. As a consequence, the place of religion in explaining the world declined. Bruce then discusses differentiation. As society became increasingly specialized, large organizations like the Catholic Church lost control over spheres such as education, welfare, and ethics, which were then divided up among dedicated interest groups. His third and final point centres on "societalization." As large-scale, global society grew, local communities declined. This negatively affected the capacity of religious institutions to work at the local, grassroots level, where they had historically been so successful. Bruce is only one of many theorists to hypothesize the causes for decline. For the early Peter L. Berger (1969), Protestantism was a significant causal factor in secularization. Berger contends that Protestant thought created a more individualistic and rational world, one divided into secular and sacred spaces. As the secular sphere grew, the sacred became increasingly marginalized (Berger 1969).[2] For the influential Canadian philosopher Charles Taylor (2007), however, humanism is a key factor. Over the years, other theorists have put forwarded diverse and wide-ranging hypotheses to explain secularization. These range from scientific advances and urbanization

---

2   Peter Berger changed his mind after the publication of his seminal book, *The Sacred Canopy* (1969). He no longer holds modernity, or even pluralism, responsible for secularization (Mathewes 2006).

to individualism, consumer choice, and religious pluralism. What is evident is that, while there has been little agreement on the causes of secularization, there is general agreement among proponents of the secularization theory that modernity, in some form or another, is implicated in religion's decline.

However, towards the end of the twentieth century it became increasingly obvious that secularization had not taken place in the way that early- to mid-twentieth-century thinkers had predicted, and more nuanced analyses emerged. These led to a reconsideration of the phenomenon. Charles Taylor (2007), for instance, has drawn an important distinction between the secularization of public and private space. Regarding the former, he argues that in the contemporary Western world we "can take part fully in political life without ever meeting God," and he claims that religion no longer has the right, or the power, to impose itself on every part of the political, economic, and social spheres. He notes, though, that secularization is far less pronounced in the private sphere. While he recognizes that we no longer inhabit an "enchanted world of spirits, demons and natural forces, where the natural world was a proof of the actions of some form of God and atheism was inconceivable" (42), he contends that religion has not disappeared. Instead, it has taken a subjective turn. For Taylor, Grace Davie's oft-cited term "believing without belonging" (1990) now dominates the Western world. What this means is that personal spiritual quests are now taking precedence over institutional affiliation. Whether Davie's "believing without belonging" holds for Italy is one of the critical questions this book ventures to answer.

The assumption that religion is in inexorable decline has been brought into question by recent post-secular thinkers. Theorists like Rosi Braidotti and Jürgen Habermas note that, despite the rise of secularization in the West, religion has not gone away. On the contrary, at the time of writing, one of the most glaring fault lines in the contemporary world – the perceived divide between absolutist, extremist Islamic faith and liberal but Christian-inflected secular values – has religious traditions at its core. The political underpinnings of religious tensions flare up too in the American culture wars as well as in current conflicts like the Israeli-Palestinian conflict, the war in Syria, and international terrorism. Contemporary malaise regarding religion's place in society is evident in the questioning of what constitutes Western moral and ethical values and in the debates over whether it is legitimate to wear a burka, sing carols in school, or place a crucifix in public buildings. That malaise was evident as well in the hard-fought arguments over whether religion was to be inserted into the ultimately abortive 2004 Constitution of the European Union. Rodney Stark in "Secularisation RIP" (1999) argues that religion is far from losing its grip, at least as far as personal piety is concerned, and points to the non-linear and non-universal nature of the demise of religion. Citing the example of the former Soviet Union, he also notes that secularization is far from irreversible:

the suppression of religions failed to stamp them out, and they resurfaced with the fall of the communist regime. He argues that religion is not set to die out equally and everywhere: modernization and certain religions, such as Islam, appear to be compatible.

The recent return of religious discourse from the margins of Western society to a decidedly more central position is a sign of what Jürgen Habermas (2006) has defined as the post-secular condition. Habermas, and other theorists in his wake, have put into question what most people in the West had, up to a few years ago, taken for granted: the unstoppable forward march of secularization and the concomitant marginalization of religion. Since 2001, several key theorists have reframed secularization in discursive terms as an "ideology" or "myth," thus withdrawing from it truth-claims that until recently had seemed obvious, familiar, and natural. For instance, in *Secularisms* (2008), Janet R. Jacobsen and Ann Pellegrini define secularization as a myth that hitches religion to backwardness and the secular to progress and modernity, a linkage these critics contest. Moreover, in their introduction to *Transformations of Religion in the Public Sphere* (2014), Rosi Braidotti and colleagues, citing Tariq Modood, declare secularism an *ideology* and go on to specify that it is an ideology that "spells danger" for European democracy because it does not "sufficiently recogniz[e] the importance of religious and multicultural identities and their implications for active citizenship" (1).

Braidotti and her co-editors present a global triptych of motivations for the post-secular. First, they cite the dominance of neoliberal values and consumerism after the fall of communism. Then they mention globalization, which has led to "strong movements of resistance in the form of resurgent nationalisms" and to a "resurgence of civilisation discourses about Western traditional values which in turn produce, once again, hierarchies of identities, cultures, and even ethnic belongings." This has led to a "rise of a perpetual state of 'new' wars against terror" (6). Finally, they point to the new digital technologies, which enable new connections and allow networks, such as Islamophobic ones, to flourish. The focus of Braidotti and her colleagues tends to fall on Islam as the decisive factor in post-secularism. Tariq Modood (2014) concurs, putting forward a "triple contingency" of reasons for the change in direction of secularism in Europe. First, the arrival of Muslims, which not only brings greater numbers of religious believers to Europe but also stimulates Christian identity. Second, the contemporary multiculturalist sensibility, which respects "difference" and so enables a certain openness to religious others. Third and finally, moderate secularism, which "offers some of the resources for accommodating Muslims" (30).

While there is little consensus among critics regarding how to define the post-secular condition – indeed, Modood (2014) even questions whether the post-secular is (already) in crisis – several key points emerge from the debates, and these will underpin my own analysis in this book. The first is that the post-secular turn presupposes that the secularization myth must be challenged and critiqued: the assumption that the secular is automatically a sign of progress and that religious practice is necessarily backward must be unpicked, and religious identity, or identities, must be acknowledged. This is important, and it informs my own theoretical approach in this book. The second is that religious mobilization must form part of any account of contemporary culture, for religion has remained, or again become, a player in the public sphere. Braidotti and colleagues (2014, 3) note how the "most pertinent critiques of globalization and advanced capitalisms today and of the structural injustices of globalization are voiced by religiously driven social movements." As a feature of modern society, this has only increased in Catholic countries like Italy since the election of Pope Francis. Analysing the effects of religious mobilization and the efforts of religious organizations to remain visible in the public sphere is therefore essential to my own work in this book (see especially chapter 1). Finally, following Braidotti and colleagues, the Eurocentric founding discourses of post-secularization need themselves to be challenged. Habermas and Joseph Ratzinger (2005) first conceived of post-secularization in relation to Christianity. Braidotti and colleagues, and most other recent theorists of the post-secular, see it as a multiple, diverse, and multi-religious space in which Islam is an important feature. In a book written about Italy, a country in which Catholicism is the dominant religion, this means exploring and deconstructing "Catholo-centrism" as well as giving space to the peninsula's other religions and especially its screening of Islam.

Secularization and the Post-Secular in Italy: The Italian Anomaly

Across Europe, the picture of post-secular society is not as homogeneous as the one posited by Rosi Braidotti, Charles Taylor, and others. While many of the trends, such as a marked secularization of the public sphere, traverse the continent, the significance of religion in both the private sphere and the public one differs substantially from nation to nation. Among all Western nations, the place of religion in Italy is especially curious. Italy's religious exceptionality in the post-secular Western world is the result of several features that set it apart.

First, and most obviously, the Italian peninsula is the headquarters of the largest religion on earth, one that boasts one and a quarter billion members. The seat of the Catholic Church has been in Rome for the greater part of two millennia. This is not without consequence. The Vatican is a place where Italians work: it has drawn most of its popes, cardinals and officials, secretaries, and cleaners from the local Italian population. Karol Wojtyla, elected Pope John Paul II in 1978, was the first non-Italian pope in 525 years. All of this means that for Italians, the Vatican is not a distant institution. The Vatican cupola dominates the architecture and skyline of Italy's capital city; every day, Italians move in and out of its grounds. Moreover, the Church consolidated a Catholic subculture throughout the Italian peninsula. At the start of the twentieth century, the Church developed networks of banks, publishing houses, workers' unions, the Azione Cattolica, and various cultural organizations. Since then, this subculture has, according to Franco Garelli (2014), "retained its vitality and solidity" while "the country's traditional subcultures (Communist, Socialist, Liberal, Republican, Right-Wing) have dissolved" (1). Thus the Vatican as an institution, together with a well-developed Catholic subculture that spans the peninsula, has long had a living, networked presence in the lives of Italians.

A second anomaly is that the Vatican and the state are more evenly matched in Italy than they are in other Western countries. This has resulted in a complex rivalry. A key factor in the creation of the modern Italian state was the head-to-head confrontation between the emerging nation of Italy and the Papal States: for Italy to complete its unification, its newly formed government had to attack the Papal States, which were forced to surrender in 1871. The ensuing relationship between the Church and the new state was marked by power struggles over the place of religion in education, welfare, and local communities. The state attempted to reduce the Church's powers; the Church strove to regain them. In contemporary Italy, this tension continues. The Catholic Church is no longer the established religion of Italy. As a result, in theory at least, the Vatican is not directly answerable to the state that encircles it, nor is the state answerable to the Church. Thus the relationship between Church and state is not marked by incorporation of the Church into the state or by submission of the Church to the state, but by independence, tension, and even rivalry between equal players. Given that the Church stands as a (global) counter-power to the state, the workings of power and politics are key to understanding how religion works in Italy. The peculiar rivalry between politics and the state is inscribed on the very structure of Italy's sociocultural ecosystem.

Italy's exceptionality means that even for the most hardened defenders of the secularization thesis, there is no easy, linear tale of secularization to be told.[3] The power of the Church in Italy has not steadily declined; rather, it has waxed and waned and has been surprisingly resilient. For example, even after the Papal States were defeated, the Church strengthened its grassroots position: local support for the Church grew as Italians mobilized against the new liberal state and set up alternatives to the rising communist subculture (Pollard 2008). Under the early years of fascism the Church lost a great deal of its temporal power, but then the Lateran Pacts of 1929 consolidated and thereby strengthened its – albeit

---

3 The clearest English-language history of twentieth-century relationships between church and state is John Pollard's *Catholicism in Modern Italy: Religion, Society, and Politics since 1861* (2008). Franco Garelli's *Religion Italian Style: Continuities and Changes in a Catholic Country* (2014) provides an interesting analysis of why religion has the place that it does in Italian life.

weakened – position.[4] For more than forty years (1948–92), the success of the Democrazia cristiana (Christian Democrats) ensured that Catholic positions were voiced in government; even so, under its watch a number of laws were passed that countered the Catholic emphasis on the sanctity of marriage and of life.[5] In 1984, even though the Christian Democrats were in power, the Church, which had been established as the state church under the Lateran Pacts, was disestablished, and other faiths began to be recognized.[6]

By the third millennium – the period examined in this book – Catholicism as a state religion had been abolished, the ruling Catholic postwar political party had been disbanded, and certain parts of the grassroots, subcultural network of Catholicism had died away. Moreover, several significant Catholic teachings on abortion, contraception, and divorce had been overturned by state legislation. The religious education hour still existed in schools but was no longer compulsory. These signs of secularization in the public sphere were compounded by a notable level of anticlerical protest on parts of the peninsula – protests that had a strong, if minority, following during the first decade of the millennium. While the Catholic Church has never been without its detractors, the annual anti-Vatican "No-Vat" protests, contesting the continuing place of the Catholic Church in Italian politics, and the emergence of bitter debates around the Church's position on LGBTQ rights and civil partnerships, saw criticism of

---

4   The 1929 Lateran Pacts reversed some of these trends and finally recognized and formalized the relationship between state and church, restoring some of the Vatican's temporal power by establishing the Vatican state as sovereign, independent, and neutral and by reinstating ecclesiastical immunities and privileges; restoring some of its economic power by compensating the Vatican for losses and allowing it to purchase property again; and restoring some of its socio-political power by nominating Catholicism the state religion. While the Catholic Church had failed to create a political presence in Italy, these pacts – which are still the basis of the relationship between church and state today – restored some lost privileges and halted further erosions.

5   The laws on divorce and abortion (in 1970 and 1978 respectively) were a significant blow for the Church, as were the ensuing referendums (1974, 1981), which tried unsuccessfully to get these laws repealed. In 1971 the law forbidding propaganda in favour of contraception was declared unconstitutional.

6   In the new agreement, the phrase "the sole religion of the state" was abandoned, marking the first legal recognition of other faiths in Italy. While the Concordat gave the Church some concrete advantages, such the establishment of *otto per mille* funding (whereby Italians can elect to give 0.8 per cent of their income tax directly to a religious organization rather than the state), other special privileges the Church had been enjoying were ended: church property was now to be taxed; the Vatican Bank, which had been subject to scandals, was to be regulated under Italian law; and the idea of the sacred character of Rome was abolished during the same period. Concordats with the minority religions in Italy, while not providing them with the privileges held by the Catholic Church, formally recognized their existence on the peninsula and permitted them some degree of parity. Italy was now giving formal legal recognition to religions other than Catholicism – the exception being Islam, which to this day has been unable to establish a concordat for its recognition in Italy.

the Church rise steeply (see chapter 4). At the same time, though, the scandal surrounding clerical sexual abuse, so widespread in the United States and Ireland, gained little traction in Italy, for reasons I will discuss later in this book. The year 2013 saw the election of the charismatic Pope Francis, whose conciliatory pronouncements on sexuality and profound expressions of care for the poor and the marginalized (a position that chimes with the social left in Italy) resulted in, or at least coincided with, a decline in the level of protest and a rise in the number of people attending mass (Hooper 2013). However, in 2014 declines in attendance resumed (ISTAT 2017).

As Luca Diotellevi (2002), Franco Garelli (2014), and others note, while secularization of the public sphere has undoubtedly been growing, various indicators demonstrate that the Catholic Church in Italy is especially tenacious. While the Catholic voice has become more fragmented since the break-up of the ruling Christian Democrats in 1992, it is far from absent in politics. Indeed, its ongoing presence is so strongly felt that it has been subject to protest (see chapter 4). Italy has now no major Catholic political party, but this has not stopped the Church from developing an outspoken political voice, which makes itself heard though Catholic ministers working across parliamentary parties, through the CEI (Conferenza episcopale italiana), through the pope's interventions, and through the national and local media, which broadcast and discuss religious opinions as a matter of course. Through these and other channels, the Church has spoken out on key arguments in Italian society, from inequality to migration, from Italy's part in the 2003 Iraq War to bioethics and gay rights. The result of this political intervention is that legislation on civil partnerships, on adoption rights for gay couples, on stem cell research, and on in vitro fertilization, all of which have recently been adopted across much of Europe, has met with strong resistance not just from the Vatican and clerical representatives but from Catholic parliamentarians and lobbyists.

While Catholicism is overwhelmingly *the* religion on the peninsula, and most Italian nationals "don't seem to contest the bond between the prevailing religious denomination and national identity" (Garelli 2004, 3) even if they do not regularly attend mass, Italy is nonetheless becoming religiously plural. Islam is now Italy's second religion; according to the Pew Research Centre (Hackett 2017), the country is home to an estimated 2.87 million Muslims – around 4.8 per cent of the population – as migration to Italy from countries with large Islamic populations continues. This makes Italy's Muslim population the fourth-largest in Europe (after France, Germany, and the UK). Mosques were built in Catania (1980), Milan (1988), and Rome (1995) before a ruling made the building of further mosques in Italy unlawful. In their place, prayer houses have sprung up across the country (Saint-Blancat and Schmidt di Friedberg 2005), a phenomenon captured in Farborz Kamkari's comedy *Pitza e datteri* (2015). A political voice for Islam in parliament was established in 2005 in the form of a consultative body (Consulta per l'Islam italiano); after initially folding, it has recently been relaunched (Polchi 2015). Other minority religions have also been growing. The Waldensians, for example, have benefited from the political and economic recognition provided by the 1988 Concordat. Their tiny community now sees nearly a quarter of a million Italians contribute to its social work through *otto per mille* personal tax donations. Modood, Braidotti, and others link post-secular society with the return of religion due, in large part, to the rise of Islam; yet Italy's Islamic community is, at the time of writing, too small and too marginal to overhaul the concept of "Italianicity." The resistance of religion in post-secular Italy has as much to do with the survival of the dominant religion as the arrival of alternatives.

From this preliminary sketch, it should be apparent that religion, *in primis* Catholicism, has a far greater presence in the public sphere than it does in other European countries. Catholic processions and events are still held in piazzas and streets across the country; the Church plays a role in key state ceremonies; despite heated challenges, crucifixes and religious statues are still displayed in schools and in other public buildings. The Church appoints chaplains to public institutions such as prisons and hospitals. It continues to own banks, publishing houses, radio stations, television stations, newspapers and magazines, and an extraordinary wealth of cultural assets. It runs its own universities and institutes, including the Università Cattolica del Sacro Cuore in Milan. It is a significant provider of health and welfare facilities and is at the forefront, claims Pollard (2008), of tackling drug abuse and managing Italy's rapidly expanding immigrant populations. Charles Taylor's point (2007) that we could move within the culture without ever meeting God simply does not hold for Italy.

That such a powerful religious player made its headquarters on the peninsula has created, according to Carlo Falconi, a "levitical people, a nation whose essential function and raison d'être is to be in the service of the church" (cited in Pollard 2008, 186). While Falconi's view may be overstated, the expectations and pressures placed on the Italian state and its people by the Vatican have undoubtedly resulted in a complex range of individual and national responses, expressed through government legislation, individual and collective protest, and cultural production. These responses have ranged from overwhelming support for official Vatican teachings right through to angry resistance. Religion in contemporary Italy is contested, multidimensional, and complex.

A post-secular picture of Italians' personal attitudes towards religion could certainly be assembled from polls such as Eurobarometer, Eurispes, and the European Values Survey, all of which point to a high level of personal belief in Italy and significant levels of church attendance, especially when compared to the European average. This picture could be made more accurate by analysing figures for the *otto per mille* personal contributions to the Church, which remain steady. It might be amplified by ethnographic, historical, and sociological comment by the likes of John Pollard and Franco Garelli. All of these are valid approaches. However, a reading of Italy's contemporary cultural production – and especially Italy's cinema, which has long been a barometer of societal change – opens a path to a particularly enlightening and nuanced understanding of the role religion plays in the public sphere.

Methodology, Key Questions, and Organization of the Book

This is the first book-length study to tackle the question of religion in contemporary Italian filmmaking. It addresses two questions: *how* Italian filmmaking reflects and constructs the continuing position of religion in the public sphere, and *why* religion persists on Italian screens. This book's hypothesis is that the post-secular "subjective turn," which results in religion leaking from public into private space, creating "believing without belonging," may not have happened in Italy, or may have happened there only partially. This would mean that Italy's post-secular experience, as reflected and constructed on screen, is itself partial. It is this hypothesis that the book will test. I will therefore be making a case for the exceptionality of religion in Italian public space and will show how the approximations of much international criticism regarding the place of religion in cinema do not hold in that country. This will help balance the many critical discussions of religion in the United States that compress the difference between the American and European religious experiences. I will also address a more recent problem – that publications on religion in Europe tend to compress the differences across this complex continent. Most of the chapters in Braidotti and colleagues' important edited volume on post-secularization in the public sphere (2014) presume that a Northern European secularism of the public sphere speaks for religion in Europe as a whole. That is not the case. This book will also balance current European discussions of religion, which typically stress the rise of Islam and overlook the continuing place of indigenous religion on the continent. In so doing, I voice the concern raised by Cornel West in his debate with Judith Butler in *The Power of Religion in the Public Sphere* (Butler et al. 2011) that "some of the conceptual frameworks we have for linking secularization with modernization actually assume certain kinds of religions as the relevant ones" (104).

The temporal focus of this book runs from the turn of the new millennium to the time of writing (2017). The year 2000 marks a neat watershed: it was the year of the Catholic Church's Great Jubilee, a particularly large and significant event, centred in Rome, that marked the beginning of the third millennium of Christianity. The choice to focus on contemporary Italy rather than on mid-twentieth-century filmmakers whose names are traditionally linked to religion in film (Roberto Rossellini, Vittorio De Sica, Pier Paolo Pasolini, Federico Fellini) is motivated by a number of factors. First, contemporary Italy is facing a particularly complex set of post-secular challenges as it absorbs many of the effects of secularization and turns to confront a multi-religious future. For a country with a historically high level of engagement with religion, the aftershocks of these changes have been particularly deep and challenging, and even traumatic. Second, in the wake of the Church's increased intervention in political and social affairs, it is a period in which new kinds of tensions have emerged between the Catholic Church, the Italian state, and protest groups, the latter often explicitly anticlerical and/or professedly atheist. Third, it is a time in which faiths other than Catholicism have been struggling to become visible in a cinematography deeply influenced by Catholic symbology. Whether they can gain such visibility is a subject of this book. Fourth and finally, despite the distribution of important films and miniseries in the new millennium whose very titles speak of religion (*Habemus Papam*; *Corpo celeste*; *L'ora di religione*; *The Young Pope*; *Si accettano miracoli*; *Come Dio comanda*; *La terra dei santi*), research on religion in contemporary cinema has remained sidelined. Italian film studies has given attention to religious aspects of mid-century filmmaking, including censorship and other forms of Church intervention, but there has been little critical work on films made since 2000.

It is essential, however, to make two clarifications regarding the timescale. First, by choosing to focus on the films of the new millennium, I am not suggesting there was an unexpected rupture in Italian cinematic trends in 1999. In fact, I see some lines of continuity connecting films distributed at the very end of the last century to those released at the beginning of the new one. The boundary between the films of the new and old millennium will therefore be treated with a degree of porosity. Second, while the focus of this book is firmly on the films of the new millennium, at times I have deliberately contextualized these in relation to earlier filmmaking practices, especially, as a point of contrast, with the cinema of the 1960s and 1970s, which was vocal in its challenges to the institution of the Church. Contextualizing contemporary cinema in relation to an earlier period of politically engaged contestation, in which highly critical views of the Church were often expressed, is crucial for gaining a historical perspective on contemporary concerns and filmmaking attitudes. This context also helps make sense of the rapid and significant changes that have taken place in the on-screen construction of religion.

In this book I am working with a corpus of more than two hundred fiction films. My primary focus is on films distributed across the cinema circuit. However, my investigations also encompass television fiction as a critical point of reference, given the key position the small screen holds in the circulation of religion in the public sphere. It is easy to underestimate the number of religious-themed miniseries and films screened on prime-time Italian television; it is also impossible to ignore those productions. Bringing television fiction film into the picture enables me to explore how the different visual media enable and disable the circulation of religion in the public sphere. There is a notable difference between what can be, and is, scheduled on Italian television and what can be, and is, screened in Italy's cinemas. The often-conflicting picture of religion presented by television on the one hand and by cinema on the other needs to be taken into account in a country in which control of television is highly concentrated: the government-owned RAI possesses three of the seven main terrestrial channels (RAI 1; RAI 2; RAI 3). RAI and Mediaset (owned by ex-premier Silvio Berlusconi) together control 70 per cent of the television airwaves. The films I have selected for discussion encompass not only different media (TV and cinema) but also a variety of genres, from art-house to the *film medio*, from drama to comedy, from television fiction to experimental cinema. I also open a window on the subterranean film cultures of low-budget horror. This corpus *must* be inclusive if we are to piece together a broader picture of how religion is being constructed in post-secular Italian filmmaking. The wide range of genres demonstrates the tentacular reach of religion, from the most obscure underground films to the buffed and soft-focused television hagiopic. Given the diverse nature of the construction of religion in Italy, only a wide-ranging set of genres can hope to provide a meaningful analysis.

I am well aware that my analysis of religion in contemporary Italy could have been brought to bear on a wider cultural context – including, for instance painting, fiction writing, and music – and that doing so might provide a more representative picture than the necessarily fragmentary one this book will offer. My choice to focus more narrowly is motivated by two key factors. First, from a pragmatic point of view, concentrating on one artistic medium allows a depth and rigour of analysis that would be absent from a wider overview. Second, and more importantly, over the course of the twentieth and twenty-first centuries the visual media, including cinema, have attracted the Catholic Church's attention more than any other, both in terms of the censorship of material seen as inappropriate and in terms of the Church's support for films that present positive or challenging moral messages. Exploring filmmaking, especially across a range of media, therefore seems apposite.

This book's methodology is firmly post-secular. It sets out neither to laud the place of religion in Italian cultural production nor to mock the "residues" of religion or attack the institution of Catholicism, Islam, or any religion on the peninsula. My aim is to investigate by means of an open-minded, curious, and post-secular frame the peculiar phenomena of religion in twenty-first-century Italian cinema, in line with the research questions outlined at the start of this section – that is, *how* Italian filmmaking reflects and constructs the continuing position of religion in the public sphere and *why* religion persists on Italian screens. I propose to achieve this by focusing attention on Catholicism above all. Catholicism unquestionably towers over other religions in Italy in demographic, historic, social, and political terms. It also dominates debates in the Italian public sphere and representations on Italian cinema and television screens. This does not mean that I ignore Italy's minority religions. On the contrary, throughout this book I draw these into my argument where appropriate, and I dedicate chapter 5 to them. Islam in particular has been growing enormously in importance and is key to any discussion of the post-secular. As the religion that has been expanding most rapidly across Europe and is now the second-largest in Italy, it is a source of unease and anxiety on Italian screens. No discussion of the post-secular in Italy would be complete without it.

My use of the concept of the public sphere has its roots in Habermas, whose seminal book *The Structural Transformation of the Public Sphere* (1962) was foundational to subsequent debates. For Habermas, the public sphere, which was created in the eighteenth century by the public monitoring of the state on the part of the bourgeoisie, expanded to include other parts of society. In his 1962 work, Habermas neglected the place of religion in the public sphere; subsequently, however, as outlined above, he rebalanced his argument by drawing questions of religion into the debate. In contemporary social welfare state democracies, the public sphere is now a fragmented field of competition among conflicting interests. It is a societal space in which diverging opinions can be expressed, matters of shared interest discussed, and solutions collectively weighed. It is therefore the space of communication within any given society.

This book's stated aim is to investigate how the film industry reflects and constructs religion and to assess the part played by the industry in the ongoing circulation of religion in the public sphere. Chapter 1 examines the space available for the production and distribution of religious films in Italy. I explore how religious organizations gain, and maintain, control over their media messages. I assess what kinds of religious mobilization exist and the degree of control exercised by religions on the peninsula. I examine Catholic filmmaking policies and infrastructure as well as the policies and infrastructures of minority faiths, taking Islam as the case study. It is not surprising that minority religions have failed to gain any significant foothold in the industry; what *is* surprising is that Catholicism's hold over the production and distribution of films has been strengthening rather than weakening since the 1990s. I explore what is behind this as I assess the importance of Catholic mobilization in contemporary filmic production.

Chapter 1, then, centres on the mechanics and management of the production and distribution of religious messages. The chapters that follow it examine the form and content of the films. Together these chapters explore the narratives, imagery, rituals, and values that lie behind the continued circulation of religion on screen. Throughout this investigation I ask why religion persists in Italy's public sphere. What is keeping it there? What can we learn from filmmaking about the persistence of religion? In chapter 2, I begin to answer these questions by addressing the attraction of Catholic iconography, rituals, and settings for filmmakers. I select filmmakers who are professedly agnostic or atheist and who are working outside the Catholic sphere of production in order to demonstrate just how strong the lure of Catholicism is. Countering thinkers like Stig Hjarvard (2011) and Stewart Hoover (2006), who argue that contemporary uses of religious iconography are little more than superficial spectacle, I argue that in Italy attachment to the imagery and ritual of Catholicism is in fact deeply rooted. While Italian directors often recognize that religion sells both at home and on the global market (the *"Da Vinci Code* effect"), and this does underpin their use of spectacle, its use is often also motivated by deeper factors, from implicit or explicit religious belief, to a dialogue with Italy's plastic and performance arts, to the fostering of collective national belonging, sharing, and remembering. Ultimately, in a reversal of Grace Davie's "believing without belonging" catchphrase (1990), Italian filmmaking demonstrates the importance of icons and ritual in "belonging without (necessarily) believing."

In chapter 3, I focus on Catholic values. Here, I investigate how and why certain contemporary filmmakers bond religious values to countercultural discourse. I argue that through the fusion of religious values and countercultural rhetoric, the on-screen twenty-first-century Catholic Church has been remodelled as a *Chiesa della minoranza* (minority church). This new paradigm has replaced the former one whereby Catholicism was the powerful hegemonic faith of the peninsula. This has enabled ethical paradigms – the battling priest and Saint Francis – to emerge as relevant to contemporary post-capitalist life in Italy. In an era in which ethical models are few and problematic, these models have gained widespread circulation, thereby enabling an ethics grounded in religion to regain a place in Italy's public sphere. This investigation of how Catholic values circulate helps explain why Catholicism remains so deeply embedded in Italy's public sphere and why it has been so difficult for the peninsula's other religions to emerge. The corpus of films in this chapter centres on hagiopics, Lux Vide's miniseries for television, and *film di qualità* (quality films), all of which position emblematic clerical figures against capitalism and fascism.

In chapter 4, I investigate another piece of the puzzle: protest. Here, following the seminal work of Michael Lipsky (1969), I hypothesize that protest against the Church is one of the reasons why religion remains an object of interest and discussion in Italy's media. Without protest, religion risks being seen as an "old" story. A series of conflicts over the position of the Church in secular life have marked the twenty-first-century debate and are reflected on Italian screens. In particular, filmmakers have recently protested the Vatican's relationship with Italy's political and economic ecosystem (the banks, the Mafia, and the political sphere) and its control over the lives and bodies of its citizens through legislation on civil partnerships, euthanasia, and in vitro fertilization. The films I discuss in this chapter include Giuseppe Ferrara's *I banchieri di Dio* (The God's Bankers, 2001), Paolo Sorrentino's *Il divo* (2008), and Roberto Faenza's *La verità sta in cielo* (2016), as well as Gustav Hofer and Luca Ragazzi's *Improvvisamente l'inverno scorso* (Suddenly Last Winter, 2008), Marco Bellocchio's *Bella addormentata* (Dormant Beauty, 2012) and Carlo Verdone's *Manuale d'amore 2* (Manual of Love 2, 2007). My analysis here will show that the line marking what belongs to religious and what belongs to secular space has shifted radically over the last seventy years. In the conclusion, I look at what the diminishing levels of protest mean for the circulation of religion.

In chapter 5, I explore the position of Italy's minority faiths on screen. Given the extent to which the Catholic Church and Catholic iconography, narratives, and values still dominate Italy's film production, the emergence of Italy's minority faiths on screen is destined to be fraught. In this chapter, I examine how Italian filmmaking for the big and small screen approaches the religious other. I examine the paths of assimilation and expulsion as well as emerging signs of a third way in which acceptance of difference is possible. The chapter draws on a wide range of genres, including comedies like Fariborz Kamkari's *Pitza e datteri* (2015), horror movies like Dario Argento's *La terza madre* (Mother of Tears, 2007), conspiracy thrillers like Martinelli's *Il mercante di pietre* (The Stone Merchant, 2006), and the work of Italo-Turkish filmmaker Ferzan Özpetek.

Finally, in the book's conclusion, I explore several films that deliberately foreground post-secularism. These films are investigative and attempt to understand the place of religion in Italy, chronicling change and crisis. My aim is to identify the specificity of twenty-first-century post-secularism on screen and understand how this differs from portrayals of religion in the mid-twentieth century and in relation to contemporary post-secular portrayals elsewhere. The films on which I focus include two big-budget auteur works, Nanni Moretti's *Habemus Papam* (2011) and Paolo Sorrentino's *The Young Pope* (2017), as well as Alice Rohrwacher's low-budget debut, *Corpo celeste* (Heavenly Body, 2011). In the chapter's conclusion, I endeavour to outline this volume's findings, drawing together the main threads of my argument and sketching future directions.

This study does not claim to be exhaustive. Religion is too integral to Italian filmmaking and too all-pervasive on big and small screens for me to treat every instance in the space available. In this book, what I hope to do instead is provide a roadmap, indicating some key directions in Italy's curious and anomalous filmic response to its complex, post-secular existence.

1 The Space for Religious Filmmaking: Policy and Infrastructures

Introduction

Contemporary filmmaking is the site of a struggle over the control of public and private images and narratives. Political parties, lobbies, religious leaders, protest groups, and fans are fully aware of just how crucial it is, in a media-dominated world, to consolidate and communicate their perspectives and their versions of events.[1] These groups and individuals typically engage in tactics to render visible their vision, or to gain supremacy, in a crowded media environment. When challenged by a film or other media event that threatens their narrative, they emerge into the public sphere to underscore, or impose, a different version that is more coherent with their own. For contemporary religions in Italy, it is crucial to maintain a public voice and a place in the culture industry, given that the Catholic Church's influence in the world is no longer tied to a leading economic, military, or political presence, and given that the position of minority religions is far from assured. Gaining or retaining this public voice allows for control of the message, and this message is at the heart of the proselytizing religions, especially Christianity and Islam. For minority religions in Italy, breaking into this public space, which is dominated by competing Catholic and secular concerns, is a demanding but essential undertaking.

In this chapter I explore whether the filmmaking industries are contributing to the decline of religion in the public sphere, or whether they are successfully mobilizing to resist decline, and if so, how successfully. My focus is on

---

1 Imposing one's image of events is not confined to hegemonic power structures, of course. In 2003, *Buongiorno notte* (Good Morning, Night), directed by veteran filmmaker Marco Bellocchio, put forward a rather two-dimensional image of the male terrorists who kidnapped and later murdered the leader of the Christian Democrats, Aldo Moro. This image was challenged by ex-members of the terrorist organization portrayed, who invited the actors to come and discuss their version of events and experiences with them in the wake of the film's release.

the Catholic Church's control of the industry, given that it is the main player. Towards the end of the chapter, however, I draw in Islam as an instance of minority religious filmmaking, investigating whether growing minority faiths have any meaningful access to the media in Italy – a question that is key to the post-secular debates forwarded by Braidotti and her colleagues (2014). In order to answer these questions, I provide an overview of the tactics used both by religious organizations and by individuals for controlling media messages, and I examine how successful they have been. I work on the critical assumption that control over the media is not simply a matter of a hegemonic Catholic Church exercising its power. While the Vatican's position on cinema and media is of course crucial (and for this reason, I will be exploring its policies later in this chapter), it is imperative to assess the plurality of Catholic voices that weave across the peninsula, as well as the presence, or absence, of production and distribution circuits for films dealing directly with Islam and other minority religions. In this chapter I challenge the commonly held view that the interventions of religions in Italy's mediasphere are repressive and punitive – a view that stems from the early interventions of the Catholic Church in the cinema industry, which typically were both. While the legacy of censorship certainly casts a shadow, I will show how many contemporary interventions are instead creative and open. This is not to deny the long history of Catholic censorship in Italy, but rather to emphasize how in contemporary Italy it is no longer censorship that defines the Church's relationship with cinema and other media. In the first part of the chapter, I provide a brief overview of the Catholic Church's campaign for media presence. I then sketch major Catholic policy positions regarding film-making and the infrastructure it has managed to build. Finally, taking Islam as a case study, I investigate whether minority religions have mobilized and been able to enter the public arena, assessing what support both the Italian state and their own religious institutions and infrastructures have provided.

Catholic Media Presence in Italy

The Catholic Church has for some time invested in a broad international media presence to ensure that its voice continues to be heard. There are the key Catholic news agencies like ACI Prensa, which prepares news for the Spanish-speaking world, and ZENIT, which provides stories across Catholic and secular media, as well as international organizations like Catholics in Media (CIMA), EWTN (the global Catholic television network), and the Catholic Media Council (CAMECO), which promotes the work of the Church in developing countries. There are around five hundred official Vatican reporters in the world today (Paoluzi 2009). The Vatican has its own newspaper, the *Osservatore romano*, and a TV production company, Centro Televisivo Vaticano (now Vatican Media), founded in 1983, which makes many documentaries and prepares news footage. It also has its own website (www.vatican.va), established in 1995 and containing a wealth of material, including a repository of official documents and statements that allows people direct access to documents so that they can "judge by themselves if mass media coverage is adequate or somehow biased" (Catoni 2010, 23). It has a radio station, Radio Vatican, which broadcasts in thirty-eight languages. It publishes videos of the pope on YouTube and has myriad Twitter accounts. Since the early 1960s each national bishops' conference worldwide has maintained its own media office. The Catholic Church is increasingly involved in product tie-ins, in licensing arrangements for merchandising, and in contracts with advertising and public relations firms – a trend that, given the relatively limited nature of its own media presence, is set to continue (Budde 1998). For instance, the global communications firm Saatchi & Saatchi had a contract with the Italian Catholic Church worth €4 million euro annually, to promote campaigns such its *otto per mille* drive, which encourages Italians to nominate the Catholic Church on their tax returns (Budde 1998). The Church's contemporary attitude towards the media is summarized in the late Pope John Paul II's apostolic exhortation, *Christifideles laici*: "The pastoral responsibility among the lay faithful does not stop with this work of defense. It extends to everyone in the world of communications, even to those professional people of the press, cinema, radio, television and theatre. These also are called to proclaim the gospel that brings salvation" (30 December 1988, no. 44).

Beyond the official media engine put in place by the Vatican, a great multiplicity of media, some of which have official links to the Vatican and some of which do not, have emerged, representing the plural voices of Catholicism internationally and amounting to a large and "formidabile famiglia" (formidable family) (Boffi 2007, 177). SIGNIS, the World Catholic Association for Communication, is recognized by the Vatican, although independent of it. It brings together Catholics working in film, radio, and television and has a history of clashing with the Vatican over its choice of films: when it was still known as OCIC, it assigned prizes to morally controversial films such as John Schlesinger's *Midnight Cowboy* (1969) and Pasolini's *Teorema* (Theorem, 1968). Various media channels have been established by religious communities, dioceses, or individuals, and some of these have achieved a significant national or international dimension. Communion and Liberation, for instance, first set up a website in Italy; its Web presence has since expanded to eighty countries and draws sixty thousand visitors a month (Arasa, Catoni, and Ruiz 2010). Catholic print titles have recently been estimated at around ten thousand worldwide (Paoluzi 2009).

The Church's media presence is particularly strongly felt in Italy, relative to other European countries. The Catholic Church retains a significant voice and visibility across a range of media, and many major international media publications, broadcasts, websites, and production companies are based on the peninsula. While Italy's major national TV and radio stations are secular, five hundred of the thirty-five-hundred local radio stations and fifty of the four hundred to five hundred TV stations are Catholic run (Boffi, 2007). The print media also have a significant Catholic presence: around three thousand Catholic titles are available in Italy, just under one third of the worldwide Catholic print output (Paoluzi 2009, 149). The Catholic-run *Famiglia cristiana* sells 1.2 million copies a week and has maintained its position as the most popular weekly magazine in Italy, beating all secular offerings. The Catholic-oriented daily newspaper *Avvenire*, with a circulation of 106,826 in 2011, is small but growing and according to Italy's *Marketing Journal* is one of the more solid titles in Italy's editorial panorama (Editors 2011).

This overview of Catholic media in contemporary Italy might suggest that the Church holds a hegemonic position in the public sphere. The reality, though, is more complex. For a start, the link between media circulation and faith is not straightforward: increases in circulation, like that reported for *Avvenire*, cannot be read as indicating either a (re)turn to faith or an increased ability to broadcast a message. *Marketing Journal*, for instance, attributes *Avvenire*'s recent success to marketing techniques, including customer relations management, rather than to growth in religious engagement. Moreover, increased circulation can result from a *decrease* in the quantity or specificity of religious material, in order to render the magazine, newspaper, blog, or website more palatable to a broader range of secular media consumers. A reduction in the impact of the religious message may therefore accompany an increase in circulation.

Data on the circulation of Catholic messages across the media therefore need to be interpreted in relation to the wider context of contemporary secular media. Michael L. Budde (1998, 85), discussing the presence of the Catholic message on the international market, claims that the secular press dominates in such a way as to make the Catholic Church's efforts seem "inadequate and minuscule." While "minuscule" is certainly not an appropriate adjective to describe the Italian position, and the presence of Catholic messages on national television is significantly higher than in other European countries, the communication of Catholic stories appears rather less impressive when alternative comparators or indicators are used. Franco Garelli reports that in a 2007 analysis of television broadcasting, "a bishop or member of an ecclesiastical office intervened in some way (interview or reported declaration) in the evening news broadcasts on 227 out of 365 days" (Garelli 2014, 88). This frequency is very high in European terms, but it must be pointed out here that the official voice of the Vatican is not heard on news bulletins for one third of the year, that only one story in every six or seven on the television news has a Catholic angle, and that the Catholic story or viewpoint does not always make it to the main headlines. In addition, Garelli claims that the presence of other faiths in Italy's media is "disproportionate" (Garelli 2014, 190). He further claims – without, however, providing evidence – that this is especially true of Oriental religions (Buddhism and Hinduism), New Age practices, and Islam, the latter attaining a high media profile due to reportage on terrorist threats. As I will show later, Garelli's claim regarding the elevated media visibility of minorities does not necessarily generate a stronger voice for these religions. Minorities find it an almost insurmountable challenge to raise their own voice.

Catholic media presence also needs to be viewed diachronically, that is, in a way that maps its current presence in Italy against its historical performance. In the early years of the twentieth century, religion played a central role in the media. Peter Elvy (1990) notes that at the beginning of the wireless era there were twenty daily Catholic newspapers; today there are only two. He argues that after the First World War, the Catholic Church never managed to regain its lost ground. The broadcast time given to the Catholic Church in Italy, and indeed across Catholic Europe, has been steadily diminishing since the advent of television. While the Catholic Church has managed to maintain visibility across the mediascape, especially through its own Catholic channels but also through Italy's secular local and national media networks, Italy's broadcasting is predominantly secular. Religious broadcasting makes up only a very small proportion of broadcasting time, and Catholic media presence, while clearly dominant when compared to other religions, is therefore far from hegemonic.

Policies for Catholic Filmmaking in Italy

If Catholic presence in the Italian media has diminished in terms of market share since the start of the twentieth century, its relative resilience is testimony to a solid cultural policy that provides clear guidelines about how the Church should act regarding the media. It is this cultural policy that I wish to outline briefly here, sketching the Vatican's policies, the support and checks the Church provides, and, as far as possible, how that support maps onto real results within Italy. My focus in the next section will narrow from the broader media context to assess the film industry.

Much has changed since Antonio Gramsci analysed the Catholic Church as an "ideological apparatus with its own institutional grassroots structure ... whose purpose was to control its mass social base ... in a somewhat repressive manner" (Allum 1990, 81). The Church's attitude towards both the media in general and film in particular shifted dramatically over the course of the twentieth century. In the very early days of cinema, the Vatican saw the new medium as an instrument of base spectacle and presumed a passive spectator who would be easily influenced and who therefore needed protection from its dangers (Chinnici 2003, 35). By the end of the 1920s the Church authorities had taken an embattled and rigorously conservative position as censorship was imposed. This position changed only slowly over the course of the century, most obviously in the years following the Second Vatican Council (1962-5) and after the election of Pope John Paul II in 1978. John Paul II, who had been an actor and a writer for theatre before becoming pope, revised the Church's positions in relation to media and cinema.

The Church has centralized authority in the Vatican, so we can turn to Vatican documents to gain an understanding of developments in film policy. Catholicism is a proselytizing religion, so communication of the Catholic message is key, and thus the Vatican has given guidance across a wide set of documents and pronouncements, from official papal documents to documents written under the auspices of the Pontifical Council of Social Communications (the body that oversees the Church's media relations, authorizes all radio and television work within the Vatican, and oversees the Vatican Film Library). It also uses speeches made on various occasions, especially, since 1967, for the annual World Communications Day. However, while noting that the official policy comes from the quarters closest to the Vatican, it is important to acknowledge that attitudes towards the media across the Catholic world are diverse and do not always reflect the official Vatican voice. Some Catholics, like the Vaticanista Giancarlo Zizola (1996), for example, have taken the view that the Catholic Church has compromised itself by its involvement with media spectacle.

In broad terms, the positions voiced through the official documents and speeches fall into two camps. On the one hand, they express concern about the dangers of film (and subsequently television and the Internet) and the need for Catholics to adopt a critical view towards them; on the other, they support film and other media in their work of communicating Christian values. In the early years of cinema, the former position dominated. In fact, the first intervention by the Church, in 1909, prohibited the clergy from watching films in Rome's public cinemas. This was swiftly followed by the 1912 Decree, which forbade the projection of films in churches (Valli 1999). The Church's concerns about film continued to grow in the 1920s and 1930s, as reflected in the encyclical *Vigilanti cura* (1936), which encouraged Catholics to fight unhealthy films and praised the repressive US Legion of Decency as well as filmmaking that was "moral, moralising and educating." During this subsequent period, the Catholic Church became increasingly interested in film. Citing Enrico Baragli's figures, Daniela Treveri Gennari (2010) notes that the documents prior to *Vigilanti cura* amounted to just ten, whereas between 1936 and 1955 the Church amassed a total of forty-four documents; by 1957 this had grown to fifty-four.

Some critics, like Bernardo Valli (1999), posit that 1955 marked the start of a swing towards a more open attitude on the part of the Church. That year, Pope Pius XII made two speeches on the "ideal film," speeches that, for the first time, demonstrated sensitivity to the film industry and took as their starting point cinema rather than the imposition of Catholic values. Pius XII's description of the "ideal film" was firmly aligned with Catholic values in that it upheld the family, traditional gender roles, and the state and encouraged spectators to remain on the "right path"; but he also moved beyond film as solely a moral educative tool, as had been proposed in *Vigilanti cura*. He instead recognized the entertainment value of film – that it provided an escape from oppressive reality – and he declared that the ideal film might show evil provided that it was portrayed in a negative manner. He warned that filmmakers must not be drawn into doing otherwise by the lure of the market. The focus in these documents was on communicating implicitly religious messages within the secular film industry, rather than producing explicitly religious films, which, as Pope Pius conceded, were rarely successful.

Pius XII's speeches on the ideal film, for all they represented a significant step forward, were still inherently conservative, rigid, and controlling and continued to lend support to censorship. Like the encyclical letter that followed (*Miranda Prorsus*, 1957), they also resisted an industrial, market-focused model of cinema and reiterated the need for cinema to be driven not by profit but by values. In the context of Europe's developing film industry, the pope's support fell not so much behind the American industrial model of cinema, which was being felt across the continent, but ironically behind the independent, art-house model, which was not driven solely by profits. Italy's art-house sector would, over the course of the 1960s and 1970s, explicitly attack bourgeois and Catholic values and express criticism of, or even downright hostility towards, the Church.

The Second Vatican Council represented a revolution in the church's teaching. It signalled a shift towards a more progressive model of Catholicism, one that placed greater emphasis on pluralism and dialogue. It marked an important step in the church's developing attitude towards modernity and ecumenicalism. The admission of media representatives to the council for the first time was significant; so was the discussion of the media's place in Church thinking. However, the decree dedicated to the media, *Inter Mirifica*, passed in 1963, continued to follow the line that the Church had been taking prior to the council: in broad terms, the media were viewed as instrumental, as subject to the Church's moral directives, and as exercising a primarily educational function. The primacy of morality over art was reaffirmed. The Church assigned the media the term "social communication," which was understood to better reflect the Church's position (Valli 1999). The invention of a specific term for the media demonstrated the Church's desire to distinguish between religious and secular use of the means of communication. The Church's "social communication" was seen as somehow less tainted by the secular and commercial values of media, and was dominated by Catholic values.

The rather backward-looking *Inter Mirifica* was, however, followed by *Communio et Progressio*, a pastoral instruction issued in 1971 that was significantly less prescriptive and dogmatic than the documents that had preceded it. It is, to date, the Church's most complete document on film, television, and the press, so it can be viewed as the cornerstone for understanding the official

Church position on film and the media. It takes a generally positive line and calls for the use of censorship only in extreme cases. There is little specific to cinema in the document; it does, though, exhort Catholics to promote spiritual values and to use the media to communicate not just with the faithful but with the whole public sphere, besides underscoring the importance of understanding the medium (and thus of media education). All of this serves as a clear and more modern message about how to respond to, and use, the media.

During the 1960s, then, the Church accepted the need to take a strong position in the public sphere and saw the media as key to achieving this. This view continues to be held by the Catholic Church today. When the Vatican published its second pastoral instruction on the media, *Aetatis Novae*, in 1992, it reaffirmed many of the principles found in the first instruction. Valli (1999), however, notes a developing concern in the document: that in a media-saturated world, the Church's voice not become marginalized. There is a clear recognition of the ever-increasing presence of the media in people's lives and of the Church's own loss of a hegemonic position as it struggles to make itself heard among a multiplicity of voices in an aggressive market. According to *Aetatis Novae*, the solution is to ensure that the Church does not rely solely on its own religious media to provide news; it must also infuse the secular media with its voice and values. According to Zizola (1996, 92) what is really new about *Aetatis Novae* is that it discusses the need to beat secularization with its own means, calling specifically for those working in the media to dedicate themselves to pastoral action. Daniel Arasa (2009, 37) notes the shift in this document towards an understanding that the media form the life of the people and the community, so it is part of the Church's mission to adapt its language, activities, and culture to the new cultural environment. This was the era of Pope John Paul II (1978–2005), a particularly media-aware and media-friendly pope, a man who had worked as an actor and who not only permitted media spectacle to develop around him but indeed positively encouraged it. Of his numerous interventions on media, the most important as far as the film industry is concerned was his *Cinema, veicolo di cultura e proposta di valori*, delivered for the annual World Communications Day in 1995: besides warning of the dangers of cinema, this speech discussed its importance in terms of education and the formation of values. In the wake of *Cinema, veicolo di cultura*, the themes picked for World Communications Days, alongside papal documents and other official speeches, demonstrate that in the 1990s the Vatican's focus shifted rapidly from cinema to television, the Internet, and social media. Collectively, these have displaced attention from cinema.[2] Neither of the two subsequent popes (Benedict XVI and Francis I) has shown a significant interest in cinema.

---

2 For a complete list of the annual World Communications Day themes, see Meneghetti (2015). These annual events, which were established by the Inter Mirifica decree, provide fascinating

It is clear from the outline presented above that the Vatican's official policy has evolved over time and adapted to the socio-political environment in which the Church has now found itself. It is clear too that in terms of the Vatican's attention, cinema has given way to television and the new media, reflecting the steady decline in cinemagoing over the past hundred years and the rise of other media. The Vatican's declining interest in supporting and controlling cinema reflects its understanding of its diminishing presence as the great purveyor of images and narratives that influence values and taste. The current official Catholic views also reflect cinema's increasing specialization as a provider of fictional accounts of the world; over the course of the twentieth century, factual newsreels and documentaries have shifted from the big to the small screen. Cinema's increasing focus on fiction has made it ever less serviceable for the promulgation of Catholic messages. Nonetheless, official Catholic documents that address the media more broadly provide a clear message to contemporary Catholics working in the film industry. Like those working across the range of old and new media, those employed in the film industry are expected to be proactive in making the Church's voice heard.

Italian Infrastructures for Catholic Filmmaking

The question that follows on from this is how the Vatican's evolving policy is being translated into concrete action across the diverse and complex Catholic network in Italy. Policy without action is meaningless. Only by exploring the Church's actions can one develop an understanding of the kind of control it has been able to exercise, and still exercises, over the peninsula's filmmaking and, through filmmaking, over the public sphere.

In the first decades of the twentieth century, controlling what people watched, rather than how they watched it, was the Catholic Church's overriding concern. The Vatican encouraged the creation of infrastructures aimed at gaining and retaining control over the cinema industry. It also encouraged Catholics to infiltrate the state censorship boards, whose classifications and cuts had the force of law. The Church was most hostile towards film between the late 1920s and the end of the 1930s, a period during which religiously inspired movements that favoured increased censorship were growing in strength in Europe (Biltereyst 2006). Daniel Biltereyst describes how Catholic film organizations

---

insights into the developing relationship between the Catholic Church and the media between 1967 and the present. They also allow us to track how the focus has shifted from cinema to mass media to the Internet and social media. The World Communications Days draw attention to questions surrounding the communication of the message; they also habituate people to hearing about the media from the pulpit, in addition to creating a funding stream through the faithful's offerings (Meneghetti 2015, 174).

railed against the "film problem" throughout Belgium, France, Italy, and Spain. In Italy, Catholic censorship was formalized through the creation of the Centro Cattolico Cinematografico (CCC) in 1935. That organization created a national classification system and then classified each film as it was released. While the CCC's recommendations did not have force of law, the Church used punitive measures, such as forbidding erring parishioners to attend communion, to encourage adherence. According to Maurizio Cesari (cited in Treveri Gennari 2011), a bad word from the CCC would affect a film's success by effectively blocking it from the then-extensive Catholic film circuit. This means that the Church at that time had significant control over what could successfully be distributed and therefore what could be successfully made.

The punitive system of Church censorship had ended in Europe by the late 1960s; even so, Church censorship did not disappear entirely from contemporary Italy. Although they are unlikely to be noticed in secular circles and have little influence over ordinary Catholics, the Church continues to provide classifications. These take the form of guidance rather than the punitive recommendations of the pre-Vatican Council period. In Italy today, two distinct and sometimes contradictory bodies provide Catholics with recommendations and classifications. The Commissione Nazionale Valutazione Film judges and classifies films; however, it is binding only for parish cinemas and a few other Catholic bodies, not for Catholic lay people. The Fondazione Ente dello Spettacolo, founded in 1943 as an offshoot of the CCC, provides guidance to individual Catholics through the columns of its *Rivista del cinematografo*, although these have no binding status (Viganò 2006). In addition to these bodies, the Vatican itself occasionally publishes official statements on individual films, especially those viewed as directly attacking the Catholic Church and its mission, such as Ron Howard's *The Da Vinci Code* (2006) and Pedro Almodóvar's *La mala educación* (Bad Education, 2004). But as Dario Viganò notes, even in these cases, boycotting and censorship are rare (2006). In fact, the Catholic Church in Italy today, unlike its evangelical counterpart in the States, deliberately fosters discussion and even "ingestion" of films that might be considered critical of its position. That approach follows Pope John Paul II's letter to artists in 1999 in which he praised artists' ability to "seek the beautiful" but also noted, in a reversal of his predecessor's attitudes, that the portrayal of evil can have a positive value: "even when they explore the darkest depths of the soul or the most unsettling aspects of evil, artists give voice in a way to the universal desire for redemption" (cited in Williams Ortiz 2003, 181). In this way the contemporary Church manages to claim as its own what Peter Malone (2009) has described as the "*De profundis* film," a film that presents a cry from the depths of moral despair. *De profundis* films are now used as a basis for discussing Christian values (Williams Ortiz 2003). Thus, Jessica Hausner, director of the controversial film *Lourdes* (2009), was invited to the Catholic Tertio Millennio festival in Rome in 2011, and Antonia Bird's provocative *Priest* (1994), which led to firebombings in the United States, had a more open reception in Europe. *Priest*, a British film about a gay priest, was discussed by the Organisation catholique internationale du cinéma et de l'audiovisuel (OCIC, later SIGNIS) at the Berlin Film Festival and scheduled for screenings in Catholic communities throughout Germany; these were followed by seminars and discussions arranged by the media office of the national bishops' conference (Williams Ortiz 2003).

Of course, influencing what a nation or indeed a continent watches, and how they watch it, is only in part down to censorship. As I have shown here, the role played by censorship in Italy has diminished rapidly since the 1960s and is almost imperceptible there today. Censorship plays little real part in what Italians see on screens today, at least outside of parish cinema billings. Where the Church's influence *is* still felt is in the infrastructure it has created and maintained to support the production and distribution of films.

Prior to the Second Vatican Council (1962–5), the Catholic Church failed to establish itself as a major player in Italian film production, in large part because it was intent on resisting the dangers of film. This is not to say that in Italian cinema history there have not been important Catholic production houses, such as Orbis (later Universalia), founded in 1943. However, the point that needs making here is that the Church's efforts in cinema production have historically been tiny relative to Italy's secular cinema production. According to Giuseppe Chinnici (2003), negative economic forces after the Second World War compelled the Church progressively to reduce its already limited involvement in cinema production and to concentrate on education. Production houses that refused to produce secular films could not survive (Sorlin 2005), and indeed, as Chinnici (2003) notes, by the end of the 1950s the only Catholic production houses still active were San Paolo and Columbianum. Clearly, expanding production capacity in cinema has not been a priority for the Church. Chinnici goes so far as to state that "una produzione qualificabile come 'cattolica' in senso confessionale o come espressione del Movimento cattolico non esiste più" (a production that would count as "Catholic" in the confessional sense or as an expression of the Catholic movement no longer exists) (Chinnici 2003, 101–2).

Chinnici is overstating matters, however, as far as contemporary Catholic production is concerned. In fact, despite the lack of a postwar infrastructure to support Catholic filmmaking, religious production has been playing an increasingly important role in Italy's public sphere as well as globally. San Paolo, founded in Italy in 1914, now has an international presence spanning thirty nations on five continents. Lux Vide, founded in 1992, produces a large quantity of high-profile religious fiction for Italian and international television. In 2016 it was Italy's biggest producer of television fiction for RAI, capturing 20 per cent of television viewers (Fontanarosa 2017). Merging the incomplete lists available on www.intermirifica.net (the Catholic online mass media directory) and on the Catholic Radio and Television Network, what emerges is that by 2011 there were more than one hundred Catholic or Catholic-leaning producers in Europe, many of which were based in Italy. While some of these are tiny enterprises and most produce television documentaries and television fiction rather than films for the big screen, what is notable is that from the mid-1990s onwards there has been a large-scale return to film production of an explicitly religious nature, especially on the part of Catholic television production companies. This has been coupled with the more recent screening of some Catholic-inspired films in both mainstream cinema (Daniele Luchetti's *Chiamatemi Francesco: Il papa della gente* [Call me Francesco 2015]) and on the film festival and art-house circuit (Giovanni Columbu's *Su re* 2012).

If the Church's control over the production of films, especially those made for the big screen, was historically limited, its control of distribution has, from the outset, proved a success. Across Italy, the Catholic Church set up cinema screens attached to parishes where "good" films could be shown. By the 1920s these were formalized into national networks of Catholic parish cine-clubs (the so-called *sale parocchiali*, later to be called the *sale di comunità*). Subsequently, these were supported by organizations such as the Società Cattolica Assistenza Esercenti Cinema, and, after this was liquidated in the 1970s, the Associazione Cattolica Esercenti Cinema (ACEC), which was set up to manage the national Italian circuit (Chinnici 2003). These cinemas were highly successful in Italy. They provided an alternative to commercial cinema and an on-tap distribution circuit for the Church. In their heyday in the 1960s, about half the screens in Italy belonged to the Church (Bettetini 2006), and even in 1998 they represented 15 per cent of the total (Chinnici 2003). Today, they still present the only alternative to commercial multiplexes in many small rural towns. While the most recent figures suggest that there are only 1,200 parish cinemas left, they are still, according to Gianfranco Bettetini, "un patrimonio prezioso per la Chiesa soprattutto nell'ottica dell'evangelizzazione, della cura pastorale e dell'azione culturale" (an important patrimony for the church, especially for evangelisation, pastoral care and cultural action" [2006, 80]). The Church's influence over the distribution circuit is not inconsequential, as it assures a market for films with so-called positive values and thus indirectly promotes both Catholic and secular productions of this kind.

The Church also supports the distribution of films through its promotion and support of film festivals and Catholic and ecumenical prizes, both of which encourage the development of quality products relevant to the Church's moral values. Some of the more significant religious film festivals in Italy are Cinema Spirituale Tertio Millennio (1997–), which has the Vatican's support, the Religion Today Film Festival (1997–), run by the Associazione BiancoNero in Trento, and Mirabile Dictu, the International Catholic Film Festival, founded in 2010 by the Pontifical Council for Culture. What is notable here is how the past twenty years have seen a significant increase in Catholic visibility on the film festival circuit. Festival outlets, such as the Religion Today Film Festival and the Festival Internacional de Cine Educativo y Espiritual, have also developed across Europe. Moreover, Catholic or ecumenical juries are now present at most of the prominent European film festivals, such as those at Venice, Cannes, Berlin, and Rome. In 2008, SIGNIS, the international Catholic media association, was present at thirty-seven international film and television festivals, twenty-five of which were in Europe (SIGNIS Report for 2008) and many of which were in Italy. The increased visibility of religious filmmaking through Catholic, ecumenical, and secular festival circuits offers significant encouragement to filmmakers who wish to explore religious or spiritual experiences in their films.

Alongside distribution, the Church's principal focus – especially in recent decades – has been on promoting film and media education. The reasons for this are obvious and, in broad terms, twofold: first, to support Catholics throughout the film and media industries so that Catholicism has a voice in religious *and* secular media; and second, to train spectators, including members of the clergy, to be critical of films and of other media, to prevent them passively absorbing ideas. As early as 1935 the CCC in Italy set up film courses for priests. The Centro Studi Cinematografici was launched in 1953 with the remit of running courses and conferences and coordinating cinema circles. Also in the 1950s, cineforums were also established to create a space where films could be viewed and discussed. These flourished during the 1960s and 1970s, when they were more successful than their secular counterparts, and they exist to this day (Chinnici 2003). The Church has also called for, and supported, university courses in audiovisual language. Since the 1970s, when the Catholic University in Milan began offering the first degree in Social Communications, degrees and diplomas have been offered in this subject at universities across Italy. The official Church policy of educating through cinema is also reflected in the presence of cultural journals, such as *Lumen, Rassegna critica del libro e dello spettacolo,* and *Rivista del cinematografo,* as well as regular film columns and articles in Catholic newspapers and magazines like *Famiglia cristiana.*

What is clear from all this is that the Church has focused its infrastructural efforts not on producing films for the big screen – a project that had failed long before the period I am discussing in this book – but in producing non-fiction and fiction for television, in ensuring that there is a distribution circuit for religiously orientated filmmaking, and in educating people to read films critically. An infrastructure has now been developed that guides ordinary Catholics' film choices using subtle, liberal, and often market-driven methods. This infrastructure also reaches out to Catholics working in the film and media industries, encouraging them to express their religious values through their work.

As the evidence I have presented here demonstrates, the Church's attention has shifted from the big screen to television, the Internet, and social media. That said, there is not a single branch of Italy's film industry that is not still influenced by the Church's presence: production, distribution, film festivals, film journals, cinema screens, cinema clubs, film prizes, and university courses all feel the influence of Italy's principal religion.

The Filmmaking Infrastructure of Minority Religions in Italy

In a country in which a single religion has been so all-encompassing, some questions need urgent attention. Is there room in the public space for the religious messages of other religions? Do Italy's minority religions attempt to make their voices heard through the media and through filmmaking, and if so, what obstacles do they face and what kind of support do they receive? Is Italy's government and its indigenous cinema industry aware of the need to reflect the new post-secular, multi-religious reality?

Answering these questions is no easy task. While some research has been undertaken regarding the relations between Italian journalism and Islam, little work has been done thus far on the relations between Italy's minority faiths and the country's filmmaking infrastructure. Current research on migrant cinema might appear a natural place to dig out the answers, given that so many of the non-Catholic filmmakers in Italy are migrants. However, while the academic study of migrants on the Italian big screen is highly developed (see, for example: Andall and Duncan 2005; Parati 2005; Duncan 2008; Grassilli 2008; Russo Bullaro 2010; Ben-Ghiat and Hom 2016; O'Healy 2009, 2010, 2012, 2014, 2015, 2016), this research has focused primarily on race rather than religion, and on the representation of the racial other rather than on filmmaking policies or the production and distribution infrastructure. This means that little of the available secondary material answers the questions I pose above. It is perhaps no surprise that for all the vast outpouring of academic material documenting Italian Catholic media and cinema policy and infrastructure, little parallel work has been done on minority religious cinema. Festival director and film producer Maria Giulia Grassilli (2008) is one of the few to discuss Italy's infrastructure from the perspective of racial minorities. She discusses what she calls the "guerrilla practices" of migrant filmmaking, but once again her emphasis falls on race rather than religion. In their monograph on European production cultures, Petr Szczepanik and Patrick Vonderau (2013) provide insight into diasporic production in Europe, but their attention is not honed on Italy.

There is therefore an abyssal gap in the secondary literature on minority religious filmmaking, even though well over one million people in Italy belong, at least nominally, to other faiths. Some of these people are Italian, but most are first- or second-generation migrants. After Catholicism, the second religion in Italy today is Islam; according to Pew Research Centre estimates (Hackett 2017), Muslims currently account for just over 4.8 per cent of the population (2.87 million people).[3] Islam is followed by Eastern and Oriental Orthodox Christianity, and then by Protestantism (especially Pentecostalism), Jehovah's Witnesses, and Mormons. There are also a smaller number of Buddhists, Hindus, Sikhs, and Jews, who together make up about 1 per cent of the population. What voice these groups collectively have in Italian filmmaking is currently unknown. What *is* clear is that almost all the wide-ranging Catholic cinema and media infrastructure outlined above does not reach them, as it is specific to Catholic interests.

In this section my focus is on Islam, Italy's second religion, for reasons outlined in this book's introduction. Islam is the most visible minority religion in the public sphere. Moreover, like Catholicism, it has a strong proselytizing mission and is therefore invested in occupying public space and circulating its message. One would therefore expect Islam not only to try hardest among minorities to find a voice, but also, due to its association with extremism and terrorism, to struggle the most and to be pushed into alternative "guerrilla" practices. I will begin by outlining the intrinsic and extrinsic obstacles that Islam has faced in joining the Italian media system before moving on to a discussion of the specificities of filmmaking.

Islam is debated in the Italian media primarily by either secular or Catholic interlocutors. Catholicism can, and often does, represent itself across a variety of both mainstream and specialist media platforms; for Islam, direct access to these platforms is sharply limited. Grassilli (2008) notes that journalists of Arab origin have managed to gain visibility in print and television news, and she points to Rula Jebreal and Gad Lerner on La7, Magdi Allam at the *Corriere della sera*, Erfan Rashid on RaiMed, and Khaled Fouad Allam for various newspapers. But the presence of a very limited number of Arabic political commentators does not

---

3 For a series of reasons, it is not easy to find reliable and accurate figures. Massimo Introvigne and PierLuigi Zoccatelli (2006) note that while it is possible to gain an overview of the number of Italians who belong to minority religions, two factors combine to make it more difficult to understand how many migrants belong to other faiths. The first reason the critics provide is that the presence of illegal migrants, whose number is unknown, makes it impossible to accurately estimate how many migrants belong to each faith. Second, one of the two most important sources of information on migrants, Caritas, pays no attention to whether migrants are active or nominal believers, and instead records migrants' religion solely on the basis of the number of believers registered in their country of origin. This necessarily distorts numbers: "quindi se in Marocco si dichiara che i musulmani sono il 99%, la Caritas conterà i musulmani il 99% degli immigrati marocchini, senza considerare quelli che si sono convertiti in Italia o che non hanno nessun rapporto con la religione" [So if in Morocco Muslims make up 99%, Caritas will count as Muslim 99% of Moroccan immigrants, without taking into consideration those who have converted while in Italy or those who have no connection with religion at all] (Introvigne and Zoccatelli 2006).

translate into visibility for Islam: while it is common for the views of the pope and the Catholic hierarchy to be reported and seriously debated in the peninsula's media, it is rare for imams or other religious leaders to be regular interlocutors on mainstream Italian radio and television or in newspapers (Cuciniello 2013). Islam has managed to gain a more persuasive voice on the Internet and in social media, but even then, that voice is fragmented and multiple:

> Si riscontrano, infatti, spazi creati e curati da immigrati, ragazzi di seconda generazione, italiani convertiti, appartenenti a gruppi dichiaratamente sunniti (non solo di origine araba, ma anche turchi e albanesi), sciiti, sufi e ad altri di derivazione islamica (eterodossi), di respiro locale, regionale, nazionale o internazionale. Ma plurali si presentano anche gli scopi, non sempre dichiarati, di queste pagine. Si passa dall'informazione alla divulgazione, dall'utilità sociale al dialogo, da forme non sempre "velate" di proselitismo (quasi sempre in corrispondenza con l'immagine di Gesù nell'islam) ad altre di evidente apologia. (Cuciniello 2013)

> In fact, one discovers spaces that are local, regional, national or international in range and which are created and curated by immigrants, children of the second generation, converted Italians, people who belong to groups which declare themselves Sunni (and not just those of Arabic origin, but also Turks and Albanians), Shi'ite, Sufi, and others of (heterodox) Islamic derivation. But the aims of these pages – aims which are not always declared – are also plural. They range from information to divulgation, from social use to dialogue, from often thinly veiled forms of proselytising (which almost always correspond to the use of the image of Jesus in Islam) to other obvious apologias.

What emerges from any survey of Islamic messages in the media is their paucity, their recency, and their fragmented multiplicity. All of these factors firmly distinguish Islam from its Catholic counterpart. Yahya Pallavicini and Abd al-Karim Turnley note that Islam is "multiraziale, multi-etnica, transnationale and multiculturale" (multiracial, multi-ethnic, transnational and multicultural) (Pallavicini and Turnley 2010, 19), and while the same might be said of Catholicism, the difference between them lies in the level of centralization. The Islamic community has always been decentralized. Catholicism, while also multiple and diverse, has its policies centralized in Vatican documents, and its variegated global voice is ultimately guided by the pope and the clerical hierarchy and by spokesmen within the Vatican. This centring has provided the Catholic Church with a long-standing and relatively coherent voice within the Italian public sphere. If, globally, Islam is a diverse community, James Toronto (2008) contends that it is particularly so in Italy. Toronto argues that Muslim communities in other European countries have typically, and until very recently, come from a restricted set of geographical areas with which the country of destination had ties during Europe's colonial period. Migrants into Italy, by contrast, come from a wide range of geographies: Morocco (about one third), followed in order by Albania, Tunisia, Senegal, Egypt, Bangladesh, Pakistan, Algeria, Bosnia, Iran, Nigeria, Turkey, and Somalia. In addition, Toronto notes that while Sunni Muslims dominate, "every major sect of Islam – Sunni, Shi'ite, and Sufi – and many derivative orders, movements, ideologies, and schools of thought can be found in the tapestry of Italian Islam" (62). This diversity is a stumbling block for the emergence of a forceful Islamic voice across the Italian media; it is also a significant factor in preventing Islam from forming a Concordat with the Italian state that would provide the religion with the benefits and rights associated with formal recognition. Another clear stumbling block is Islam's recent arrival in Italy. While Islam has existed in Italy since ancient times, significant numbers of Muslims have arrived in Italy only recently: the first Muslim migrants began arriving in Italy during the 1960s, but their numbers began to explode only in the 1990s. There have been few converts to Islam in Italy (according to Introvigne and Zoccatelli [2006], approximately ten thousand in 2005), which means that the vast majority of Muslims are first- or second-generation migrants. They are far from fully integrated into their host country and thus lack access to the media infrastructure.

When it comes to filmmaking, it is not just Islam's decentralization, recency, and plurality that raise obstacles to visibility. These factors are compounded by the faith's anti-representational tradition. That tradition, stemming from five verses in the Quran, bans the depiction of humans and other living creatures in Muslim houses (these would encourage a human-centred vision of reality and thus displace God). The distrust of images of the human body points to the fundamental dispute that a believing Muslim has regarding cinema and the visual arts (Kabakebbji 2010).[4] After a late start, the cinema industry has now successfully established itself in all Islamic countries except Saudi Arabia; but the representation of Islamic religion on film continues to present an obstacle. As the case of Egyptian director Youssef Chahine has shown, those who depict Mohammad and the prophets on screen expose themselves to the wrath of fundamentalists.[5] This means that the Catholic Church can capitalize on prime-time televisual depictions of saints and biblical characters, exploiting the lucrative and popular hagiopic genre, while acceptable depictions of Islam have a far more

---

4 There is, nonetheless, a wide range of views about what aspects of bodily representation are permitted: the four juridical schools of Sunni Islam ban only depictions of God, Mohammad, and the prophets, while some extremists contest the use of passport photos (Martini 2010).

5 Martini (2010) notes that Chahine, who is from a Christian family, suffered violent attacks by fundamentalists because he showed the biblical figure of Joseph, an important prophet for Islam, in *The Emigrant* (1994).

restrictive range, largely centred on the world of the faithful. These restrictions on iconographic and narrative material negatively affect Islam's media visibility.

So Islam's visibility is hampered by a range of obstacles internal to its own current ethos and context. But there are also externally imposed obstacles, which flow from an Italian film and media industry that offers very little space for representations of minority religion. Moreover, the spaces in which minority religions are depicted are almost always occupied by Catholic and secular voices. As a consequence, even where minority religions are debated and screened, it is almost never on their own terms. This is especially true of Islam. Cousin and Vitali (2012) contend that the dominant attitude across the media regarding Islam has been crystallized by the Islamophobic presence of Italian journalist Oriana Fallaci (1929–2006) and Egyptian journalist Magdi Allam, who in his post-9/11 writings shifted to an alarmist position in which he condemned both multiculturalism and the "death-dealing essence of Islam" (50). These high-profile Italian media presences were supported, claim Cousin and Vitali (1983), by a series of Forza Italia party organic intellectuals working in journalism, television, and universities as well as by institutional Catholicism, which under Benedict XVI expressed suspicion of and lent limited support to ecumenicalism.[6] The aftermath of Benedict XVI's papacy and of the centre-right Berlusconi era saw a notable shift towards more receptive positions in Italy. Pope Francis (2013–) has taken a decidedly more ecumenical approach that his predecessor and has thus far demonstrated greater openness to Islam. This change in political and religious leadership has gone a small way towards reining in Islamophobia across the media. Nonetheless, Islamophobia dominates the public sphere so strongly that it is hard to see how such a well-established hegemonic position could ever be countered by the raising of splintered voices from the Muslim diaspora. Moreover, unlike Britain and France, Italy lacks a cultural policy to address cultural diversity and support the development of images of migrant others (Grassilli 2008). Most images of Islam, both filmic and in the wider mediasphere, continue to be constructed by Italians without recourse to any official policy. Many of these images, as I will argue in chapter 5, express deep-rooted Islamophobia.

---

6   For more details on Islamophobia in the public sphere, see Bruno Cousin and Tommaso Vitale's chapter on Italian intellectuals and their promotion of Islamophobia in Italy post-9/11 (2012). These authors contend that intellectuals played a significant role in driving Islamophobia in Italy and list Marcello Pera, Gaetano Quagliariello, Father Gianni Biaget Bozzo, and others. Cousin and Vitale also argue that Benedict XVI "strongly limited pluralism within the Catholic Church, becoming known for his authoritarianism, his intransigence concerning orthodoxy, and his reservations about ecumenism and the possibility of shared ethics among the major religions" (53). According to the European Union Agency for Fundamental Rights, in 2009 public and institutional hostility towards Muslims stood at a record high in Western European countries.

Yet some voices do break through into the public sphere and, to use Graziella Parati's terminology (2005), succeed in "talking back" to the destination culture, "recolouring" it. Islam has carved out a certain space online, through a variety of websites and blogs, and offline, through specialist Italian-language magazines such as the *Il messaggero dell'Islam*, *The Muslim*, and the European *Famiglia musulmana*, although the circulation and readership for each of these are limited. A press agency attached to the Università Islamica d'Italia circulates information, debates, and narratives relevant to Islam and the Muslim community. There are also some signs of "talking back" in the film industry. The recent presence of film festivals dedicated to broad religious themes has provided an important distribution outlet, albeit a niche one, for films with minority religious themes. The Fajr Film Festival collaborates with the Casa del cinema in Rome and the Iranian Cultural Embassy to bring Iranian films to Italy. The Casa del cinema also runs an annual Jewish film festival, the Pitigliani Kolno'a Festival. The Med Film Festival brings together a plurality of voices and religious belongings from across Italy, Egypt, Iran, Morocco, Portugal, and the other countries of the Mediterranean region. The Festival del Cinema Interreligioso brings together diverse religions, while Catholic-run film festivals such as the Tertio Millennio Film Festival and the itinerant Religion Today Film Festival, mentioned previously, are open to voices from other religious backgrounds. There are also retrospectives, such as "Cinema e Buddismo," held at the Fondazione Cineteca Italiana in Milan in 2011. The ecumenical juries that are now present at major film festivals like Cannes and Venice, mentioned earlier, also promote visibility for minority religious cinema. There are, however, very few Italian production or distribution companies that specialize in the religious cinema of minorities. Far Out Films, a small Roman company, has a stated mission of promoting films from diverse cultural backgrounds, although this mission is focused on cultural rather than specifically religious diversity. Moreover, some "guerrilla" filmmakers are creating films independently, using personal digital cameras and editing via digital programs like Final Cut (Grassilli 2008). These films and documentaries can then be distributed via Internet platforms like YouTube and Dailymotion or on sites dedicated to minority religious causes. Nonetheless, compared to the Catholic and secular filmmaking ecosystems, with their broad access to the public sphere, the handful of film festivals and tiny production houses can do little to even out the balance.

In the absence of a clear and documented production and distribution network for Islamic filmmaking in Italy, I will demonstrate how, in two individual cases from 2015, filmmakers negotiated routes through an unsympathetic secular/Catholic filmmaking environment into the public sphere. These two cases cannot speak for every film made by minorities; they do, nonetheless, bring to light certain tactics that are employed. The two cases are *Pitza e datteri* (2015), a comedy on Islamic integration by Kurdish Iranian director Fariborz Kamkari, and the documentary *NapolIslam* (2015) by Ernesto Pagano. The latter, although directed by an Italian, gave voice to the Islamic community in Naples, especially Italian converts to Islam, through ethnographic documentary-making techniques.

From an analysis of the production tactics of these two films, several points emerge. First, both directors accessed a production model that is widespread in Italy: the tiny independent company. Kamkari used Adriana Chiesa Enterprises, AKEK, and Far Out Films; Pagano used Ladoc and L'Isola Production. Small production companies that focus on *cinema di qualità* flourish in the Italian production environment, have scope to resist the dominant culture, and typically promote civil values, including those of multiculturalism, besides supporting practices of transnational filmmaking.[7] So these independent production companies are the first important port of call for filmmakers. Second, both filmmakers successfully accessed regional funding: Kamkari applied to the Regione del Veneto and to the Venice Film and Media Fund; *NapolIslam* was part-produced by a Neapolitan company, Ladoc, which prioritizes local Neapolitan material. Rooting films with an international flavour in a very distinct, local environment is a glocal filmmaking tactic, one that provides low-budget films with an important funding source and results in recognizably regional films that emphasize local colour in tandem with international concerns. The third and final route taken by these filmmakers is that of international co-production. Pagano uses this in his accessing of Sky Arte HD. Grassilli has identified this route as one of the most important available to migrant or "accented" (Naficy 2001) cinema. It allowed *NapolIslam* to reach into deeper funding pots and out to wider international audiences.

So alternative production tactics can provide the financing for determined filmmakers to make films foregrounding religious minorities; however, these films can enter the public sphere only by successfully navigating distribution networks. The two films under discussion here accessed a range of such networks. First, they both used the secular art-house circuit, with its archipelago of small cinemas nationwide and its access to national and international film festivals: *NapolIslam* was screened at the Psicologia Film Festival in Turin, the Documentary Film Festival in Amsterdam, and Biografilm, where it won "Best Film." In other words, it accessed the alternative and less commercially oriented

---

7 Tiziana Ferrero-Regis (2009, 23) claims the following about the Italian production environment: "Data collected in 2004 confirm that the majority of Italian production companies are small, artisan-like enterprises, as the companies employing between one and four people constitute 65.4% of the total of production companies ... In a capitalist economy, this small-scale system of production implies that artisanal production 'lies outside the dominant system'" (Pam Cook, cited in Elsaesser 1989, 42).

screening network in Italy, where alternative voices are welcomed. Second, both films accessed religious networks. For *NapolIslam*, this consisted of screenings, often in the open air, to largely Muslim audiences during the month of Ramadan. The less controversial but thought-provoking comedy *Pitza e datteri*, surprisingly perhaps, made it onto the Catholic *sale di comunità* network, where it provided mainly rural and often Catholic audiences a rare glimpse of an Islamic narrative perspective honed on Italy. Finally, each film had a limited run in a small number of commercial cinemas.

There is no triumphalist narrative to be written here. In the main, the avenues available to minority religions for production and distribution are not mainstream, and this has significantly limited their visibility and impact. The reliance on the Catholic *sale di comunità* or religious festival circuits is problematic, especially as the latter, while apparently ecumenical and open, are nonetheless run in large part by Catholics. Also, films about minority religions rely for larger-scale distribution on companies that produce *cinema d'impegno* (politically engaged cinema-making), which, as I have argued elsewhere (Brook 2017), is itself inflected by Catholicism. The mainstream media and cinemas continue to be dominated by messages and images of religious minorities created by secular or Catholic media. However well-meaning these are, they are not sufficiently informed and tend to reproduce stereotypes and, as far as Islam is concerned, phobias. The distribution network is fragile and easily alarmed, especially by Islam. For instance, Italy's biggest cinema chain, UCI, pulled *NapolIslam* from scheduled screenings after the terrorist attacks in Paris in November 2015. Although the screenings were subsequently reinstated, the speed with which a pro-Islamic film was taken out of mainstream circulation demonstrates just how precarious Islam's access to the public sphere really is. International co-productions, transnational film festivals, and low-budget digital filmmaking with online distribution are possible and proven ways to access that sphere. Even so, it is not hard to see why minority religions struggle to find a voice when mainstream avenues used by many Italian filmmakers are in large part closed.

Conclusion: Religious Mobilization

Patrick Eisenlohr (2014) writes that for two key thinkers of the post-secular – Charles Taylor and Taral Asad – the notion of religious mobilization is critical. Indeed, mobilization is key to understanding the very concept of post-secularism. Eisenlohr notes that while Taylor and Asad have different theoretical frames, they come to similar conclusions about the "co-presence of deeply secular and highly salient religious activism and mobilization" (Eisenlohr 2007, 196). For Asad, the nation-state is no longer divinely legitimized; it moulds its citizens through its regulatory framework, and Islamists in Europe must contend with this. For Taylor, religious mobilization is crucial because in an age of "disenchantment," in which religion is no longer required, religions need to distinguish themselves from competing ideological systems in order to attract members. While the reasons the two theorists provide for mobilization differ, both focus on the rise of religious mobilization in a world now dominated by secular discourse.

My research in this chapter suggests that Taylor's and Asad's thinking about the co-presence of religious mobilization and secularization rings true, at least in part, for Italy. At the precise point when the secularization of Italy's public sphere intensified, the apparently inexorable decline of the presence of the peninsula's main religion in the media was unexpectedly halted. During the 1990s, as secularization advanced, Catholic players determinedly turned to the production and distribution of films. They focused especially on filmmaking for television, the medium that attracts the largest audiences.[8] Since then, producers like Lux Vide have forcefully entered both RAI and Mediaset, and the infrastructure for Catholic filmmaking has expanded and transformed as new festivals, university courses, retrospectives, and forums for debate emerge. Lux Vide now occupies the top position in the public broadcaster's (RAI) fiction scheduling, attracting 15 per cent of RAI's fiction investment and 20 per cent of its audience share (Fontanarosa 2016). Its success has strongly influenced the secular production company Taodue, which has copied Lux Vide's formula by producing its own religious fictions for Mediaset. The twenty-first-century shift towards Catholic-oriented series and miniseries, documentaries, and news items for state television, as well as for Silvio Berlusconi's Mediaset and independent Catholic television stations, has caught some commentators by surprise. It implies that Catholicism has an exceptional position in Italy's public sphere. It is unlikely that this is a coincidence. It seems that, faced with the ever-receding space for religion in the public sphere, the Church is engaged in a determined mobilization. Ellen E. Moore's analysis of the media system in the United States does not therefore hold for the Italian peninsula. Moore argues that Evangelical Christians in North America find themselves in the rather fragile position of repeatedly "reframing secular media to have a religious message" (2017, 124). However, on Italian television, Catholic players have recently gained the power to actively frame the media. They have been busy developing an active position, one with far greater leverage.

So Catholic mobilization shifted up a gear as the millennium approached. Islam, meanwhile, has attained only the tiniest, most fragile foothold in Italy's mediasphere. Nor is it easy to see how it could occupy a more substantial position, given the number of impediments it faces: the absence of its own

---

8   In 2015 only 49.7 per cent of people had attended the cinema, compared to 92.2 per cent who habitually watched TV (ISTAT 2017).

production and distribution network, internal religious differences, Islam's ambivalent views of the use of religious images, and the lack of proactive support from the Italian media hierarchy. As a result, most filmic portrayals of Islam in Italy are constructed by non-Muslims, with inevitable consequences for what is, and can be, shown, as I will discuss in chapter 5. While early signs of openings for minority religions are now beginning to be seen, these fade into insignificance when compared to the opening that Catholicism has long enjoyed. As far as filmmaking on the part of minority religions is concerned, there is still nothing that can possibly be termed mainstream mobilization in Italy. Minority religions need to find ways to mobilize if they are to find a voice for themselves and not be left simply reframing secular and Catholic messages.

It remains to be seen what the future will bring. Twenty-first-century changes, such as the launch in 2004 of digital terrestrial television, which introduced a range of new channels, and the growth of satellite pay TV now monopolized by Rupert Murdoch's secular Sky-Italia (95.3 per cent of satellite market share in 2012), have shifted patterns of consumption (Noam 2016). There has been a recent shift towards a model of global secularization shaped by Sky-Italia and Netflix. This has been flanked by the rise of new modes of access to films through mobile devices. All of this affects, and will continue to influence, what is, and can be, consumed. It also affects *how* it is consumed. Italy's increased dependence on the Internet and on global producers of fiction is altering the context in which religion circulates on the peninsula. This presents new opportunities and challenges for the peninsula's faith groups. However, Italy's religions will need to be agile if they are not to fall back into peripheral spaces in an emerging global market in which Catholics do not wield the extraordinary control they wield in Italy.

2 The Persistence of Religion on Screen: Icons, Rituals, and the Arts

Introduction: The Post-Secular Persistence of On-Screen Catholicism

The sheer quantity of priests, monks, saints, bishops, popes, and Christs who still pace across Italian big and small screens will come as a surprise to some people. Given the Catholic Church's influence over television, revealed in the previous chapter, we might expect these characters to be concentrated in Lux Vide's productions for the small screen. Nothing is further from the truth. Catholic-produced series and miniseries for the small screen do, of course, play a significant part in ensuring that religious iconography circulates in Italy's public sphere. The long-running and popular prime-time crime series *Don Matteo* made by Lux Vide (2000–present), for instance, features a priest in the title role. Moreover, a glut of hagiopics, again largely produced by Lux Vide, successfully fill key viewing slots: these include *Don Gnocchi: L'angelo dei bambini* (2004), *Don Bosco* (2004), *La buona battaglia: Don Pietro Pappagallo* (2006), *L'uomo della carità: Don Luigi di Liegro* (2007), *Don Zeno – L'uomo di Nomadelfia* (2008), *Santa Barbara* (2012), and *Francesco* (2014). However, some of the most iconic recent performances have not been produced by Catholic production companies. Jude Law's performance as Pope Pius XIII in Sorrentino's television series *The Young Pope* (2017) was transmitted by the global and secular Sky Television. The octogenarian pope in Nanni Moretti's *Habemus Papam* (2011) and the iconic monk played by Toni Servillo in Roberto Andò's *Le confessioni* (The Confessions, 2016) appeared in films that were co-produced by small, independent Italian producers alongside RAI and secular European television channels (Canal+; France 3 Cinéma).

What is immediately evident is that there is no necessary and close link between Catholic production and Catholic iconography. Nor, as I will argue in this chapter, are personal faith and Catholic iconography synonymous. The secular outlook of production houses and the agnostic, anticlerical, or atheist positions of directors have not blocked Catholic figures from appearing in droves on the big screen. These range from the old priest in Ermanno Olmi's *Il villaggio di cartone* (The Cardboard Village, 2011) to the Sardinian Christ in Giovanni Columbu's *Su re* (The King, 2012); from a young Pope Francis in Daniele Luchetti's *Chiamatemi Francesco: Il papa della gente* (Call me Francesco, 2015) to Pope Benedict XVI in Stefano Sollima's *Suburra* (2015). Striking too are the vast numbers of cupolas, pious paintings, sacred sculptures, crosses, and religious processions that crowd the mise en scène of so many twenty-first-century Italian films. To mention just a few, we have the mysterious Venetian monastery in Saverio Constanzo's *In memoria di me* (In Memory of Me, 2007), the rural church in Giorgio Diritti's *L'uomo che verrà* (The Man Who Will Come, 2009), the baroque façade dominating a Sicilian piazza in Roberto Faenza's *Alla luce del sole* (Come into the Light, 2005), the concluding funeral procession in Marco Tullio Giordano's *I cento passi* (One Hundred Steps, 2000), the mystery play in *La scomparsa di Patò* (The Vanishing of Patò, 2010) and the mother-Madonna in Marco Bellocchio's *L'ora di religione* (My Mother's Smile, 2002). Except for *Su re*, which was co-produced by the Pontificia Facoltà Teologica della Sardegna, the production houses for these films are secular; they include big entertainment producers like Medusa Film, Sky, and Taodue as well as independent producers (Filmalbatros; Mikado Film; Aranciafilm) and television (Rai Cinemafiction; Tele+; Mediaset). Catholic imagery has wide circulation on both secular and religious circuits. In no sense, then, are Catholic themes and iconography being censored, curtailed, or restricted by Italian secular production forces.

Striking too is the breadth of Catholic iconography. It crosses swathes of genres, from the television hagiopic to thrillers and crime fiction, from undemanding sentimental comedy to melodrama and horror, and from lavish costume drama to low-budget experimental film. Its tonal range encompasses light entertainment, middlebrow *cinema di qualità*, and complex art-house offerings. Nor can it be argued that it is just the old guard of Italy's directors who are hooked, having grown up in a more religious time: young directors have also been discovering it. There are no corners of Italy's film production that this iconography does not reach. Even romantic comedies and *cinepanettoni* (Christmas films) occasionally light upon it. The sentimental comedy *Si accettano miracoli* (Alessandro Siani, 2015) and Neri Parenti's Christmas film *Colpi di fulmine* (Lightning Strike, 2012), are clear examples of this. The visual dominance of Catholicism across Italy's film production is especially striking when compared with other European countries and the United States, where such elevated levels of visual saturation are inconceivable. Unsurprisingly, as indicated in the last chapter, Catholicism eclipses the other religions on the peninsula, which struggle to emerge. The continued dominance of Catholic iconography in contemporary Italian cinema confounds the secularism thesis that predicted that religion would abandon the public sphere. In Italy there is little sign of Catholic imagery losing its foothold and retreating into a private world.

The Catholic Church is a great purveyor of spectacle. With its rites and rituals, its sumptuous settings and its icons, it embraces the visual. It roots the invisibility and immateriality of spirit in the materiality of the seen. In this chapter I argue that under the surface of even the most anticlerical filmmaking, the spectacular nature of Catholicism acts as a lure. It lures even the most hardened of its critics – filmmakers like Marco Bellocchio, who has attacked the Church throughout his filmmaking career, and Nanni Moretti and Alice Rohrwacher, both of whom are professed atheists. It is precisely, and perhaps ironically, through the filmmaking of agnostics, atheists, and anticlerical directors – directors who question the very imagery they put on screen – that Catholic imagery continues to circulate.

The questions this chapter attempts to answer are as follows: Why do so many religious icons, rituals, and settings persist on Italian screens? And what do they collectively say about how religious imagery circulates in Italy's public sphere? The persistance of a certain spectacular Catholic imaginary in Italian cinema is not necessarily a sign of the persistence of Catholicism as religious practice; it does, though, point to the extraordinary symbolic power of its visual presence and legacy. In this chapter I set out to uncover the source of the iconographic lure by exploring two forms of Catholic imagery: the icon and the religious ritual. The static characteristics of the former reflect the art of painting and the photographic close-up. Ritual, by contrast, is operatic, theatrical, and deeply cinematographic. The ways in which icon and ritual function on screen point to their roots in the plastic and performance arts, respectively. I argue here that the relations between icon and ritual and these two categories of the arts facilitate the continuing circulation of religious imagery in the public sphere. This chapter concentrates on films made by directors who either define themselves as atheist (Marco Bellocchio; Nanni Moretti) or agnostic (Paolo Sorrentino) or, while believing, have taken up positions against the institution of the Church (Ermanno Olmi). I have chosen films made by some of Italy's most religiously resistant directors in order to test the hypothesis that the visual nature of Catholicism provides an almost irresistible "lure." If even these filmmakers can be lured by this imagery, then its hold on Italian society is deep and assured.

The Spectacular Icon and Italy's Plastic Arts

Several contemporary Italian films fix the camera on a religious icon that appears to captivate and enthrall it. In this section I examine three such icons: the mother-Madonna in Marco Bellocchio's *L'ora di religione* (2002), the cross in Ermanno Olmi's *Il villaggio di cartone*, and the iconic pope in Paolo Sorrentino's *The Young Pope* (2017). My aim is not to provide a definitive reading of the meaning of each of these icons but rather to investigate what might have attracted a sceptical, contemporary camera eye to its visual surface. Each one fulfils Martin Kemp's (2011) contemporary definition of an icon as an object both memorable and exceptionally well-known. Each defies the nature of contemporary cinematography by requiring the camera to be still and to fix on a single object of contemplation. In so doing, the camera aligns itself with the photographed or painted picture over cinema's fluid and moving image.

In Bellocchio's *L'ora di religione*, a bourgeois Roman family contrives to have their murdered mother declared a saint in order to cement their position in society. They falsify miracles, indoctrinate family members, create elaborate publicity materials, and present their case to the Vatican. The protagonist, Ernesto Picciafuoco (played by Sergio Castellito), is the last of the siblings to know of the plot. He discovers it only when a mysterious emissary of the Vatican knocks on the door of his studio. Ernesto, the film's focalizer, is an artist and atheist and steadfastly refuses to engage with his family's scheme. It is through his sceptical eyes that we learn his mother was not a saintly martyr but a "finta martire e reale assassina" (fake martyr and real assassin) (Cruciani 2003, 19). Her emotional coldness drove one of her four sons mad, and it was this madness that resulted in her murder.

It is the film's construction and deconstruction of the beatification campaign's images that is of interest to my argument here. As Ernesto investigates the family's mysterious plot, he visits his aunt's aristocratic residence. It is she who has designed the family's elaborate public relations strategy. Upstairs, he is met by an overwhelming icon of his mother's face, the epitome of an empty sign. Ernesto gazes up at a vast, surreal photographic print of his mother that has been stretched out on a canvas across the French windows and that now, although still, stirs mysteriously in the air, as if animated. The female face, unadorned by kohl or mascara, signals the world of early modern art and creates a classic image of the sacred beyond the trappings of the material and the modern. The film positions this portrait within Catholic artistic iconography: the ambiguous smile mirrors that of Leonardo da Vinci's Madonnas and so sets up an explicit analogy between the earthly mother and the mother of God.

Bellocchio is not playing things straight here. In this scene, the filmmaker has taken an iconic image and deconstructed it, showing just how charismatic religious images can be even while revealing them as fraudulent. He is questioning and satirizing the Marian cult, with its idealization of an undifferentiated icon of the mother as good, pure, and *sine macula*, an idealization that – according to the film – is as deceptive as the photo shoots and paintings produced by the family to promote the case for beatification. The gigantic canvas points to the Baudrillardian interpretation of spectacle as dealing "with the human in inhuman ways" (Kershaw 2003, 594). In other words, it acts as a great canvas on which to address the complex relation between mother and son in one potent and transcendent visual symbol. The image of the mother is framed so as to engulf the cinema screen, emphasizing the mother's dominance over her son: she stares past him towards the spectator, overlooking him entirely. This image is beautiful and charismatic but ultimately fraudulent. The scene highlights the lure of the religious icon while simultaneously pointing to its role as an unreliable narrator of the human relationships it reifies. The real mother-son relationship is not captured in the idealized relationship of Madonna and child that has been enshrined through centuries of papal documents and Italian painting.

What emerges from this scene is the aligning of two processes usually seen as distinct – the creation of images for the cinema, and the creation of images for the Catholic Church. Given that Ernesto has just witnessed a photoshoot downstairs in which the scene of his mother's murder is re-created by the photographer in the style of a Baroque painting of martyrdom, complete with fake blood and the urging of the actress to feign a "sorriso da santo" (saintly smile), the film is underscoring the meta-artistic process of image creation. Indeed, the icon of the mother-Madonna dominates Ernesto in precisely the same way that the cinema image dominates the spectator in the cinema space, a parallel that seems explicitly to forge a link between the processes of filmmaking and the creation of religious images. The mythmaking process of the Church is being aligned with the artistic process of image-making. Art and religion here share the process of creating visual material from abstract or elusive matter. They share the aspiration of making the intangible tangible and so need images for their very existence. These scenes show that the Church, the camera, and the plastic arts all have the capacity to enlarge images into universal, still, outsized forms, and that this size, alongside their apparent universality, renders them potent and charismatic whether they are true or not. The intense, still, frontal close-up of a face, which has its roots in devotional medieval iconography, is here absorbed into the medium of cinema and reflected back to its audience as an enormous, fraudulent presence. So in this film, Bellocchio both questions the validity and truth of the religious icon and shows how it comes to have power over those whom it visually dominates.

In the second illustration – Ermanno Olmi's *Il villaggio di cartone* – another religious icon is captured, and held, by the filmmaker's gaze. Again, the camera becomes transfixed by its lure. This film tells the tale of an old priest whose plain, post-conciliar church has been deconsecrated, its interior brutally dismantled, and the space reinstated as a shelter for migrants caught in an ill-defined war. The film provocatively attacks the institution of the Church, positing it as decaying and irrelevant to an emerging multicultural Italy. However, it repeatedly exposes a deeply submerged attachment to Catholic icons, which, however irrelevant and outdated, are nonetheless full of pathos.

The attraction to the icon can be seen in the film's opening scene, in which a large crucifix is taken down from its dominant position above the altar. The aerial cross is captured initially in a long-shot, entangled in a crane that lowers it to the ground. It is, in other words, an object to be removed from a deconsecrated church like any other. However, as the camera zooms in to provide a close-up of the downcast face of Christ, the cold blue light catching bleakly on the crown of thorns, the sequence reveals its nostalgia for the loss of this central icon of Christianity. This visual effect is supported by the soundtrack, in which the metallic clanks of a building site are slowly supplanted with the deeply nostalgic pealing of church bells. By the time the African migrants flood into the sheltering church, the Christian iconography has been dismantled. The migrants replace it with a new iconography: the cardboard boxes with which they form a temporary shelter inside the church's protective walls.

On the surface, then, Olmi dismantles the cross – a sacred, long-standing Western icon of suffering and redemption – and replaces it with a cardboard box, which provides a contemporary image of suffering and fragile salvation. An icon representing two thousand years of European history, with its roots embedded in centuries of Italian art, has been replaced by an *objet trouvé*. Centuries of sacred sculpture have been set aside for a piece of secular twentieth-century conceptual art that references today's homeless people. What is significant about this is not so much the dismantling and replacement of an icon, but the failure of its substitution. Christian iconography continues to exercise power in the film despite being explicitly deconstructed in the opening scene. Later, almost inevitably, the repressed returns. A migrant gives birth to a baby within the walls of the sheltering church, and she goes to see the priest. At this point, the film explicitly draws on iconography of the Christian nativity scene, which is emphasized in the posture of the black mother as she cradles her child. The scene interpellates Italian Renaissance religious art and reproposes it for a twenty-first-century multicultural world, in much the same way that Paul Gauguin reproposed the Madonna and child with his once-controversial painting *Hail Mary* (1891), in which the characters are depicted as Tahitian. In other words, Catholic iconography though questioned is never abandoned. Moreover, while Olmi shows nothing of the migrant's religion, which is, by implication, Islam,[1] his referencing of the nativity collocates the migrants within a Christian iconographic universe.

The alternative to the religious icon the film proposes – a cardboard box – proves to be inadequate: it possesses neither the long artistic legacy nor the striking uniqueness necessary for attaining auratic power. Ultimately, the movie camera decentres both Islam and alternative secular iconography

---

1   While one of the film's migrants is shown preparing a terrorist attack, which implicitly links him to Islamic terrorists, there are no indications of an Islamic belief system. Islamic beliefs are reduced to politico-religious terrorism, while Christian belief is the subject of fascination and attention.

(the cardboard box), while Catholic iconography remains firmly if sometimes subterraneously at its heart. Marian iconography and the symbol of the sheltering church, do, ultimately, provide an answer: together they propose a Church that can still protect its flock. While the film's message appears iconoclastic (for Italy to modernize, Christian icons must be challenged and dismantled), it turns out that preventing the icons from returning to circulation is impossible.

My final illustration is Jude Law's performance as Pope Pius XIII in Sorrentino's *The Young Pope*. Taken from Episode 5 of the US Sky series, the much-cited "Sexy and I Know It" scene playfully shows the self-conscious construction of a pope as the icon of the Church. To LMFAO's musical track, which provides a humorous and iconoclastic commentary on the visual display, Pope Pius XIII dramatically dresses. Lenny Belardo had begun his pontificate dressed in contemporary papal garb. However, as his increasingly traditional perspectives emerge, and in preparation for his long-awaited speech to the cardinals, he re-creates himself in the likeness of a medieval pope, with embroidered slippers, an ornate red mantum, gloves, and heavy rings. As a final touch, he places on his own head a flamboyant tiara last worn by Pope Paul VI (1963–78) and recreated for the scene by one of Italy's greatest costume designers, Carlo Poggioli (Zucherman 2017). In a pop-video-like montage that lasts little more than a minute, the pope undergoes an extraordinary transformation from a handsome, bare-torsoed actor to an iconic figure of a pope, a figure that could have stepped out of a painting by Giotto or Raphael, the artists who inspired Sorrentino's vision (Zucherman 2017). The dressing scene brings together consumer choice, American rap, sacred Italian art, and fashion (indeed, Jude Law went on to model Catholic-inspired fashion for Dolce & Gabbana's Fall 2017 season). Like Bellocchio's Madonna-mother scene, it exposes the processes of icon-making and the way contemporary icons are bound up with public relations strategies and consumerism.

The scene that follows, however, drops the humour associated with the meta-artistic creation of the icon. The exhibition of the icon becomes deadly serious. Held high, transported on the papal litter into the Sistine Chapel, his body still, his face impassive, and his gaze firmly tilted up towards Leonardo da Vinci's magnificent ceiling, Pope Pius XIII gains the static look of an icon whose mystery induces awe and fear. His entrance is accompanied by John Tavener's moving "Song for Athene," which merges twentieth-century lyrics, written by an Orthodox nun, with an *a cappella* Byzantium soundscape. The sound world and the iconography fuse to create an emblem of the pope as terrestrial prince and godlike leader: an emblem of symbolic power, in other words. The anachronistic, medievalized pope joins together art and religion: nothing is left of his human form except his emotionless face. The rest of him is a static, embroidered, and jewel-encrusted artwork. Art and religion have swallowed his human form. He is the auratic icon.

This self-consciously created icon inspires awe in the upturned faces of the cardinals who witness Belardo's transformation. In an instant, the spectator is transported back from the world of twenty-first-century fashion to a pre-conciliar, pre-Enlightenment world in which the pope acts as a sublime emperor and the cardinals are his subjects. Indeed, these cardinals will now be required to bow and kiss his pointed shoe. As the doors to the Sistine Chapel are thrown open, the spectator is plunged into a world in which premodern sentiments of awe and mystery are reawakened. To use Charles Taylor's terminology, the television series, in an unexpected twist, now turns to re-enchanting the world. While *L'ora di religione* retains an ironic and distanced focalizer (Ernesto Picciafuoco), and by so doing maintains the lure of the Catholic Church at an almost safe distance, here, unexpectedly, the series capitulates, and screens all the uneasy, premodern and undemocratic pleasures of enchantment. From this point on, it becomes increasingly clear that Pope Pius XIII *can* perform miracles. While ultimately the enchanted medieval pope conjured in this scene is set aside as too anachronistic and fundamentalist to provide an answer, the enchantment awakened in this scene remains a key trope for the rest of the series. In fact, one question this series poses is what would happen if a church that has sidelined enchantment in favour of the pope's proximity to the flock (as embodied by a pope like Pope Francis) were to reach back into pre-conciliar tradition in order to reappropriate mystery. What, asks the series, would the Church's place in the public sphere be then?

It should now be clear that icons provide a striking lure to three of the most important auteurs working in the contemporary Italian film industry: Marco Bellocchio, Ermanno Olmi, and Paolo Sorrentino. In each of the films discussed above, the camera pauses to gaze upon a religious image, suspending the sense of movement that defines the very medium of cinema and applying the frontal camera work used by Pasolini, Carl Theodor Dreyer, and others as a sign of the sacred. Neither exposing the construction of an icon (Bellocchio, Sorrentino) nor dismantling it (Olmi) diminishes the icon's power. While Bellocchio keeps the icon at a safe distance through an atheist focalizer, Olmi's tormented priest still desperately desires it and Sorrentino's Pope Belardo is so entranced by it as to actually become it, embodying the inaccessibility and mystery of a church without Vatican II.

The question that then arises is why this iconography presents such a strong lure, particularly among the most sceptical and questioning of directors. In answering this, I beg to differ from critics such as Stewart Hoover (2006) and Stig Hjarvard (2011), who argue that the deployment of religious imagery in secular cinema and media is straightforwardly superficial and banal. It does not draw spectators to God, they argue, and its spectacle is reductive and simplistic. This is not necessarily the case in Italy, nor is it quite the point. It is true that religious icons in Italian cinema can be, and are, employed in a stereotyped way, serving as a denotative shortcut, an easily accessible metonymy. However, while this is *among* the functions of cinematic religious images, any reading that suggests this is *always* the case misses the complexity in works that deploy such imagery. It also misses the contemporary questioning and remediation of these icons in Italy, a process that is far from simple or simplistic and that raises important questions about the continuing place of religious iconography in a public sphere that is not as secular as might be expected.

The first explanation I offer here for the camera's attachment is that religious icons provide filmmakers with large, luminous images that are more intense than those in everyday reality and that they provide material images to convey complex human realities. Christ's suffering on the cross presents the message that salvation is possible for those in distress, especially among the underprivileged social and economical social strata (Weber 1978); the icon of a pope reflects the human aspiration to the enchanted life and provides a striking image of a contemporary but timeless spiritual guide; Marian iconography reflects and rediscovers maternal and filial love and the value of maternity. Filmic images rooted in icons of the Madonna, the crucifix, or the pope therefore harbour meanings that have a wide resonance within the national frameworks in which they have long survived. To survive they must have continued to provide meaningful material images to convey complex, invisible, or ungraspable ideas and emotions. That all icons would suddenly fall into disuse is inconceivable, even if their religious signifieds were to be found false or fraudulent. As André Malraux explains, "[u]ne civilisation qui rompt avec le style dont elle dispose, se trouve en face du néant" (a civilization which breaks with the style to which it has access, finds itself in the face of nothingness) (2004, 498). Images, then, survive not just because they belong to the religion that promotes them but also because they re-present religious ideas in human frames that continue to be meaningful in mass culture. These icons carry within them the power of myth, which provides a universal frame for individual human stories. This is essential to the process of filmmaking. As Malraux explains: "Le cinema s'adresse aux masses, et les masses aiment le mythe, en bien et en mal. Le mythe commence à Fantômes, mais il finit au Christ" (Cinema addresses the masses, and the masses love myth, for better or for worse. Myth begins with phantoms, but it ends with Christ) (2004, 16).

Malraux's reading has a great deal of truth to it, but it does not go far enough in explaining why icons have retained their power in Italian filmmaking while they have lost their centrality in other Western nations. This can only be explained by exploring a further, and key, point: the legacy of Italy's visual arts in the peninsula's cultural identification with Catholicism. The plastic arts, which have long been "an inexhaustible spring for artistic creation" (Weber 1978, 608), have provided contemporary filmmakers with a visual toolbox full of images. The works of the golden ages of Italian art (late medieval, Renaissance, and baroque especially) are infused with religious imagery, and these works form part of Italians' sense of national belonging (Janni and McLean 2003): Giotto, Masaccio, Leonardo da Vinci, Michelangelo, and Caravaggio are part of the fabric of Italian education and the shared national cultural frame of reference. That over several centuries, Catholicism was woven so intensely into the country's artistic fabric means there is a significant national body of artworks ripe for reworking and remediating. Pier Paolo Pasolini's mid-century use of religious iconography has been widely commented upon as if it were in some way anomalous. This is not the case. In the twenty-first century, iconic Italian paintings are still being remediated in Italian cinema: Masaccio's *Dead Christ* has been reworked not just in Pasolini's *Mamma Roma* (1962) but in Roberto Andò's *Le confessioni* (2016); Leonardo da Vinci's Madonnas are visually cited and reworked in *L'ora di religione*; Leonardo da Vinci travels as a subtext in *The Young Pope* (as reflected in Lenny Belardo's name), and Giotto and Raphael underpin the iconography of Pope Pius XIII. Relics and artworks are foregrounded iconographically across many contemporary films. They attain so much power that they can set plots or subplots in motion: a stolen relic of a saint's tongue sets in play the comic plot in Carlo Mazzacurati's *La lingua del santo* (Holy Tongue, 2000); the search for a *croce figurativa* (figurative cross) forms the subplot in Alice Rohrwacher's *Corpo celeste* (Heavenly Body, 2011); the weeping statue of Saint Thomas provides the plot's fulcrum in Alessandro Siani's *Si accettano miracoli* (2015).

What is unique to Italy, then, is the continued contemporary engagement with a Catholic treasure trove of material objects and the plastic arts – relics, sculptures, painting – through their remediation. In the Italian world of arthouse cinema especially, this remediation is tightly interwoven with a process of deconstruction and re-presentation of the iconographic work. This self-conscious grappling with religious images on screen has been present in Italian filmmaking at least since Pasolini's "La ricotta" (1963). "La ricotta" is, of course, the cinematic urtext for the remediation of religious iconography. In it, a film troupe attempts to re-create through cinema two Mannerist depositions of Christ (by Pontormo and Rosso Fiorentino respectively) by keeping perfectly motionless while decrying their lines. The attempt is marked by struggle and failure, and finally one of the "paintings" giddily collapses.[2] "La ricotta" – and

---

2 In "La ricotta," Pasolini emphasizes the struggle created by the effort required to remediate images. Pasolini's intermediality is explicit, deliberate, and personal. In an interview for *Il Giorno* in 1962, he says,

> Il mio gusto cinematografico non è di origine cinematografica, ma figurativa. Quello che io ho in testa come visione, come campo visivo, sono gli affreschi di Masaccio, di Giotto – che sono i pittori che amo di più, assieme a certi manieristi (per esempio il Pontormo). E non riesco a concepire immagini, paesaggi, composizioni di figure al di fuori di questa mia iniziale passione pittorica.

Pasolini's cinema more widely – is haunted by the static and sacred plastic art forms he loved. He repeatedly struggled to bring the motionless, sacred auratic form into a moving picture that, according to Walter Benjamin (1936), lacks the aura.

Like "La ricotta," the three cases I have described above demonstrate how the remediation of art forms undergoes a process of postmodern questioning, deconstruction, and re-presentation. This is a telling sign of the post-secular, of a recognition that both the place of religious icons in the public sphere, and that of the still icon in the ceaseless movement of a film, are under question. In each of the examples above (the Madonna, the cross, and the pope), the remediated icon is revealed as real only to the extent that it is performed in the public sphere. This construction and performance of the religious icon plays out differently in each of my examples here: it is dealt a cynical card in Bellocchio's film; it is playful in Sorrentino's and nostalgic in Olmi's. But despite the overt critique of its constructed nature, its irrelevance or fraudulence, in none of the three films does the religious icon lose its aura. Perplexingly for *The Young Pope*'s viewers, the construction of a pope as fashion icon does not lead to the emptying out of the religious sign seen in Italian cinema's other famous religious fashion show: the clerical catwalk in Fellini's *Roma* (1972). Instead, as the miniseries developed from week to week the pope-sign was revealed as increasingly complex; by the final episode, in a thoroughly post-secular twist, it was shown to be inhabited by mysterious, unearthly, and saintly powers – fraudulence, performance, and mystery co-exist.

The triangulation between a powerful static icon, its dynamic mantling and dismantling, and its circulation within a late-capitalist *habitus* (where it comfortably rubs shoulders with secular public relations campaigns and fashion parades) signals the post-secular. Bellocchio's, Sorrentino's, and Olmi's icons are emblematic of the cohabitation of the secular and the religious within the

---

My cinematographic taste is not of cinematographic origin, but figurative. What I have in my head, as a vision, as a visual field, are the frescos of Masaccio, Giotto – who are the painters I love the most, together with certain mannerists, like Pontormo, for example. And I am unable to conceive of images, landscapes, compositions of images, outside this original painterly passion of mine. (quoted in Rumble 1996, 16)

In this scene, the director's striving for the external vestments of piety appears forced and unnatural. Only when Christ is dropped and the *tableau vivant* collapses do the actors finally come to life. Their laughter is rich and whole-hearted; their piety is not. From this perspective, "La ricotta" is about the performance of religious identity in Italy and the detachment of that performance from the reality of the personal feelings and social roles of the poor of Rome's suburbs. Their performance of piety is imposed on them; it is not a natural expression of their selfhood or experience. In Pasolini's reading these people are not cynical post-Christians, but *pre*-Christian. They cannot perform Christianity because they do not *know* Christianity.

public sphere. The agnostic, aesthetic, and anticlerical questioning that underlies these films paradoxically permits icons to continue to circulate.

Catholic Spectacle: Rituals and the Art of Performance

I turn now from the religious icon to the performance of religious rituals, sacraments, and festivals in contemporary Italian cinema. The difference between a spectacular icon and a spectacular ritual or sacrament inheres in a shift from a single shot to a scene, from an individual auratic image to an image of the collective, from the static object to the sacred-in-motion, and from the plastic to the performance arts. This shift is not insignificant. Many critics interpret the cinematic close-up (Botta and Prinzivalli 2010) and the fixity of the image (Schrader 1972; Brent Plate 2008) as the ultimate expression of the sacred. The shift away from the still photographic image to a moving sequence will thus affect how the sequence functions and is received.

From the screening of religious weddings (*Il regista di matrimoni*; *Io e lei*; *Manuale d'amore 2*), to funerals (*La stanza del figlio*; *I cento passi*), from the inauguration – or not – of a pope (*Habemus Papam*; *The Young Pope*) to local religious festivals (*Il regista di matrimoni*; *Corpo celeste*; *Alla luce del sole*; *Amiche da morire*), from the mass (*Manuale d'amore 2*; *Il villaggio di cartone*; *I banchieri di Dio*) to the confession (*Le confessioni*; *Il divo*), Italian cinema returns to the spectacular rites and rituals of Catholicism across a wide range of filmic genres. Even where the spectacle is dismissed or undermined – as is the case, for instance, with the Catholic funeral imposed on the family in Moretti's *La stanza del figlio* (The Son's Room, 2001), and the pathetic religious festival in *Corpo celeste* – the ostensible dismissal only serves to emphasize the centrality of the ritual itself. This is a largely Catholic phenomenon on Italian screens; only very occasionally – and very briefly – are the rituals of minority faiths screened, and these are usually peripheral to the plot. The Hare Krishna procession in Moretti's *La stanza del figlio* occupies just fifty-three seconds of screen time, for instance, before vanishing without a trace. In Renzo Martinelli's *Il mercante di pietre* (The Stone Merchant, 2006), a sufi whirling dance is observed by an Italian couple during their holiday in Turkey, but no further reference to it is made. In Bellocchio's *Fai bei sogni* (Sweet Dreams, 2016) Buddhist chanting occupies a similarly reduced space and is incidental to the plot. While there are exceptions (see chapter 5), rituals practised by minority religions are most often peripheral to the plot, exotic, anecdotal, and quickly set aside. Ritual in Italian films is, in other words, overwhelmingly Catholo-centric.

To provide some concrete examples of religious spectacle as performance, I will take the papal balcony scenes found in Sorrentino's *The Young Pope* and Moretti's *Habemus Papam*. In both, the dominance of the spectacular elements of Catholic ritual and performance becomes explicit. Both the film and the miniseries deliberately signal theatrical motifs and reserve a central symbolic place for the dialogue between balcony and piazza, between stage and stalls. Both point to the inherent theatricality of the interplay of pope and public and problematize the ensuing show.

In Moretti's film, the balcony scene appears twice. On the first occasion, the elderly and recently elected pope approaches the heavy red curtains of the balcony-stage and hears the thundering cheers rising from the crowd below. As he waits in the wings to go onstage he suffers an extreme attack of something that resembles stage fright and cries, "non ce la faccio!" (I can't do it!), before making a hurried and breathless exit from the scene. In the final scene of the film, the interplay of balcony and piazza is repeated. This time the pope steps out onto the balcony only to reject the role thrust upon him, creating an apocalyptic scenario that shows the collapse of ecclesiastical leadership and perhaps of the entire Church.

In *The Young Pope*, the balcony scene is repeatedly and almost obsessively rehearsed and revisited until the film's final scene. We first see it in Episode 1, when a dream sequence colours it in demonic and apocalyptic tones. The young, assured, and confident Pope Pius XIII steps forward onto the balcony, through the heavy theatrical curtain, to face the cheering crowd. After performing a dramatic meteorological miracle, he delivers a blasting "What have we forgotten?" speech in favour of masturbation, gay marriage, nuns reciting mass, and – in short – absolute freedom, to the horror of all those assembled. In his second balcony appearance, the pope is backlit so that his face cannot be seen by the assembled crowd in the square below. He resumes the dreamt "What have we forgotten" speech but takes a distinctly different approach. This time, he accuses his again horrified audience of having forgotten God. He fractures the modern connection between pope and believer-spectator by stating that he is close to God but will never be close to his people. In his third appearance, during Episode 8, he takes a pre-conciliar stance and stands with his back to St Peter's Square, intoning the mass in Latin. The square is virtually empty, apart from a few members of the media flicking through magazines as he recites. He has lost his audience. After an interlude in Africa during which he refuses to appear on stage, but instead projects his voice acousmatically into the arena, astounding his public, the long-deferred "normal" public address takes place. The final scene of the ten-episode series sees the pope facing his real audience and addressing them frontally, in the vernacular and from his heart. It ends with him collapsing on the ground, ostensibly breathing his last. In other words, finally, he becomes the role, and the embodiment is so intense and perfect that it not only succeeds in conjuring the ghostly parents, who had abandoned him in childhood, but also thrusts him to the ground.

If *Habemus Papam* deals with the balcony in terms of stage fright and the refusal of a role imposed by others, *The Young Pope* envisages the balcony as a series of dress rehearsals, as Pope Pius XIII gradually negotiates the steps towards becoming a fully embodied actor and pope. Moretti's pope grows out of the role – and into himself – as the film proceeds. Sorrentino's pope, by contrast, grows into the role – but also into himself – through his rehearsals. Acting is at the heart of the spectacle in both films. It encompasses stage fright, rehearsals, dressing, overcoming unsuccessful performances, exposing the actor's toolbox of gestures and the paraphernalia of theatre with its heavy, red curtains and its waiting in the wings. If the lure of the static icon reveals Italy's plastic arts, here the lure is unswervingly theatre.

While it may be tempting to interpret the conjoining of theatre, cinema, and religion in these works as a profession of the falsity and insincerity of religion as a mere staged performance, this is not the message of either film. It is not the superficiality of Catholicism that attracts these directors, so much as its theatricality.

Like the icon, theatrical spectacle lures the Italian film industry. The reasons are many and varied. The first is simply economic. Since the millennium, religious spectacle has proved particularly lucrative. The enormous success of Ron Howard's Vatican-set films, *The Da Vinci Code* (2006) and *Angels and Demons* (2009), provided Italy with an attractive economic precedent and model. What these American films made clear was that a sumptuous Vatican setting, coupled with secretive chambers and arcane rituals, could turn the spectacular nature of Catholicism to significant financial gain. Even more interestingly for Italy, films that interpellated both the secular market (through Vatican spectacle) and the large international Christian market that Mel Gibson's *The Passion of the Christ* (2004) had tapped, were set to make enormous profits. Natalie Dupont (2015) dubs these dual-market blockbusters "Godsploitation" films. Glossy Italian films made in the wake of the American "Godsploitation" genre that foreground Catholic spectacle need to be read in this light. Moretti's *Habemus Papam*, Sorrentino's *The Young Pope*, Roberto Andò's *Le confessioni* (2016), Dario Argento's *La terza madre* (Mother of Tears, 2007), Saverio Costanzo's *In memoria di me* (In Memory of Me, 2007), and even Stefano Sollima's *Suburru* (2015) can be interpreted in this context.

Theatrical spectacle also serves a second and linked purpose: cultural prestige. In the highly meta-cultural world of art-house cinema, the stage provides a space for reflecting on performance. Catholicism – with its highly theatrical surface – then becomes a key part of such reflection. Both Sorrentino's television series and Moretti's film reflect on the role of religious theatricality in cinema and, by extension, in the world. This use of meta-theatre deliberately interpellates a cultivated and intellectual cinemagoer and positions the films within an international production circuit – the art-house circuit – that despite filmmakers' disavowals is prestigious and lucrative (see Bourdieu 1980; Neale 1981; Wilinsky 2001). This is also the case with films like *Corpo celeste*, which foreground a despectacularized version of Catholic ritual-as-theatre to great critical acclaim among the international intellectual press.

Money and prestige are, however, clearly not the sole motivations for making cinema, and the lure of theatrical spectacle goes beyond a clever eye for marketing. A third explanation for the endurance of rites and rituals on screen is that they create excess through spectacle. In both Moretti's work and Sorrentino's, the papal balcony provides a stage set excessively high above a crowd who are in its thrall. The pope emerges in sumptuous ecclesiastical vestments in saturated reds and pure white and is surrounded by cardinals; in Moretti's film, he is accompanied by a standard bearer with an ornate gold cross held high. From the aerial stage, there are choreographed entries and exits, entries keenly awaited from below and greeted with ecstatic pleasure from the crowd, with flag-waving, cheering, and clapping. The intercutting of the high balcony, with its beautifully adorned cardinal and pope, and crane shots of vast crowds offers "the pleasures associated with the enjoyment of 'larger than life' representations, more luminous or intense than everyday reality" (King 2000, 4). Or, as Brent Plate observes, "the altar and the screen offer an alternative to the everyday world, and there are semi-permeable passages between the two worlds so that everyday life is transformed" (Brent Plate 2008, 41). In the *habemus papam* scenes, the excitement of revelation, the sumptuousness of the vestments, and the pomp and solemnity of the occasion provide an opportunity for the crowd, and cinema audience, to cast off banality and immerse themselves in the emotion of a great event. Moreover, the pleasures of established order, authority, and repetition bring relief in a disestablished, postmodern world. Even in films where ecclesiastical rituals do not forestall ordinariness, but instead represent it – as they do in the early scenes of *Si accettano miracoli*, in *Corpo celeste*, and in Giorgio Diritti's *Il vento fa il suo giro* (The Wind Blows Round, 2005), for instance – they signal, in part at least, a lost otherness and opulence. In other words, they denote the occasional failure of spectacle rather than no spectacle at all.

Finally, the spectacular theatricality of the Church is rooted in ritual, and ritual is rooted in time and memory. Deep connections inhere between ritual, repetition, and remembering.

Ritual fosters the sensation of stopped time. It creates an eternal present rooted in hundreds or millions of reiterations in the past. This past-present typically transcends modernity and puts it briefly aside. Rites and rituals are unchanged and almost unchanging (*Corpo celeste*'s tawdry modernization of rites proves the exception to the rule). These on-screen rituals thus not only transcend modernity but also transgress it. In doing so, they provide the image of a less fragmented past in which community and collectivity reigned supreme over the individual and security and stability were guaranteed. Rituals brush over the differences between people and offer a temporary illusion of consensus and shared social codes (Bertetto 2010). Rituals at the Vatican bring together a community, a community of strangers from many different continents and from many different language groups, united only by a cultural form they understand and share. For a brief moment, these strangers share social codes. The distinctions between lay and religious, rich and poor, Italian and other, are put aside. Their shared humanity and communality means that the community thus created appears both harmonious and stable. Even if this turns out to be illusory.

The prevalence of religious ritual in Italian filmmaking reveals a great deal about Italy's uncomfortable relationship with an unstable modernity. It uncovers a half-hidden nostalgia for an imagined simplicity, collectivity, and order, for a premodern way of life that was swept away with industrialization and is glimpsed now only in moments of unchanging practice. It overvalues the past. The stable familiarity represented by religious ritual is deeply conservative, and its emergence in the work of even politically oppositional directors like Marco Bellocchio and Nanni Moretti is the very opposite of progressive political change.

Conclusion: Cultural Catholicism and Collective National Belonging

At the end of Marco Bellocchio's *L'ora di religione*, the protagonist, Ernesto Picciafuoco, takes his son to school instead of joining the family at the Vatican. In so doing, father and son escape the family's scheming to make his mother a saint. As Ernesto waves goodbye to his son on the school steps, a European Union flag flaps conspicuously in the corner of the screen. The implication seems to be that secular Europe is the escape route from a densely Catholic Rome (Brook 2009).

The happy ending brought about by Ernesto's lucky escape belies the nuances and complexities of the relationship that Italian filmmakers have established with the Catholo-centric peninsula. If Ernesto and his son can leave the Vatican behind, his creator – Marco Bellocchio – cannot survive without the icons and rituals the Catholic Church affords. Ernesto is finally able to escape his family's plotting; even so, both he and Bellocchio are bewitched by the vast icon of the mother-Madonna that flaps across the screen earlier in the film. Icons and ritual are critical to the weaving of Italian filmmaking into Italy's long artistic history, legitimizing the seventh art and rooting it firmly into local and national identity. A great number of contemporary Italian films draw on collective national or local identity and memory, weaving together Catholic spectacle and Italian sacred painting.

The extraordinarily dense, indeed mesmerizing presence of Catholic icons and rituals on Italy's screens suggests that they tap into collective national belonging, sharing, and remembering. That Catholic iconography and ritual is so tightly bound to Italian national identity supports the thesis that the domination by a single church has a defining impact on a nation. Andrew Greeley (2011) argues that the most religious societies are those which, like Poland, Greece, Ireland, and Italy, are dominated by one religion. He contends that the "enveloping religious culture" of these largely mono-religious cultures provides "metaphors and stories and devotion which incline the whole human person to religious assent" (Greeley 2011, 158). Belonging is constructed through an iconography shared across a vast swathe of the population, even where it is felt to be fraudulent and is contested as such. That most of the directors discussed in this chapter define themselves as atheists, agnostics, or anticlerical, but are nonetheless unable to detach themselves from the rituals and icons of Catholicism, points to the "enveloping religious culture" of Italy's public sphere. The Italian filmmaking industry plays an important role in sustaining this. It absorbs Catholicism, and then, through its remediation of images and rituals, plays its part in the continued circulation of "cultural Catholicism." What happens to those from other faiths who do not share the same iconography or rituals is the subject of chapter 5.

The wide range of religious icons and the lure they exert on even the most sceptical of filmmakers means that one needs to revisit Grace Davie's claim that religion in the contemporary world is founded on "believing without belonging" (Davie 1990, 135). While Davie argues that many people believe in God without being involved in, or belonging to, any church, my findings in this chapter imply that her argument does not hold for Italy. In Italy, a sense of religious belonging is still critical. In fact, one might reverse Davie's axiom and argue that across significant parts of Italian filmmaking, "belonging without believing" is a better way of expressing it. The cultural identification with Catholicism in Italy – an identification that is deeply lodged in the legacy of Italy's religious painting, architecture, theatrical spectacle, and sculpture – is perhaps better described by what Tariq Modood terms "Christianist sentiment," a sentiment best expressed by, "I never go to church, but Europe is a Christian continent" (Modood 2014). The religious imagery that infuses Italian filmmaking indicates that belonging to Italy means understanding its Catholic heritage. This on-screen imagery cannot simply be declared "trivial" or "banal," to cite Stig Hjarvard (2011), since it is so deeply rooted in Italian culture, so profoundly felt, and so widely shared. That several recent publicity posters in Italy chose to foreground Catholic imagery (*L'ora di religione*; *Habemus Papam*; *Le confessioni*; *Chiamatemi Francesco*; *Si accettano miracoli*) reveals that the Italian filmmaking industry can take for granted that Catholic imagery is shared. In this environment, integrating the religious "others" – who may not necessarily use the Catholic signs, identify with them, or even find them interesting – proves particularly challenging.

3 Countercultural Catholic Values in the Public Sphere

Introduction: The "Chiesa di minoranza": From Hegemony to Opposition?

On 12 May 1974, a referendum on divorce took place in Italy. Despite the strong backing of both the dominant Catholic-backed political party, the Democrazia cristiana (Christian Democrats), and the Catholic Church, the 1970 law that had permitted divorce was not repealed. Widely interpreted as a significant blow to the power of Catholicism in Italian society, the result of the referendum sparked a heated debate over the position of the Church and the Christian Democrats in the light of what was interpreted as rising secularization. This debate centred on concepts of "chiesa di maggioranza" (majority church) and "chiesa di minoranza" (minority church). The former alluded to the Catholic Church as a ruling institution of the nation-state, represented politically through the Democrazia cristiana, which had dominated Italian politics since 1944. The *chiesa di minoranza*, on the other hand, was the term chosen to underscore the weakened position of the institutional church after its failure to block the Divorce Law (Giovagnoli 2006).

Pier Paolo Pasolini's contribution to the *minoranza–maggioranza* debate is pivotal to the arguments in this chapter. In response to Pope Paul VI's pessimistic speech at Castel Gandolfo, in which he stated that the Catholic Church had been overtaken by a world that no longer needed it, Pasolini wrote a letter to the *Corriere della sera* newspaper in which he asserted that the pope's admission was "historic," signalling the end of the Church, at least in its traditional form. Pasolini wrote that if the Church was to avoid "una fine ingloriosa" (an inglorious end) (1975, 68), it would have to step into a countercultural position, distancing itself both from political parties and from consumerism:

[la Chiesa] dovrebbe passare all'opposizione [...] contro un potere che l'ha così cinicamente abbandonata, progettando [...] di ridurla a puro folclore. Dovrebbe negare se stessa, per riconquistare i fedeli (o coloro che hanno un "nuovo" bisogno di fede). Riprendendo una lotta che è peraltro nelle sue tradizioni (la lotta del Papato contro l'Impero), ma non per la conquista del potere, la Chiesa potrebbe essere una guida, grandiosa ma non autoritaria, di tutti coloro che rifiutano [...] il nuovo potere consumistico, che è completamente irreligioso; totalitario; violento; falsamente tollerante, anzi, più repressivo che mai; corruttore; degradante. È questo rifiuto che potrebbe dunque simboleggiare la Chiesa: ritornando alle origini, cioè all'opposizione e alla rivolta. O fare questo o accettare un potere che non la vuole più; ossia suicidarsi.

[The Church] needs to shift to the opposition ... against a power that has so cynically abandoned it, and plans ... to reduce it to pure folklore. It must deny itself in order to win back the faithful (or those who have a "new" need for faith). Taking up the fight again, which is, in any case, part of its tradition (the battle of the Papacy against the Empire), but not in order to take power. The Church could be a magnificent, but not authoritarian, guide for those who reject ... the new consumerist order, which is totally irreligious, totalitarian, violent, falsely tolerant, more repressive than ever, corrupting and degrading. And this rejection could therefore symbolize the Church: the return to its origins, and thus to opposition and revolt. Either the Church does this or it must accept a power which does not want it: in other words, suicide.

The historical facts demonstrate, of course, that the leadership of the Catholic Church did not take up Pasolini's battle cry. There was no attempt to *passare all'opposizione* (shift to the opposition). The Church firmly opposed neither capitalism nor the political status quo. Its links with the Democrazia cristiana remained in place until that party's demise in the early 1990s. Moreover, it continued to use the commercial media, as detailed in chapter 1, to market its message, a tactic that Pasolini interpreted as inherently bound up with consumerism. This is not to say that the Vatican does not oppose significant hegemonic aspects of contemporary culture, especially its moral relativism and defence of individual freedoms. Nor is it to say that the Church leadership does not make uncomfortable socio-political interventions: the papacy of Pope Francis (2013–), for instance, has been widely interpreted as challenging aspects of global capitalism, defending those excluded from its benefits, and expressing concern over its neoliberal values. Moreover, some Catholic grassroots organizations, such as Azione Cattolica (Catholic Action, 1867–present), are decidedly activist. Nonetheless, the institutional Church has attempted to maintain its terrestrial power base and normally works with, rather than against, the major institutional forces in Italy today.

This chapter places Catholic values at its heart. Here I investigate how and why some contemporary filmmakers have taken up the cry to *passare all'opposizione* and, by bonding religious values to countercultural discourse, support the circulation of Catholic values in the public sphere. My investigation is carried out in the light of claims, made by a wide range of sociologists, cultural theorists, and theologians, that the contemporary Western world is witnessing an increasing personalization of morality. These claims imply a loss of churches' control over an aspect of human existence that has until very recently been dominated by persistent religious influence. Paul Crittenden, for instance, boldly argues that "morality has become a personal concern" (1990, 78). Loek Halman and Ole Riis write, somewhat more cautiously, that "the tendency seems to be for modern people to be less prone to accept the churches as moral authorities" (2003, 5). While I do not deny that the Catholic Church's authority over personal morality has declined in Italy, there are questions about which areas of ethics and morality have been affected and whether there exist elements that have remained untouched by secularizing trends. As I will argue in chapter 4, divergence from, and personalization of, Church teaching on moral and ethical issues is encountered especially with regard to the central teachings on family (especially with regard to heteronormativity and divorce) and the sanctity of life (abortion, euthanasia, and in vitro fertilization), teachings that have long been subject to strident dissent from within the Italian cinema industry. However, dissent from, and personalization of, other aspects of ethics and morality is not as obvious, especially (as I will argue here) in light of a peculiarly Italian blend of left-wing political engagement, or *impegno*,[1] and Catholic values.

The exploration of values is the third piece of the puzzle that dominates this book and will occupy me in both this chapter and the next. In tandem with explorations of Italy's religious filmmaking infrastructure (chapter 1) and of the circulation of Catholicism's iconographic and performative surface (chapter 2), an investigation of how religious values circulate will help explain why Catholicism remains so deeply embedded in Italy's public sphere and why there is so little space for the peninsula's other religions to circulate. In this chapter my corpus includes films made for the big and small screen, especially hagiopics and *film*

---

1 "*Impegno*" is usually translated into English as "political engagement," but it also has an ethical dimension. It is a crucial aspect of modern and contemporary Italian culture – "one of the generative conditions of Italian intellectualism," says David Ward (cited in O'Leary 2009, 221) – and it continues to exercise influence over Italian culture despite the rise of a so-called post-ideological Italy. As Jennifer Burns explains, "the monolithic notion of commitment to a usually communist agenda in writing began in the 1950s to reveal cracks of dissension, and the long-term effect of this is a break-up of the commitment to a single, overarching social agenda into a fragmentary attention" (Burns 2001, i). The contemporary form of "impegno" has been variously described as "fragmented" (Burns 2001), "postmodern" (Antonello and Mussgnug 2009), imbued with Vattimo's "pensiero debole" (weak thought) (Stellardi 2009) or Bauman's "liquid modernity (Innocenti 2009). Alan O'Leary claims that cultural figures become intellectuals in Italy "to the extent that they are impegnati in the process of defining the nation and its proper direction" (2011, 221) and that *impegno* is fundamental to filmmaking in Italy.

di qualità (quality films). In the first section I focus my attention on television miniseries and films that pit the Church against fascism (*La buona battaglia: Don Pietro Pappagallo*; *Don Gnocchi: L'angelo dei bambini*; *Don Zeno – L'uomo di Nomadelfia*; *Shades of Truth*; *Sotto il cielo di Roma*). Here I explore a "David against Goliath" ethical model that pits a battling and heroic religious figure against a violent society. In the second section I investigate in more detail a particularly unexpected turn in Italian filmmaking: the use of Saint Francis as a model for a post-capitalist age (*Le confessioni*; *Chiamatemi Francesco*; *Francesco*). My objective here is to understand how and why Saint Francis has been constructed as countercultural, especially by directors positioned on the political left. I look too at the dangers that inhere in the countercultural repositioning of the Church on big and small screens. Throughout this chapter my focus is on the consequences of the circulation of Catholic values through countercultural carriers.

The Battling Priest (or David against Goliath)

In the final, emotional scenes of the television miniseries *Don Pietro Pappagallo: La buona battaglia* (Gianfranco Albano, 2006), Don Pietro, the heroic priest who has hidden resistance fighters and Jews from the authorities, is bundled into a lorry and driven to the Fosse Ardentina outside Rome, where he will be shot, together with 334 others, as part of a brutal Nazi reprisal. In the lorry, sitting alongside those he has failed to save, with tears running quietly down his face, he softly says, "ho combattuto la buona battaglia; ho terminato la mia corsa; e io ho conservato la mia fede" (I have fought the good fight; I have come to the end of my line; and I have kept my faith).

Don Pietro is one of the many battling priests who grace Italian television – one of many who are positioned positively in the face of the Nazi-fascist regime. In this section I investigate the construction of priests like him, exploring how Catholic producers employ a countercultural model in the face of powerful and violent political forces. My corpus of films here centres on miniseries made for RAI and Mediaset that feature embattled wartime priests or popes in title roles. Towards the end of this section I broaden the corpus to look at further instances of the battling priest, including those who stand up to organized crime (*Alla luce del sole* [Come into the Light]). My question here is how a "David against Goliath" model, in which a weak priest counters a strong societal force, functions to promote the circulation of Catholic values on screen. I ask what the effects are of positioning as countercultural a Church that was not actually so at the time of the events these films depict. In other words, I investigate the consequences that arise when Catholic values are closely associated with heroic countercultural positioning.

Questions about the Church's responsibility for the events of the Shoah bubbled to the surface in the early 1970s, and Pope Pius XII (1939–58) suddenly came under public criticism for his public silence. Critics argued that during the Shoah, the Church did not speak out loudly and unequivocally against events it knew were happening. The protest centred on Pope Pius's cautious and publicly neutral position during the Second World War and his avoidance of comment as the first racial laws were put into place. Since then, the question of whether his actions were adequate has generated considerable literature on both sides, much of it polemical. John Cornwell's hugely controversial book, *Hitler's Pope*, published in 2000, fired up the dispute for the twenty-first century,[2] and the debate was stoked further in 2009 when Pope Benedict declared Pius XII "venerable," a step towards making him a saint. Pope Benedict's decision was met with anger by many Jewish groups, including the World Jewish Congress; it was decried as "inopportune" and "premature" by France's chief rabbi and as "untimely" by Giuseppe Laras, President of the Assembly of Italian Rabbis (Butt 2009).

The Italian filmmaking industry responded to the public debate by making two international hagiopics on the pope's life. Christian Duguay made the Italo-German *Sotto il cielo di Roma* (Pius XII: Under the Roman Sky), (2010), a Lux Vide and RAI Fiction production that was broadcast in two prime-time slots on RAI Uno in 2010 and captured a fifth of the viewing public (Lux Vide 2010). Some years later, Liana Marabini directed the low-budget flop *Shades of Truth* (2015). Both films defend the pope's actions. *Sotto il cielo di Roma* manipulates the narrative frame to support its argument. The miniseries begins with the armistice on 8 September 1943 and ends with the liberation of Rome. By setting the film entirely in Rome and omitting any discussion of the Jews of northern Europe, it tailors its argument towards a particular outcome. By focusing its attention on the four thousand Jews of the Roman ghetto and the Vatican's part in sheltering them, it implicitly posits Pius's relationship with the Roman Jews as a metonymy for his care of all Jews. This ignores the six million Jews who perished during the Shoah and shuts down debate about the Vatican's wider role during the war.

The second film on Pius XII to be screened was Liana Marabini's *Shades of Truth* (2015), produced by Marabini's own company, Condor Films, and presented out of competition at Cannes. Marabini claims for the pope a role more important than that of Oskar Schindler (1908–1974), adding that "Schindler saved only 8,000 Jews while he saved millions" (Condor Administrator 2015). The film employs a classic conversion narrative and a sceptical frame, carefully acknowledging its audience's suspicions by embodying them

---

2 In *Hitler's Pope*, John Cornwell made some very strong allegations, including that the Pope was an anti-Semite. His allegations, many of them unsubstantiated, were then challenged by other writers, including Rabbi David G. Dalin (2005), who took Cornwell to task with *The Myth of Hitler's Pope*, laying the blame instead on an Islamic mufti. Confronted with these challenges, Cornwell retracted some of his arguments. See Bottum and Dalin, *The Pius War: Responses to the Critics of Pius XII* (2004).

in the figure of a Jewish American journalist who comes to Rome to investigate Pius's case. The journalist's initial scepticism falls away as he comes across "irrefutable" proofs of Pius's innocence through his encounters with priests, nuns, and Jews as well as his researches in the Vatican Secret Archives. The film's focalizer, in other words, attempts to win the audience over from doubt. The quality of the acting and screenwriting was such that the self-financed film was subject to universally disparaging reviews from both the secular and Catholic press and had limited circulation.

That the film industry's response to the most controversial pope of the last twelve decades was to defend and eulogize him may seem curious, but it is simple to explain. First, that Pius XII is exempt from serious criticism within the film industry signals the mobilization of pro-Catholic voices, such as Liana Marabini's, in the public debate, at a time when alternative, critical voices are subdued. Second, it reflects the powerful tendency to portray papal figures as heroic and saintly in contemporary television fiction – think here of *Papa Giovanni* (Giorgio Capitani, 2002); *Il Papa buono* (Ricky Tognazzi, 2003); *Karol: Un uomo diventato Papa* (Giacomo Battiato, 2005); *Giovanni Paolo II* (J.K. Harrison, 2005); *Papa Luciani. Il sorriso di Dio* (Giorgio Capitani, 2006); *Karol. Un Papa rimasto uomo* (Giacomo Battiato, 2006); and *Paolo VI: Il papa nella tempesta* (Fabrizio Costa, 2008). While the film industry has attacked corruption and worldliness in the Catholic hierarchy on both big and small screens, the pope remains practically untouchable.[3] Finally, and rather unexpectedly, in *Sotto il cielo di Roma*, Pius XII – leader of a powerful global Church – is positioned counterculturally. Reflecting a hallmark of the Lux Vide brand, he is humanized, and the regal trappings of his papacy – his obsequious courtly entourage; his use of the papal litter – are deleted. The courtly nineteenth-century pomp of Pius XII's reign is gone, as are almost all the vestiges of pre-Vatican II life. This is more than simply a case of rendering him more palatable to a contemporary audience. His detachment from the worldly splendour of the papacy makes possible his repositioning as an ordinary, if exemplary, person, and it is from this position that he can counter an odious dominant culture. Moreover, the film, somewhat improbably, aligns the pope with a left-wing partisan who is sheltered within the walls of the Vatican. The partisan and the pope are shown to share the battle against Nazism and fascism, and their relationship helps kill off the "black myth" that the pope was a Nazi sympathizer who harboured a personal hatred of communism (in 1949, Pius XII published

---

3   Marco Bellocchio's *Buongiorno, notte* (Good Morning, Night, 2003) mounts sustained criticism of Pope Paul VI's actions, or lack of them, after the Red Brigades kidnapped Aldo Moro, the leader of the Christian Democrats; Roberto Faenza's *La verità sta in cielo* (2016) hints that Pope Francis knows the answer to the riddle of the Orlandi case but will not share it. These exceptions aside, however, there are clearly defined limits to attacks on the Church, and the pope appears exempt from them.

a decree stating that all Catholics collaborating with communist organizations were to be excommunicated). Since the resistance fighter is portrayed as weak, mounting only inconsequential or unsuccessful attacks, the alignment also serves to establish Catholicism, rather than the resistance, as the decisive force against Nazism and fascism. Ultimately, Pius XII is portrayed as a most powerful kind of resistance fighter, one who is armed with strong diplomatic skills and the grace of God.

The establishment of an on-screen countercultural, anti-fascist Church has been reinforced in the new millennium through portrayals of the priesthood on television. Since the arrival on screen of the iconic Don Pietro, the resistance priest of Roberto Rossellini's *Roma città aperta* (Rome, Open City, 1945), countercultural priests have had visibility on screen in a way that the church hierarchy, until recently, has not. Three two-part miniseries screened on RAI and Mediaset provide exemplary illustrations. The first, made for Mediaset's Canale 5 by Nimar Studios and Together Production International, is Cinzia TH Torrini's *Don Gnocchi: L'angelo dei bambini* (2004). This film tells the story of Don Carlo Gnocchi (1902–1949), who volunteered as a chaplain on the Greco-Albanian and Russian fronts, helping mutilated soldiers and children. The second miniseries, Gianfranco Albano's *La buona battaglia: Don Pietro Pappagallo*, is another secular co-production (11 Marzo Film and RAI Fiction). It was broadcast on RAI in April 2006 and rebroadcast in a shortened version on RAI in 2008. It traces the work of the Roman priest Don Pietro Pappagallo (1888–1944), who hid Jews, deserting soldiers, and resistance fighters from the regime before being caught, and was killed by the Nazis during the brutal massacre at the Fosse Ardentina. Finally, *Don Zeno – L'uomo di Nomadelfia* (Gianluigi Calderone, 2008) recounts the story of Don Zeno Saltini (1900–1981), who worked with impoverished children during the later years of fascism and throughout the Second World War.

The three miniseries present their priests as heroes, or exemplary priests (Perugini 2011). In each, a priest is positioned against dominant forces in society in a battle in which he risks his life. Don Gnocchi, Don Pietro Pappagallo, and Don Zeno share a set of values, encapsulated best, perhaps, in the words taken from a Carthusian monk's sermon at the end of Roberto Andò's *Le confessioni*: "giustizia e pietà" (justice and mercy). Courageous and committed, these religious figures dedicate their lives to justice, treating those around them with compassion. However, the defining feature of the narratives is the courageous and peaceful stand they take against violent and evil powers in society. Their masculine resistance is heroic, especially as their tools – such as Don Gnocchi's makeshift communion table in the trench – seem inadequate for times of war. Indeed, as Don Gnocchi raises high the chalice during the mass, it becomes the target of the enemy forces and is pierced by a bullet.

The battling religious figure is a curious phenomenon in Italy. It can easily be distinguished from what Leandro Castellani (1994) terms the philanthropist priest, a feature of American cinema during the 1930s and 1940s and found in films like *Boys Town* (1938), *Men of Boys Town* (1941), *Angels with Dirty Faces* (1938), *Going My Way* (1944), and *The Bells of Saint Mary's* (1945). The contemporary Italian version of this character is decidedly more engaged, forceful, and political than its mid-century American antecedent. It does not stop with priests who defend Italians against the regime. There is a fleet of films lauding monks, nuns, priests, and saints who work unflinchingly to protect the poor, the ailing, and the socially disadvantaged. These include *Padre Pio* (Carlo Carlei, 2000), *Madre Teresa* (Fabrizio Costa, 2003), *Don Bosco* (Lodovico Gasparini, 2004), *L'uomo della carità: Don Luigi Di Liegro* (Alessandro Di Robilant, 2007), *Chiara e Francesco* (Fabrizio Costa, 2007), *Don Zeno – L'uomo di Nomadelfia* (Gianluigi Calderone, 2008), and, of course, *Francesco* (2014), which I will discuss below. Moreover, the enormously successful television detective series *Don Matteo*, a Lux Vide production first broadcast on RAI in 2000 and currently in its eleventh season, has put before the public a priest who works for the public good and who defends those who cannot defend themselves: Romanian factory workers, the socially disadvantaged, and the poor. *Dio ci aiuti!*, another Lux Vide and RAI Fiction co-production (2011–), now in its fourth season, is an attempt to harness the lucrative battling-priest market by featuring a nun with detective capacities (Suor Angelina). Then there are the retellings of the story of Don Pino Puglisi, a priest murdered for his opposition to the Mafia. A trinity of twenty-first-century films narrate the life, and death, of this high-profile figure: Roberto Faenza's prize-winning *Alla luce del sole* (Come into the Light, 2005), Gianfranco Albano's TV miniseries *Brancaccio* (2001), and the docu-film *L'ultimo sorriso* (2017), directed by Rosalinda Ferrante. Another big-screen film tells the story of a fictional priest battling the Camorra in Naples: Vincenzo Marra's *L'equilibrio* (Equilibrium, 2017). Sergio Perugini (2011) writes that in 2010 the *Osservatorio sulla fiction italiano* reported that between 1989 and 2009, heroes of the faith held the top position in Italian TV fiction, with 43.4 per cent of market share. Heroes of liberty and justice and heroes of art and science, at 13.4 and 12.4 per cent respectively, were a long way behind. Clearly, the David-against-Goliath model has been enjoying extraordinary success in Italy, especially on the small screen. In no other Western country have positive religious characters, carrying positive religious values, enjoyed such privileged access to prime-time television.

What is it about the battling priest that allows this model to be such a successful carrier of values? One answer relates to Fredric Jameson's "strategy of containment" (1981), a process whereby events in a story are organized in a way acceptable to its spectators, while insights that might be reached by examining the evidence in chronicle form are repressed. In other words, battling-priest stories are constructed in ways that appeal to their audience, whatever the consequences for narrative accuracy. Pre-conciliar trappings that might alienate contemporary viewers are moderated. Less heroic attitudes are omitted or suppressed. Priests are rendered approachable and liberal (Don Pietro Pappagallo allows deserting soldiers to get away with sexual innuendo; Don Puglisi accepts his young parishioners' foul-mouthed swearing). The evil they are pitted against – war, Nazism, fascism, poverty, organized crime – is unequivocally and uncontroversially bad, which renders worthier the cause of those who are fighting it. Moreover, the television programming does not set the heroic priest against an army of evil ones, a jarring contrast that might reignite questions. Italy now produces very few films in which priests and popes are portrayed in a negative light, and critical films made elsewhere, such as Costa-Gavras's *Amen* (2002), which denounces Pius XII, can take a decade to find space on the national broadcaster (*Amen* was first screened on RAI in 2012, ten years after its release). Contrasting perspectives internal to the story or external to it are thereby suppressed, and this makes it easier to integrate the religious model into contemporary broadcasting.

Moreover, the model of the battling priest taps into one of the most popular narrative forms in contemporary Italy: the *impegnato*, or engaged hero. It shares a great deal with the left-wing heroes of politically engaged cinema, stalwarts of Italian national production, who range from Peppino Impastato (*I cento passi*), a murdered left-wing anti-Mafia activist, to Giorgio Ambrosoli, a lawyer murdered during his investigation of the notorious banker Michele Sindona. Ambrosoli's life is described in Michele Placido's *Un eroe borghese* (Ordinary Hero, 1995). The priest who fights injustice and poverty draws on left-wing cinematic models that have proved peculiarly marketable. By adopting an especially popular narrative formula, the priest has found an uncomplicated path towards success.

The promotion of religious values through the figure of the battling priest comes at a cost, however. In the first place, these heroic portrayals whitewash the relationship between the Church and other power bases in society: especially fascism, but also organized crime.[4] Any position between the two extremes of

---

4 Much has been written about cases of collusion between the Mafia and the Church and about the Church's tardiness in speaking out as directly as it might have done against Italian organized crime (Lodato 1994; Chillura 1999; Stabile 1996; Ceruso 2007; Dino 2008). Vincenzo Ceruso (2007) lists concrete, high-profile, if isolated, cases in which priests were directly involved in crime alongside the Mafia – cases such as that of Fra Giacinto, who after his murder in 1980 was found to have owned a (legally held) revolver and four million lire in cash secreted in the seven cells he occupied in his monastery. Alessandra Dino in her 2008 book *La mafia devota* paints the portrait of a Mafia that uses church rituals, such as baptisms, weddings, and funerals, to legitimize itself and exercise its power. Sergio Quinzio (1993) in *Corriere della sera* summarizes the commonly held view that "saremmo fuori dal mondo se pensassimo che il sistema delle connivenze abbia coinvolto politici, imprenditori, amministratori e persino magistrati per arrestarsi di colpo dinanzi ai preti e ai muri della chiesa" [we would be completely out of touch if we thought that the system of connivances which involve politicians, entrepreneurs, administrators and even magistrates suddenly stopped in front of priests and the walls of the Church].

good and evil is lost, and as a result, productions like *Sotto il cielo di Roma* and *Alla luce del sole* create an overdetermined dichotomy between fascism and the Church, in the first case, and between the Mafia and the Church, in the second. This suppresses debate on how they might be linked. To the degree that the Church's indifference or complicity needs to be addressed, its depictions in television fiction fail to enable this.

Second, the sheer repetition of the battling-priest model risks fossilizing a set of ethical values – bravery, justice, compassion, self-sacrifice – on screen, and especially on the screen that most Italians watch most of the time: the small one. Fossilized values cannot be deconstructed to test their validity in contemporary Italy. Reopening the space for the discussion of values would quickly reveal the ethical issues that filmmaking brushes into the corners and out of sight, issues including the church's role in political regimes and in paedophilia cases (see chapter 4); it would also uncover the rootedness of these ethics in problematic values such as self-sacrifice and martyrdom as the basis for group identity and nation-building. Moreover, the heroic religious figure, as the most important carrier for ethical values on the small screen, repeatedly excludes from heroism great swathes of those living on the peninsula, especially those belonging to minority religions, ethnicities other than Italian (except in the case of re-enactments of the Bible), and women.[5] When women do take on the role of saintly hero, it is their idealized virginity and submission that is promoted, not how they fight the good fight.

The "Francis Turn" in a Post-Capitalist Age

Of all religious figures engaged counterculturally on screen, Saint Francis is among the most revered in Italy today. To this figure I now turn in order to understand what it is about him that leads him to be repeatedly proposed, especially by secular directors, as an ethical model for contemporary Italian society. The most high-profile of recent films to draw on the saint are *Francesco* (2014), by veteran filmmaker Liliana Cavani, Daniele Luchetti's *Chiamatemi Francesco: Il papa della gente* (Call Me Francesco, 2015), and Roberto Andò's *Le confessioni* (The Confessions, 2016).[6] The films' protagonists all take decisive "minority"

---

5   Sergio Perugini (2011) notes that between 1996 and 2006 only five protagonists from the twentieth century were women: Mother Teresa, Maria Goretti, Soraya, Maria José, and Edda.

6   Two other films are miniseries for Mediaset and RAI respectively. The first is Michele Soavi's *Francesco* (2002) made by TaoDue for Mediaset. It was first broadcast on Canale 5 during prime time and transmitted again in a shortened version in 2010 on Canale 4; in 2013 this shortened version was broadcast again on Canale 5 to mark the election of Pope Francis. Fabrizio Costa's *Chiara e Francesco* (2007) was the produced for RAI by RAI Fiction, Lux Vide, and Rai Trade. It was rebroadcast by TV2000 in 2017.

positions against the contemporary status quo and propose alternative ethical lifestyles. In itself, there is nothing new or remarkable about this: hagiopics have been produced since the dawn of Italian cinema, and they continue to be made today and screened on prime-time television to large audiences. What is more surprising is that these films are made by producers and directors who do not define themselves as religious. Rather, their directors are secular, agnostic, and engaged on the political left. Why this apparent paradox? That is, why are directors who do not believe in God bringing religious heroes to Italian screens? What kind of ethical model do such heroes present in contemporary Italy? To answer this, I focus on works by secular directors, first exploring two of the "Franciscan" films: *Le confessioni* and *Francesco*. I then draw in the biopic of Pope Francis, Daniele Luchetti's *Chiamatemi Francesco*, to give the Franciscan tale its papal twist.

The first of the films I treat here, Roberto Andò's *Le confessioni*, tells of a G8 meeting at Germany's Grand Hotel Heiligendamm, where the G8 actually held talks in 2007. A monk (the iconic white-robed Carthusian, Roberto Salus) has been invited at the behest of the director of the International Monetary Fund, Daniel Roché (Daniel Auteuil), along with a famous author and a rock star, to provide an artistic and spiritual counterbalance to the cold world of finance. Not long after their arrival, Salus hears Roché's confession. Some hours later, the IMF director is found dead. As the film unfolds, it emerges that Roché and the eight international finance ministers had been planning a secretive economic move that would severely damage the poorest countries of the world. Salus sows doubt among the ministers about the ethics of their race for global economic power. One by one the ministers back away from the plan, leaving the G8 talks in crisis. In the film's finale, Daniele Roché's funeral is held. Salus provides a compelling homily on "giustizia e pietà" (justice and mercy) to the assembled ministers before leaving the hotel, trailed – in a Franciscan touch – by one of the ministers' dogs. While Salus is a Carthusian monk, not a Franciscan one, his sharp critique of a neoliberal system that privileges the rich and powerful hints at the less attractively attired monk, Francis. Moreover, his passion for recording songbirds and his taming of the German minister's dog signal Francis's intense love for the natural world and point firmly to the Umbrian saint's presence in the film.

The second production I explore here is Liliana Cavani's *Francesco* (2014). This is the director's third exploration of the saint's life. Her first, *Francesco D'Assisi* (1966), was RAI's first telefilm and starred a rebellious Lou Castel in the title role, "una specie di beatnik che si porta dietro le stimmate di Rossellini, Pasolini e dei cattolici del dissenso" (a kind of beatnik who carries with him the stigmata of Rossellini, Pasolini, and dissenting Catholics) (Grasso 2014). Her second, in 1989, shifted the emphasis away from an overtly political message and provided a more mystical interpretation. It starred the American actor

Mickey Rourke. The 2014 version, a two-part miniseries for RAI, stars Polish actor Mateusz Kościukiewicz and repositions the tale for young, contemporary audiences. It narrates the saint's life through the eyes of two of those who were closest to him, Saint Claire of Asissi and Brother Elias. Like the earlier versions, it chronicles Francis's wealthy upbringing, his conversion, his embracing of poverty, his turbulent relationship with his father, the birth of the Franciscan movement, the problems with its organization, and his death. Unlike earlier versions, it dedicates significant screen time to Francis's part in the Fifth Crusade, his meeting with Sultan Al Malik-Al Kamil, and his failed efforts to stop the battles between Muslims and Christians. This additional material draws on new research about Francis's travels and implicitly repositions the saint's plea for peace between religions in the context of contemporary Muslim–Christian tensions.

The characters who emerge from these two filmic productions – Salus and Francis – are carriers for a set of values that blend religion and politics into a single countercultural discourse. This is not to say that the characters are identical: Salus is canny and ambiguous; Francis, by contrast, is a simple and loving free spirit. The status quo they both counter is similar. It is founded on a damaging rift between rich and poor, advantaged and disadvantaged. Both films fashion a hero who encapsulates an ethical alternative to the status quo and who seeks to occupy a revolutionary "minority" oppositional position. In *Le confessioni*, the status quo is explicitly identified as global neoliberal capitalism, an economic system in ethical crisis to which negative attributes adhere: chiefly, greed and callousness.[7] In Cavani's *Francesco*, it is against wealth and material comforts in the broadest sense that her saint campaigns. The medieval status quo that Francis counters has much in common with the contemporary West: its proponents are captivated by expensive fashion, rich food, and even house restoration. Cavani's medieval Francis is clearly meant to be read in the context of contemporary neoliberal, consumerist Italy.

The religious hero these filmmakers create as a means to expose wealth inequality and social disadvantage is strikingly countercultural. Screenwriter Pasquini's elaboration of *Le confessioni* (2016) makes it clear that Salus, whose

---

7 Pasquini's discussion of his screenplay (2016) also defines the enemy against which the hero is constructed. Roché, who embodies the enemy, is a reigning semi-divine magician ("il principe dei giocatori," "potere divinatorio," "illusionista" [the prince of players; soothsaying power; magician]), head of a politico-economic system that recalls Enlightenment deism: "la politica come sfera separata, come puro esercizio del potere, emanazione tecnocratica di una realtà economica sovranazionale, indifferente per sua natura alle regole della democrazia" [power as a separate sphere, as the pure exercise of power, a technocratic emanation of a supranational economic reality, by its nature indifferent to the rules of democracy]. The new neoliberal enemy represents a power of divine proportions – an Enlightenment God who does not care for his creation.

name signifies salvation, is a hybrid character modelled on politically committed monks like the Catholic Thomas Merton and the Buddhist Thích Nhất Hạnh, both of whom were active in non-violent countercultural activism during the 1960s; Saint Francis is named as another influence (Olivieri 2016). The decision to dress Salus as a Carthusian may signal the wish to present him as contemplative observer but is more likely to have resulted from scenographic considerations: the striking cream colour of his robes lends the monk a statuesque and unblemished air and creates maximum contrast with the dark-suited business environment. Liliana Cavani's saint, by contrast, is a thoroughbred Francis. In *Francesco*, she founds her saint on Saint Francis's concepts of peace, brotherhood, and fraternity as well as on a revolutionary "rifiuto all'omologazione" (rejection of homologation) (Chiani 2013). Cavani's saint refuses to compromise his ideals or to permit his vision of religious life to be ossified within the strictures of official teachings. The 2014 Francis takes forward the countercultural ethos that inspired Cavani's earlier 1966 version: while less blatantly political than her first version, it nevertheless builds on this earlier culture, while reinscribing the Francis figure onto the template of twenty-first-century post-capitalist activism.

In both films, monastic life – above all, the figure of Saint Francis – encapsulates a contemporary countercultural lifestyle. Salus's protest is epitomized by stillness and silence that places "giustizia e pietà" at its heart and is contrasted with the noisy and ineffectual protests of the no-global activists who scale the wall of the hotel and are swiftly dealt with by the guards. The monk's meditative stillness, which owes something to mindfulness as well as to monasticism, is powerful. It is statuesque, defiantly unresponsive and unnerving, inverting expectations of silence as subservience and instead performing "a statue's stillness as an act of passive resistance" (Getsy 2014, 13). Francis's protest, by contrast, lacks such mature control, or attachment to silence, deriving its power instead from a lively, instinctive resistance to conformity and a joyful collective energy. In other words, one might say that the (counter)cultural model that Salus provides seems set to resonate with contemporary practitioners of yoga and meditation, whereas Francis's appeal is to the world of post-capitalist collectives and ecologically minded members of Generation Z. In other words, while they share a model, the kind of resistance they present is nonetheless distinct.

In some ways there is little new in this religious model. Saint Francis as a model for ethical values has, of course, a long history in Italian filmmaking, going back to Enrico Guazzoni's short film *Il poverello d'Assisi* (1911). Some of Italy's best-known filmmakers, including Roberto Rossellini (*Francesco, giullare di Dio* [The Flowers of Saint Francis], 1950), Franco Zeffirelli (*Brother Son, Sister Moon*, 1976), and Liliana Cavani herself, have made films about the saint, often for television. However, since the millennium, Saint Francis has become increasingly visible in the public sphere. TV hagiopics on Saint Francis have been regularly broadcast and rebroadcast by Mediaset and RAI (Michele Soavi's *Francesco* (2002); Fabrizio Costa's *Chiara e Francesco* (2007; rebroadcast by TV2000 in 2017), Liliana Cavani's *Francesco* (2014), and the saint has made his way into big-budget, big-screen productions like *Le confessioni* and *Chiamatemi Francesco*. Steven Healy (2016) observes that interest in the saint has grown not just among religious thinkers but also among secular ones. Michael Hardt and Antonio Negri, Healy notes, make Francis the last word of their book *Empire* (2000), and Giorgio Agamben conspicuously features him in his "engagement with the eleventh and twelfth-century explosion of monastic movements grounded in the communal practice of the highest poverty: use without ownership" (Healy 2016, 368). The relevance of Francis to contemporary life in the West is observed by Liliana Cavani as she defends her controversial decision to make a third film on his life:

> La vita di Francesco è di sconcertante attualità e lo è ancora di più oggi, che la crisi ci costringe a fare i conti con una decrescita e con una crescente diseguaglianza [...] Lui è l'unico pensatore autentico e poetico sulle questioni economiche e finanziarie. (Cavani 2014)

> The life of Francis is disconcertingly topical; it still is, and is even more today, as the crisis forces us to face declining growth and increasing inequality ... He is the only authentic and poetic thinker on economic and financial inequality.

If Francis is returning to Italian screens as an exemplary saint not just for Catholic filmmakers but for the secular left as well, the reasons are as clear as they are complex and multiple. Francis's return rests on his being a "central archetype in the Western spiritual imagination" (Reno 2015, 29), one that can be remobilized at any point to crystallize values of joyful simplicity, poverty, and compassion, as well as those of collective life, radical protest, and ecology. His return to Italian screens is bound up with several contemporary concerns. The first has to do with wealth inequality and the failings of capitalism, which were underscored by the 2008 economic crisis. As neoliberal capitalism has come increasingly under question, the Umbrian saint has come to embody "the tremendous power of humility and renunciation – an alluring, bewitching possibility in our age of grasping accumulation" (Reno 2015, 30). Saint Francis, in other words, provides a radical alternative to the accumulation of wealth on the part of the few. This alternative is at the core of both Cavani's and Andò's films.

A second reason for Francis's return is the model of collectivity he supplies. This emerges intensely from Cavani's miniseries. This model aligns with mainstream ideas about the shared economy and with more radical alternatives promoted by post-capitalist activists. The "Francis model" therefore has both

pertinence and applicability. Francis's tale is not simply about the renunciation of wealth – it is about the place of collective life, shared goods, and community values in an alternative lifestyle that renounces overconsumption. In
this it reflects the "explosion of social movements and scholarship focused on a
post-capitalist politics: solidarity economies, economic democracy, peer-to-peer
economies, degrowth economies, buen vivir, indigenous economies, transition
towns, downshift and simple-living movements, and cooperative economies."
(Healy 2016, 376). The multitude of new movements whose adherents attempt
to live "differently, simply, lightly" and who embrace a "thoughtful and deliberate" view of consumption (376) reflect Franciscan themes of care for nature
and his efforts to find a joyful and meaningful life by living with as little as
possible. In this regard, Rosi Braidotti notes that "the most pertinent critiques
of advanced capitalisms today and of the structural injustices of globalization
are voiced by religiously driven social movements" (2012, 195).

In this reading, the saint is particularly relevant to contemporary ecology
movements and environmental theory, a connection that has been widely
noted by recent scholars (Applebaum 2015; Healy 2016; Zhang 2016; Beerman,
Dienburg, and Warode 2017). The saint that John Paul II nominated as the
"heavenly patron of those who promote ecology" provides radical answers to
present-day quests for sustainable alternatives to energy consumption. While
blame for the ecological crisis has often been laid at the door of Christianity
for its emphasis on the dualism of humanity and nature and humankind's
divine mandate to dominate the earth (White 1967, cited in Viviers 2014),
Saint Francis's saw nature as the "lettering" in which God expressed his love
(Armstrong 1973, 107), the familial interrelatedness of nature found in his
"Canticle of the Creatures," and his shared, communal, frugal living have been
cited as models for redressing the abuse of natural resources in the developed world. Pope Francis in his encyclical letter *Laudate si'* (Bergoglio 2015)
notes the saint's "radical refusal" to relegate the world to an "object simply to
be used and controlled." Stephen Healy finds in Saint Francis's "form of life"
a way of "understand[ing] the postcapitalist project of pursuing a different
'mode of humanity' in which we might develop the capacity to survive in the
Anthropocene" (370). Cavani's film, which places particular emphasis on the
collective and the sharing economy, drives these messages home. That Cavani's
Francis remains so popular with his friends, and so well-groomed and physically attractive despite depriving himself of fine food, expensive clothes, and
upmarket shelter, provides a model for the social media generation: key targets
of good looks and popularity can be met despite or even *through* renunciation
of consumerism.

Because of the ways in which Saint Francis has been recycled in contemporary
Italy to combat consumerism and provide a paradigm for post-capitalist collectivity and ecology movements, he provides a legitimatized model for left-wing

filmmakers. This is why, in contesting the status quo, Francis – or monks who owe much to him – can supplant a protagonist from the political left (whether an activist, a Nanni Moretti-style socio-democrat, or an old-style communist). In this context, Cardinal Bergoglio's appropriation of Saint Francis's name in 2013 was propitious. The curious choice of name has enabled the pope to align himself, and to be aligned by others, with the Franciscan values outlined above. The final film I explore here, Daniele Luchetti's *Chiamatemi Francesco*,[8] deals with this crucial twist in the Francis tale.

Chiamatemi Francesco's title highlights both Bergoglio's warmth and informality ("call me Francis") and the role of the medieval saint in the pope's mission. Cardinal Bergoglio chose the name in memory of "the man of poverty, the man of peace, the man who loves and protects creation" (Bergoglio 2013). Daniele Luchetti, a director best known for political films such as *Il portaborse* (The Yes Man, 1991) and *Mio fratello è figlio unico* (My Brother Is an Only Child, 2007), focuses in the film on several episodes from Bergoglio's life as a Jesuit priest. He is shown in his role as Provincial Superior (1973–7) during Argentina's "dirty war," during which the right-wing military dictatorship, under General Jorge Videla, "disappeared" (i.e., murdered) as many as thirty thousand people. While the Catholic Church officially supported the regime, Bergoglio's institute hid people on the run from Videla's police. Later on, the film describes the period during which he was Auxiliary Bishop of Buenos Aires (1992–7). During those years, he worked among the city's poor and disadvantaged, a mission encapsulated in scenes narrating how he halted the bulldozers in a stand-off between a cold property speculator and the poor who were inhabiting the houses to be levelled. Thus Bergoglio faced two distinct antagonists: Vidala's brutal right-wing dictatorship, which "disappeared" those who challenged it, and 1990s neoliberalism, with its heartless property speculation. Bergoglio emerges from the film as a firm and peaceful protester against injustice, a role that comes into sharp focus in an episode that forms the centrepiece of his work as Auxiliary Bishop: the stand-off between the poor and the property speculator's bulldozers. Here he quietly, and powerfully, uses his religion to stand up to capitalist interests and in so doing positions Catholicism firmly on the side of the poor. Luchetti's Francis is a hybrid figure, one who is moulded from the biography of Pope Francis but who is also imbued with the values of Saint Francis. Moreover, Luchetti draws on traditional narratives used for committed left-wing heroes (a point I will deal with further in the following section). In a word, this character embodies a Church that has taken up Pasolini's battle cry and moved to the opposition.

---

8   Luchetti's subsequent two-part miniseries was broadcast during prime time on Mediaset's Canale 5 in 2016. It was based on the film version and filled in some of the narrative gaps.

There is a final reason why Francis has returned to Italy's big and small screens: the election of Pope Francis. Pope Francis, a controversial figure, and one who was especially popular at the beginning of his papacy, especially among non-believers,[9] has drawn attention to the values of Saint Francis through his unusual choice of name and his ministry. While subject to criticism, some observers contend that he is renewing the Church and providing an ethical model for twenty-first-century life (Murphy 2014; Reno 2015). The pope's popularity, especially initially, and his media-friendly persona have enabled his image to circulate widely in the public sphere and to reach secular quarters more easily than his predecessor, Pope Benedict XVI. Between the date of his election in 2013 and the date of writing, he has appeared in twenty-nine television documentaries, series, and specials in Italy. He has tapped themes of consumerism, poverty, and ecology in ways that have enabled his message to resonate with the secular left in Italy. Oskari Juurikkala (2015, 257) remarks of the reception of *Evangelii Gaudium* and *Laudato si'* that some commentators "praised the critique of so-called unfettered capitalism and libertarian economics" while others "labeled the pope a leftist, even a 'Marxist.'" While Pope Francis is not a Marxist, his Franciscan outlook has garnered him favour among those on the political left, including those in the filmmaking industry, some of whom, as I have outlined here, apparently see in the Saint Francis/Pope Francis nexus the crystallization of a new ethical model.

The rise of Saint Francis/Bergoglio must be read, in part at least, in light of the fall of a political model that had dominated Italy since the mid 1990s: Berlusconianism. Andrea Minuz in his e-book on left-wing cinema, *Quando c'eravamo noi* (2014), stresses the importance of the enemy in constructing a sense of identity for the post-ideological left, defining Silvio Berlusconi as "un'incompatibilità essenziale che funziona come un feticcio per poter rivivere un 'noi' ideologicamente compatto" (an essential incompatibility that functions as a fetish in order to be able to bring to life an ideologically compact "us") (2014). If Minuz is correct that the Berlusconi phenomenon helped keep the Italian left intact by providing it with an enemy against which to define its own (superior) identity, then the post-Berlusconi era poses a problem. As the Berlusconi-enemy that has functioned to keep the left compact since 1994 vanishes, so too does the certainty of the value system held on to by the left, a certainty founded on, according to Minuz, a "nostalgia del comunismo – non di quello reale, ma di quel sogno collettivo che mobilitava un 'noi'" (a nostalgia for communism – not for the real one, but for that collective dream which

---

9   Pope Francis was exceptionally popular in Italy, especially when he first took up his position. According to the Pew Research Center (2014), 97 per cent of Italian Catholics and 71 per cent of non-Catholics had a favourable opinion of him.

mobilized an "us"). It is in the context of a Renzi-Gentiloni era in which the politics of the left are no longer founded on a collective communist dream that we can read the hero-protagonists of three recent films and the further versions of the saint broadcast on RAI and Mediaset in recent years. If neoliberalism provides an enemy, a fictionalized Saint Francis/Pope Francis provides a hero with which to counter it.

Conclusion: The Impact of Fictional Catholic Values on Post-Secular Italy

The Manichean dichotomy between Salus and neoliberal leaders in *Le confessioni*, between the young Jorge Bergoglio and a corrupt political system in *Chiamatemi Francesco*, between Pius XII and the Nazis and fascists in *Sotto il cielo di Roma*, between a real priest and the Mafia in *Alla luce del sole*, confirms how deep-rooted the countercultural motif is in Italian filmmaking; it also underscores how this formula of the little man (and he is usually a man) who embraces "giustizia e pietà" (justice and mercy) and bravely strives against a corrupt system is critical to narrative structures in Italian cinema. As I will demonstrate in the following chapter, there are exceptions to the countercultural mode, but in the main, portrayals of the Church as a powerful political hierarchy no longer dominate cinema screens. Instead, the David-against-Goliath trope can indeed be read as the quintessential contemporary Italian plot form for the circulation of Catholic values. This trope, which is, of course, timeless, has nonetheless gained renewed visibility in the third millennium, during which it emphasizes the individual against the system, the politically powerless against the politically powerful, and – and this for me is the crucial part of the puzzle – the ethically powerful against the ethically weak. To a significant extent, this model has displaced the model of the Church that dominated the cinema of the 1960s, which saw the Church as a towering authoritarian institution aligned with the socio-political status quo.

The cinematic narratives that portray these ideal "David" characters owe a great deal to Catholic social teachings and suggest that ethical values, far from becoming a purely personal affair in Italy, are deeply enmeshed in the ethical fabric of one of Italy's most highly developed contemporary cultural industries: fiction filmmaking. The privatization of morality, widely seen as a key element of contemporary post-secular society, is therefore at most partial within the sector. The ethical binary of "giustizia e pietà" (justice and mercy) yokes oppositional, countercultural, and ethical values firmly together. It weaves together the threads of a watered-down Catholic social ethics and the threads of a watered-down left-wing politics. If representations in fiction filmmaking are in any way reflective of reality, this weave is critical to what it means to be Italian in twenty-first-century Italy.

That religious values are still circulating so successfully in Italy could be read as a sign of the emergence of a post-secular society in which religion has been assigned a significant cultural voice. However, such a reading would be premature as it does not take into account the multi-faith society that Italy is becoming. As we have seen in this chapter, the religious values assigned a voice are broadly Catholic. This raises the question about how other religions may voice their values. How can Italy's minority religious voices enter the film industry if it is dominated by such a well-defined sense of ethico-political identity and has such a strongly rooted narrative structure founded on a particular type of hero and a particular set of values?

Ferzan Özpetek's cinema provides a curious response to this question. Özpetek is a Turkish national who moved from a primarily Muslim country to Rome in 1976, took Italian citizenship, and has worked for decades in the Italian cinema industry. He has increasingly and visibly absorbed aspects of the religious and political matrix in which he works. If his first two films, *Il bagno turno (Hamam)* (1997), and *Harem suare* (1999), operated with an exotic, re-membered, Oriental matrix with which he blended Western European values, his later film, *Cuore sacro* (Sacred Heart, 2005), set entirely in Rome, not only cites the Catholic sacred heart in its title but also deliberately uses Catholic spectacle, even modelling a scene on Michelangelo's *Pietà*. More importantly for my argument here, it plants a Franciscan-inflected conversion narrative at its heart. A hard-working businesswoman, Irene (Barbara Bobulova), prioritizes a neoliberal economic agenda over its socio-political consequences, rather like the leaders of the G8 in Andò's *Le confessioni*, discussed earlier. In a lecture at the start of the film, she declares to her audience that

> è arrivato il momento di cercare nuovi mercati, in una logica in cui non possiamo più permetterci di considerare l'esistenza di un terzo o un quarto mondo ... cre[ando] bisogni dove apparentemente non sembrano esserci.

> the moment has arrived to find new markets, and to take an approach which no longer allows us to be concerned with the existence of the third or fourth world ... creating needs where apparently there are none.

However, faced with a profound emotional and ethical crisis, she goes in search of redemption, and gives up her riches to serve the poor. In the final scene, as she walks through a crowded Termini train station, she slowly removes her earrings, rings, and bag, and eventually strips naked, passing each item to a bewildered bystander. The scene, in its radical rejection of possessions, calls to mind the Saint Francis narrative. With its focus on Catholic-inflected alternatives to neoliberalism, it demonstrates how full integration into Catholic culture ultimately means full integration into the value system inherent in the narrative and spectacle of its dominant religion. If Özpetek's career, in which he slowly absorbs Catholic values, is anything to go by, conforming to the ethical matrix is an important part of being accepted as an "Italian" rather than migrant filmmaker. The turn towards religious models as carriers for values creates a compact *italianità* (Italianness) that results in conformity within the film industry: even the most agnostic directors (Cavani, Luchetti, Andò) are called upon to make, or choose to make, films on saints, monks, popes, and resisting priests. This leaves very little space for cinema – especially migrant cinema – that does not conform.

The second point regarding post-secular society to be made here is of another order. This centres on whether the religious voice found in Italian fiction filmmaking is being heard on its own terms. Habermas speaks of how religious citizens cannot contribute directly to the debate in post-secular societies but need to "translate" their contributions into "secular" or "public" reason, thus creating an asymmetric burden (Habermas 2006, 11). With church buildings ever less frequented, films, alongside other media, tend to provide the "real story" for many spectators, supplanting the Church's message. Stig Hjarvard (2011) contends that mediatization changes how people engage with religion: when the media become the site where people encounter religion and the sacred, the position of religious institutions is weakened. Hjarvard concludes that media, including film, "takes over the power to define and frame what religion is, and what parts of religion are considered significant in society" (cited in Lövheim and Lynch 2011, 109). As religious messages are mediatized, they are inevitably edited, recomposed, and changed. While Michael L. Budde, a media sceptic writing in the American context, says that the message about religion in media and film becomes focused on "controversy, scandal, the unusual or freakish" (1998), what I have explored here shows that this does not hold for contemporary Italy: few films today focus on Church scandal. What is happening in Italy instead may be closer to what Hjarvard discusses when he says that mediatization results in "banal religion," a hybrid form that "contains elements drawn from the texts and practices of institutional religion, but [that] merges these with elements from folk religion and popular conceptions, emotions and practices that refer to a supernatural or spiritual dimension of life" – a "bricolage," says Hjarvard, using Levi-Strauss's well-known term. This leads to the transformation of religion as the meanings of religious symbols "become[] disembedded from their context" and "reinterpreted" and "circulated into a wider range of contexts than those controlled by formal religious authorities."

The religious values I have discussed in this chapter cannot be described as banal, but they certainly can be seen as "hybrids" and "translations." The

"Francis turn" demonstrates how religious values become intermingled with left-wing politics, and particularly with critiques of capitalism. *Sotto il cielo di Roma* shows how a secular character (the partisan) and a pope can be aligned, filmically speaking. For religious thinkers, the problem with this process of hybridization and translation is that the distinctive nature of Catholic faith is in large part erased. Turning back to Salus's last sermon in *Le confessioni*, we can see precisely how this happens. In his abridged version of Matthew, Salus cites the words "giustizia e pietà." The sermon omits the third word that appears in the original biblical text: "faith." So Catholic values may circulate, but they are only able to do so when they soft-peddle on Catholic faith.

4 Protest in the Public Sphere: The Shifting Line between Religious and Secular Space

Introduction

In 2010 the radical anticlerical group Facciamo Breccia staged its last parade in Rome after five years of protests calling for the separation of church and state. In a move that was to attract the scorn of both the conservative Vatican press and the left-wing newspaper *Il manifesto*, the group transported a life-size transsexual Madonna with bleeding heart and male genitals across the city. With the then-incumbent Pope Benedict XVI in mind, they accompanied their progress with chants of "Benedetta, vecchia travestita, alzati la gonna e goditi la vita" (Benedetta, you old transvestite, lift up your skirt and enjoy life). Facciamo Breccia's deliberately provocative protest provides a glimpse of the more extreme attacks on the Catholic Church that have taken place in Italy's piazzas in the first decade of the new millennium. Furthermore, Catholicism is not the only religion under attack. In September 2017 the extreme-right-wing group Casa Pound marched through the Esquilino area of Rome carrying flaming torches and calling for the closing of a Muslim prayer house in Via San Vito. Casa Pound arrived just days after a flash-mob organized by another group on the extreme right, Fratelli d'Italia, protested outside the prayer house. The protests at Via San Vito are just a tiny fraction of the Islamophobic protests against mosques and prayer houses. There have also been protests against, and attacks on, migrants, many of whom are Muslim (Bartoli 2012; Fondazione ISMU 2017).

Protests by organizations like Facciamo Breccia, Casa Pound, and Fratelli d'Italia demonstrate that Italy's two largest religions – Catholicism and Islam – are objects of protest in twenty-first-century Italy. At the heart of anti-Catholic protest lies the angry response on the part of certain secular elements in society at the Vatican's intervention in matters judged to be beyond its jurisdiction. Central to anti-Islamic protest are Muslim places of prayer and the increasingly visible place of Muslims in Italy. In other words, while anti-Catholic protest is largely confined to Catholic interference in matters considered secular, anti-Muslim protest is existential and protests the very existence of mosques, and therefore of the faith itself, on Italian soil. My focus in this chapter is on anti-Catholic protest. I reserve my investigation of opposition to Islam for the following chapter, which deals with Italy's minority faiths.

Since the millennium, religion has persisted in the public sphere not only because of Catholicism's hold over the filmmaking industry (chapter 1), nor simply because it remains a model in iconographic and performative terms (chapter 2) or retains a significant place in the narration and circulation of values (chapter 3), but also, somewhat paradoxically, because of protests launched against it. Without protest, religion would struggle to retain its current level of visibility in the public sphere. The media coverage that a protest cycle can attract plays a critical role in the creation and circulation of debate, as outlined in Michael Lipsky's seminal analysis. Lipsky argues that protesters and the media are interdependent: "if protest tactics are not considered significant by the media, or if newspaper and television reporters or editors decide to overlook protest tactics, protest organizations will not succeed" (Lipsky 1969, 1151). This view is widely held by scholars of protest (Oliver and Myers 1999; Gamson and Meyer 1996; Gamson and Wolfsfeld 1993; Zald 1996). Mediated protest renders movements, ideas, and stories visible. The screening of protest stories, however, does more than enable protest groups to gain visibility; it also keeps the objects of protest in the public sphere, providing lasting images and narratives, even where these are negative. When religion is neither protester nor protested it risks being perceived as an "old" story and disappearing from circulation in the public sphere. Thus, one way in which religion continues to circulate and persist is through its very contestation. While most scholars of protest focus on non-fiction media reporting, in this chapter I make the case for fiction filmmaking, arguing that it is a significant player in the circulation of protest stories in Italy. Its role is crucial because *impegnato* (engaged) filmmaking is a large and prestigious part of the fiction filmmaking industry and one that commands a high audience share. Given the size and importance of engaged filmmaking in Italy, fiction provides an acute if not always accurate barometer of protest.

My argument here is that the filmmaking industry occupies its place in the contemporary public debate especially by narrativizing two key loci of conflict, each of which reflects a broader debate over the role of the Catholic Church in life on the peninsula. These two are the Vatican's relationship with Italy's political and economic ecosystem, and its relationship with the lives and bodies of individual Italian citizens through its interventions in debates on civil partnerships and medical ethics (euthanasia, in vitro fertilization, and so on). In the first section of the chapter I explore how several films take the Vatican to task for the part it plays in Italy's tightly woven economic and political life. Its enmeshment in political institutions and banking has led to it being implicated in the dark underbelly of Italian politics, from Masonic lodges to the Mafia. The films I investigate here include Giuseppe Ferrara's *I banchieri di Dio: Il caso Calvi* (The God's Bankers, 2001), Paolo Sorrentino's *Il divo: La spettacolare vita di Giulio Andreotti* (Il Divo, 2008), and Roberto Faenza's *La verità sta in cielo* (2016). In the following section, I shift the focus away from the body politic and towards the politicized body, where conflict between religious and secular standpoints has long been projected. My corpus includes a range of genres, from the re-enacted documentary – Gustav Hofer and Luca Ragazzi's *Improvvisamente l'inverno scorso* (Suddenly, Last Winter, 2008) – to Marco Bellocchio's *Bella addormentata* (Dormant Beauty, 2012) and "La maternità," a comic episode from Carlo Verdone's *Manuale d'amore 2* (Manual of Love 2, 2007). As it is fiction filmmaking for cinema, rather than television, that provides the channel for protest in Italy, films made for the big screen provide most of my examples in this chapter.[1]

At stake in this chapter is the separation of the institutions of church and state (as discussed especially in the first section) and the clash between Catholic teachings and twenty-first-century liberal standpoints regarding an individual's right to his or her body (in the second section). Together, these two loci of conflict demarcate the boundary between what many contemporary Italian filmmakers believe should reside within the arena of the secular and what can legitimately appertain to the sacred. Identifying where this boundary lies is critical to an understanding of the secular and post-secular in twenty-first-century Italian filmmaking. This is a hard-fought and constantly shifting boundary. As will quickly become apparent, there is nothing stable about the line drawn between secular and religious space.

Protesting "Diffuse Religion": The Vatican Enmeshed in Mafia and Politics

In chapter 3 I argued that a paradigm shift has taken place in Italian filmmaking. The Catholic Church, so often portrayed in the work of mid-century Italian filmmakers like Federico Fellini, Pietro Germi, and Marco Ferrari as a domineering force in society, has been emerging as countercultural on television and in much cinema. In this section I turn the tables and investigate those films

---

1 I investigate divergences between television and cinema with regard to protest in "The Cinema of Resistance: Nanni Moretti's *Il caimano* and the Italian Film Industry" (Brook 2009), arguing that during the Berlusconi governments, cinemas – especially art-house cinemas – provided a haven for films that failed to get aired elsewhere. In that article I was arguing that Berlusconi exerted strong influence over the national channels and Mediaset; in Chapter 1 of this volume I discussed how the Catholic presence on RAI, in particular, has made it a fundamentally pro-Catholic space, which limits its capacity for protest.

in which the Church is still construed as a powerful societal force. Films that construct the Church in this way generally narrate Vatican scandals, especially those pertaining to the Vatican bank. My corpus here is narrow, reflecting a significantly smaller set of examples. All three films chosen (*I banchieri di Dio*; *Il divo*; *La verità sta in cielo*) describe how the Catholic Church has insinuated itself into secular society, and all tackle the shadowy links between the Istituto per le opere di religione (the IOR, or Vatican Bank), the Vatican, the Mafia, a Masonic lodge known as Propaganda Due (P2), and the Italian political class.[2]

The first two of these films, Giuseppe Ferrara's *I banchieri di Dio* and Paolo Sorrentino's *Il divo*, draw these worlds together through the entangled, and ultimately deadly, stories of two notorious bankers, Roberto Calvi and Michele Sindona, whose relations with the Vatican Bank led to it being swept into a web of offshore holding companies that later came under intense investigation regarding tax evasion and money laundering.[3] Then in 2016, the third film – Roberto Faenza's *La verità sta in cielo* – revisits the Vatican Bank story as part of an investigation into another of Italy's unsolved mysteries: the disappearance of schoolgirl Emanuela Orlandi on 22 June 1983. While Christian Uva describes *Il divo* as "un vero e proprio 'cineglossario' dei principali 'fattacci' dell'Italia repubblicana" (a true "cineglossary" of the main "bad facts" of Republican Italy) (Uva 2011), all three of these post-millennium thrillers set out to knit together the various powers active in Italian life. It is as if these powers were threads in an intricate web that ultimately controls society and the players in it but that is too vast and complex ever to be fully grasped. In this section I illustrate how

---

2   The Vatican Bank has been subjected to unfavourable cinematic portrayals in American movies since the scandal first broke in the 1980s. A dark connection was drawn at this time between the Vatican hierarchy, the Mafia, and money. The plot of Francis Ford Coppola's *Godfather III* (1990) casts dark suspicions over the Vatican Bank's part in the collapse of Italy's Catholic Bank, the Ambrosiano. The film shows an archbishop, with suspicious links to the Mafia, murdered in the Vatican, "his corpse replicating sixteenth-century Protestant images of the defeat of the Antichrist" (Posner 2014, 363). Frank Perry's *Monsignor* (1982) portrays an ambitious American priest arriving at the Vatican and entering into dealings with the Mafia, banks, and the black market. He is made a cardinal. Peter Richardson's controversial comedy *The Pope Must Die* (1991) tells the story of a priest elected pope by clerical error in a Vatican controlled by the Mafia: his investigation of the Vatican Bank's accounts uncovers illegal gun smuggling, and although he is promptly removed from his duties because he poses a threat, he continues his anti-Mafia campaign until a good female pope is elected. The depiction of a powerful religious institution directing its attentions away from heavenly goals towards terrestrial ones is a not infrequent trope in Hollywood. Hollywood does not just attack the Catholic hierarchy in Rome on questions of financial corruption; it also targets home-grown evangelical ministers. See, for example, Stephen Gyllenhaal's *Promised a Miracle* (1988) and Richard Pearce's *Leap of Faith* (1992). Italy is much less damning in its depictions.

3   The dealings of Sindona, Calvi, the P2, the Mafia, and the political class are deeply interwoven. I refer the reader to Posner (2014), Willan (2007), Gurwin (1983) and R. Cornwell (1983) for their contrasting interpretations of events.

that web has been constructed in filmic terms in order better to understand where Church power ends on screen and other powers in society begin. In other words, by highlighting protest I attempt to map where the line is drawn today between secular and religious space.

The first of these films, Ferrara's *I banchieri di Dio*, focuses keenly on the place of the Church in the scandals, reconstructing the final period of Roberto Calvi's life, from revelations of his dealings with the Masonic lodge P2 (Propaganda Due) in 1981 to his mysterious death by hanging under Blackfriar's Bridge in London on 11 June 1982. It documents his dealings with a complex tapestry of powerful figures who reside in the banking world (Michele Sindona; Roberto Calvi), in the P2 (Licio Gelli; Umberto Ortolani), in the Italian government (Giulio Andreotti); and in the Vatican (Paul Casimir Marcinkus and Luigi Mennini), as well as Mafia figures, criminals, and fixers like Francesco Pazienza. While *I banchieri di Dio* presents an accurate account of many of the events in the Calvi affair, it sits firmly within the speculative conspiracy thriller genre, giving undue emphasis, for instance, to a rescue plan hatched by Calvi's Banco Ambrosiano on the part of Opus Dei – the organization so sinisterly portrayed in Ron Howard's *The Da Vinci Code*. Moreover, the film's finale offers a speculative account of events, narrated with studied realist precision, whereas Calvi's final days are still veiled in mystery. Ferrara's explicit framing of Flavio Carbone and Pippo (Giuseppe Calò) as Calvi's murderers led Carbone to bring a legal case against the filmmaker.

In the second film, Sorrentino's *Il divo*, the emphasis falls on the political class rather than the Church. It centres on Giulio Andreotti, one of the principal protagonists of the Christian Democratic Party that dominated Italian political life for fifty-two years. It takes Andreotti as the centre of, and symbol for, obscure power, and from this centring reveals the unravelling of Italy's corrupt political ecosystem between 1991 and 1996. The film is set against the background of the end of Italy's first republic and the "disfacimento morale di un intera nazione" (moral undoing of an entire nation) (Iannotta 2016, 6). The Vatican is implicated from the outset in the film's grotesque denunciation of the corruption of the head of the party. During the film's violent and spectacular opening, it lists among Italy's mysterious murders the deaths of two bankers caught up in the Vatican scandals, Roberto Calvi and Michele Sindona.

Of the three films, it is Faenza's *La verità sta in cielo* that comes closest to providing a denunciation, rather than simply a glamorization, of the nexus between organized crime, politicians, and the Vatican. The film slowly pieces together the puzzle of the disappearance of a fifteen-year-old, Emanuela Orlandi, daughter of a Vatican employee. An Italian journalist (Maya Sansa) is engaged by the British media to investigate the case. Through her interviews, the film concludes that Orlandi's kidnapper was Enrico De Pedis (Riccardo Scamarcio), boss of a Roman gang called the Testaccini, a rival to the more famous Banda della Magliana. The film's hypothesis is that he was trying to force the Vatican Bank to return to him money lent to it through Calvi's Banco Ambrosiano. Nonetheless, the film ends with the mystery still unresolved. Like *I banchieri di Dio*, *La verità sta in cielo* makes truth-claims and markets itself as investigative. Indeed, in 2017, it was screened during the United Nations International Day for the Right to Truth in Paris. The target of its denunciation is the Vatican's secrecy and silence. Faenza claims that the Church holds a dossier on the case and knows what happened but has never revealed the truth, a truth that therefore remains in the "cielo" (heavens) of the film's title. The investigative nature of the film is reinforced by five short promotional documentaries, in which actor Riccardo Festa plays a journalist who interviews several non-fictional characters, including Orlandi's brother, a judge, and a RAI journalist involved in the case. These semi-fictional documentaries support the feature film's truth-claims.

All three films employ elements from the crime thriller genre and foreground the interwoven institutional and criminal structures of Italy. All three present the Holy See as one element in a mosaic of power bases, equal in terrestrial power to the state, the P2 (especially in the case *of I banchieri di Dio*), and the web of organized crime. In *I banchieri di Dio*, this mosaic is presented visually in the film's rapid cutting between a radically large number of spaces, both interior and exterior, that are occupied by each key power base (the Vatican, the houses of parliament, the Banco Ambrosiano, judicial offices, American banks) and by the off-duty rich and powerful (fine houses, yachts, runways for private planes). As the film proceeds, it also weaves in spaces occupied by those whose power is threatened or lost (Gelli's bunker, Lodi jail, Calvi's cheap hotel room in London). The persistent intercutting of spaces increases rather than decreases as the plot unfolds; this runs counter to the more typical thriller structure, in which multiple spaces are gradually reduced as the links between disparate spaces become clearer as parallel plots are drawn together. This complex and often jarring mosaic, patched together through rapid cutting, is reinforced by the removal of boundaries between the spaces occupied by the powerful. This spatial porosity is sustained by a mise en scène that features an array of large windows and open doorways as well as by sequences presenting busy movement between spaces (up and down stairs, along corridors, in cars). While Calvi holds on to his power, his movement between these spaces is seamless. The loss of power results in locked doors and cages (in the jail and courtroom), unheeded requests for entry (the Vatican), and border checks (London). The ease and freedom with which the rich and powerful move between their privileged spaces is reinforced by a mise en scène that draws the fragmented spaces together under a series of visual motifs that together create a gradient from the most to least powerful: the most powerful inhabit semi-regal spaces full of high windows, heavy curtains, mahogany furniture, and leather and brocade (the Banco Ambrosiano, the Vatican, the Masonic lodge). The next tier down inhabits plain late-1970s-style offices: functional buildings such as judicial offices. At the bottom of the pecking order are enclosed, almost windowless, spartan spaces such as Lodi prison, Gelli's bunker, and Calvi's London hotel, with its narrow, ill-lit corridors, peeling wallpaper, and plywood doors. In other words, in this film spaces are divided into types according to the level of power that they reflect.

This same intermingling of worlds that might otherwise be considered distinct is seen in both *Il divo* and *La verità sta in cielo*. In *Il divo*, visual parallels are put in place between the spaces inhabited by the powerful. Whether religious or political, they share an opulent, courtly atmosphere. There is a striking scene that captures the arrival of Andreotti's men (the "brutta corrente," or bad tide) in menacing slow motion: politicians, a businessman, and a cardinal all exit their cars in identical fashion, as if there were no distinctions to be made among these societal segments. In *La verità sta in cielo* the Italian political system, bosses of organized crime, and the Catholic Church again move within the same Italian power system: a Mafia boss has privileged access both to the legal system and to the Vatican Bank. By knitting the Vatican together with the corrupt elements of the Italian state and the dark underbelly of Italian organized crime, these films demonstrate anxiety about the entangled and compromised position of the Church in Italy. The Vatican is a sovereign state in these films, but it is far from being independent of the Italian political system and other worldly matters and is deeply enmeshed in Italy's affairs.

This enmeshment strengthens the Church's terrestrial powers rather than weakening them. The enmeshed Vatican is resilient, immutable, and enduring. The buffeting it receives from the Sindona and Calvi and Orlandi cases leaves it unscathed, while around it others fall. In *I banchieri di Dio*, American Bishop Marcinkus provides the metonymy for this power. Rutger Hauer, the Dutch actor who plays him, transforms Marcinkus's Lithuanian features into Teutonic ones: blue eyes and a strong, square jaw. The trope of the Teutonic man is used here – indeed, repeatedly in Italian cinema – as a signal of superiority, foreignness, and cold brutality. His immense physicality is set against that of Calvi, a man with weaker facial features, who is portrayed as neurotic and infantile. In the film's epilogue, a slow pan reveals the inner sanctum of the Vatican – heavy marble columns, thick red brocade curtains, cardinals motionless on their golden thrones, the pope kneeling with his back to us, and Marcinkus wearing a mitre and vestments. The bold solidity of the mise en scène and the resistant, statuesque characters – none of whom will challenge Marcinkus's doctored account of Calvi's death – provides an allegory for the strong silence of the Church. Marcinkus's brand of strong but mobile masculinity – which dynamically links the Church to banks, politics, and ultimately the Mafia – provides a key to the film's construction of the Church as an invincible Darwinian survivor, persisting through its ability to weave its way into society.

The key observation to be drawn from the Vatican Bank scandal stories it that they reveal anxiety about the fragility of the national democratic process and the Church's role in bringing about that fragility. The chaotic and porous relationship between state, Church, bankers, and criminal gangs has the effect of presenting Italy's political ecosystem as systemically weak: attacked on one side by a supra-national network of criminals, on another by bankers, and on a third by a glob-ally networked Catholic hierarchy. In these films, democratic decision-making is displaced to spaces outside the national political sphere: the Vatican, crimi-nal dens, bank board rooms, Masonic lodges. In this vision, the dualistic par-adigm of church and state that has long dominated cinematic thinking about Catholicism has been replaced by a model of interlocking and multiple worlds that together form a mobile and networked force. While these films purportedly investigate or present crimes from the 1980s (Calvi died in 1982, and Sindona in 1986; Emanuela Orlandi disappeared in 1983), their vision of interlocking, tentacular forces is distinctly contemporary and reflects recent critical interpre-tations of the place of Catholicism in the public sphere. John Pollard (2008) and Tom Bailey and Michael Driessen (2016), for instance, describe the Catholic Church in the third millennium as no longer rooted in politics through a single political party (the Democrazia cristiana, which collapsed in the mid 1990s). Instead it has developed a diffuse, cross-party presence. Moreover, the Church has entered directly into debates in the public sphere on immigration, bioethics, gay marriage, and so on, bypassing political parties. Pollard (2008) argues that this has far from weakened the Church; indeed, this diffuse Catholicism has never had such a strong influence over Italian politics as it does today. While the films detailing the Vatican Bank scandals deal with the historic scandals, rather than their recent reiterations, their positing of the Church as a strong, tentacular presence owes much to anxieties about the contemporary re-embedding of the Vatican in Italy's political life in the new millennium.

Contesting the Body in the "Age of Authenticity"

The second bastion of protest in Italy today has to do with the rights of the indi-vidual over his or her own body in the face of an institution that has historically written the rules governing it. Today, the Vatican still frequently intervenes on issues pertaining to the body (sexuality, euthanasia, in vitro fertilization, and stem-cell research) and attempts to influence Italian legislation (Fox 2008; Di Marco 2009; Grzymala-Busse 2015). This has proved a point of conflict between secular and religious constituencies and indeed at times within or between Catholic organizations. My aim in this section is not simply to identify what has been protested, but to explore how body-centred protest reflects a deeper cultural clash between religious and secular positions today. This cul-tural clash inheres between religious regulation and the wishes of the individual against the backdrop of an era labelled by philosopher Charles Taylor (2007) as the "Age of Authenticity."

In this section I explore three key issues that have provided filmmakers with material for protest. First I investigate the civil partnerships debate, drawing on a corpus of films that include comedies for the big and small screen: *Il padre delle spose* (2006), the episode on gay marriage in Carlo Verdone's *Manuale d'amore 2* (Manual of Love 2, 2007), the comedy by Matteo Vicino, *Outing: Fidanzati per sbaglio* (2013), and Maria Sole Tognazzi's *Io e Lei* (2015). The film on which I focus here is Gustav Hofer and Luca Ragazzi's *Improvvisamente l'inverno scorso* (Suddenly, Last Winter, 2008), a re-enacted documentary that weaves narrative fiction into the documentary format. Then, I explore how filmmakers have criticized the Vatican for its control over fertility, drawing on a corpus of comedies and dramas, including Paolo Virzì's *Tutti i santi giorni* (Every Blessed Day, 2012) and the episode "La maternità" from Carlo Verdone's *Manuale d'amore 2*. As "La maternità" best encapsulates the nub of the conflict, it provides my focus here. Finally, I look at euthanasia, especially as discussed in Marco Bellocchio's *Bella addormentata* (Dormant Beauty, 2012), which deals directly with the politics of euthanasia in Italy today, but also drawing on Enrico Pau's *L'Accabadora* (2015), which is set in the 1940s and describes a traditional form of euthanasia in Sardinia, and *Miele* (Honey, 2013) by Valeria Golina.

One of the most hard-fought issues in Italy in recent years has been the clash between Catholicism and LGBTQ groups. Activists in Italy have protested at Church intervention that has supported the continued exclusion of sexual minorities from the economic, personal, and societal benefits of marriage, highlighting how the Vatican's position stands in conflict with secular civil rights. For its part, the Vatican continues to emphasize that marriage is more than a sacrament – it is also a public institution that lays the foundation for the proper working of society. For the Church, marriage is not simply a private affair. While members of the Church's liberal wings have made efforts to bring these two apparently irreconcilable positions together (Heywood 2015), compromise remains difficult.[4] The activism of lay liberal Catholics involved in the global movement We Are Church and the work of theologians like Gianino Piano have not yet succeeded in bridging the gap. Despite certain conciliatory statements made by Pope Francis, there is no obvious compromise to be found between the Vatican's official position on marriage and family and that of gay

---

4   Paolo Heywood's anthropological study of the Bologna chapter of We Are Church (Heywood 2015) found that its lobbying for the Church to adopt a progressive position drew it closer to LGBTQ perspectives. But in so doing, it shifted it away from the official Church in the eyes of the LGBTQ community, and as it was unrepresentative of official positions, its effectiveness was undermined. Heywood's study found that in Bologna the middle ground between such opposing positions was impossible to maintain.

rights activists. Nonetheless, on 11 May 2016, after a long and divisive battle, Italy's parliament finally approved a same-sex civil unions bill.

Ragazzi and Hofer's *Improvvisamente l'inverno scorso* documents the tortured and finally aborted life of the DiCo legislation (Diritti e doveri dei conviventi / Rights and Responsibilities of Domestic Partners), a forerunner of the civil union bill, which was subjected to heated public, ecclesiastical, and parliamentary debate in Italy after it was proposed by Romano Prodi's centre-left government in 2007. The tale of the legislation is told through the eyes of a gay couple: two young and fashionable urban male journalists, Gustav Hofer and Luca Ragazzi. They travel through Rome attending protests and interviewing people from a wide spectrum of positions, from neofascists to members of the conservative Catholic organization Communion and Liberation, and from the centre-left Minister for Equal Rights, Barbara Pollastrini, to Franco Grillini, founder of Arcigay. As the film develops, their hopes for the legislation, and for a society in which they will have equal rights, crumble. The film concludes without the legislation being passed.

Central to the film's protest is the conflict over who, in Italy, has the right to the discourse of family. The film deliberately challenges the notion that the Catholic Church has exclusive rights to "family" and endeavours to claim that term for gay couples, portraying an alternative family in opposition to, but also equal to, the Catholic family. In a sequence documenting Gay Pride, for instance, the camera focuses on an emotive speech by a transgender MP, Vladimir Luxuria, in which she employs the category of "family" to frame her argument. She denounces the Catholic family as flawed and redefines "family" in broad, liberal terms as a place where abuse is absent and there is "ascolto, rispetto, amore" (listening, respect, love). In other words, she deconstructs the fundamentally biological and reproductive concept of family, on which the Catholic Church bases its teachings, and replaces it with a concept founded not on reproduction but on broad and contemporary values.

Of all the terms available to it – "queer," "couple," "equality," "civil rights," and so on – *Improvvisamente l'inverno scorso* selects "family" as its primary ideological frame. Gustav and Luca perform family throughout the film, from scenes depicting their ordinary domestic life (reading together in bed; eating breakfast together; minor disagreements) to their absence of sexual interest in anyone else and the co-opting of children. The imperative of assimilating children into the film's discourse seems the only possible motivation for a zoom in the film's epilogue: during the imagined wedding of Luca and Gustav, a woman carrying a baby is suddenly foregrounded. Their performance of the family foregrounds monogamy, children, a loving relationship, and duration over promiscuity, queer-ness, childlessness, and unstable relationships. What is at stake in *Improvvisamente l'inverno scorso* is the ownership of the contested family frame. Rather than focusing on equal rights, or even the freedom to love or have sex with whom one wishes, the film chooses the one thing that sets it most firmly against the Vatican's position. This distinguishes it from media discussions of civil partnerships and gay marriage that took place in countries like the United Kingdom before they passed legislation.

While the choice of a family frame, and the concomitant domestication of gay and lesbian lives, is hardly an exclusively Italian phenomenon and can be read as part of a wider trend in Western cinema and sociocultural discourse since the 1990s to legitimize homosexuality (Dyer 1993; Duggan 2002; Benshoff and Griffen 2006), it is nonetheless a striking feature of Italian filmmaking today and demonstrates a significant disparity between Italy and other Western countries. In Italy, the films mentioned above (*Il padre delle spose*; the episode on gay marriage in *Manuale d'amore 2*; *Outing: Fidanzati per sbaglio*; Maria Sole Tognazzi's *Io e Lei*) all attempt to legitimize gay relationships by employing the family frame. In the United States, France, Germany, Spain, and the United Kingdom battles with religious institutions over gay marriage have died down and expressions of gay sex on screen are increasingly acceptable.

This centring on the family paradigm excludes queer. The chaste, metonymic gay kiss found in films like *Improvvisamente l'inverno scorso*, *Manuale di amore 2*, and *Io e Lei* shares a peculiar similarity with the metonymic, heterosexual kiss in the heyday of mid-century Hollywood cinema, before the end of the Hayes Production Code, and reveals the films' protest as more conservative and cautious than it first seems. Queer, defined by Benshoff and Griffen (2006, 6) as "the vast array of human sexualities that actually exist outside of monogamous heterosexual procreative intercourse," one that "exposes the inadequacy of the straight-gay binary and the power hierarchies involved in it" (7), continues to present a problem for Italian filmmakers. Queer, with its call for fluidity, performativity, relativity, and non-monogamous practices, could not be further from Catholic discourses on the family as an absolute value, and on monogamy and procreation. The queer discourse has been silenced in order to inscribe these Italian films onto a looser discourse of the family, one that is still ultimately founded on Catholic values. What has not developed in Italy is the kind of filmmaking seen in America's New Queer Cinema during the 1990s, which was "edgy, angry and theoretically rigorous" and was "unapologetic in [its] frank look at sexuality" and "eschewed 'positive images' and 'happy endings' in favour of more complexly queer musings on the nature of gender and sexuality" (Benshoff and Griffen 2006, 220). Instead these Italian films avoid complexity in their reinscription of relationships within a family that is surprisingly close to a traditional one. Their happy ending is an imagined integration of good, unthreatening, monogamous gay people into Italian society. They repress – or conceal – queer elements of sexuality, which would necessarily foreground incompatibility with Catholicism, in order to have their voice on the peninsula. They also suppress and deny the real, and unresolved, fault line between Catholic attitudes and secular ones. While these films may appear to speak for the LGBTQ community, they actually silence queer as well as, of course, transexual and intersex experiences.[5] In other words, they only speak for a part of this community, one that is compatible with liberal Catholic theologian Giannino Piana's (2010) emphasis on the "authenticity" of a romantic partnership above the sexual orientation or gender of those engaging in it. The middle ground in the conflict between LGBTQ and the Vatican, which, as We Are Church and others have discovered, is actually almost impossible to occupy, is effectively colonized by the world of cinema fiction. The family frame positions gay themes in such a way as to make them acceptable to liberal Catholics and secular conservatives alike.

The second area of investigation is the Church's control over fertility. The Vatican opposes in vitro fertilization because it disassociates sexual from reproductive acts and fails to respect human life, since multiple embryos are created, most of which are destroyed. In 2004 a restrictive law was introduced in Italy that opposed the fertilization of more than three oocytes during reproduction and forbade the selection or cryopreservation of embryos. In 2005 a referendum was held to repeal the law, and in the heated debate that ensued, the Catholic Church appealed for Catholics not to cast their vote. In the referendum only one in four Italians voted, so the law remained in place. The Church's intervention in the debate was seen by those who opposed the result as an attack on the secular state. For instance, Emma Bonino, a former European Union commissioner, claimed that "today we have three victims: the secularism of the state, political authority, and the institution of the referendum" (Turone 2005). The outcome of the 2005 referendum resulted in 3,610 Italians travelling to other countries the following year to access fertilization treatment (Turone 2005).

Carlo Verdone's episode "La maternità" was released the year after the referendum. It recounts the story of Franco (Fabio Volo) and Manuela (Barbara Bobulova), a young couple unable to have a child, who, with the help of an Italian medical doctor, fly to Barcelona for fertility treatment unavailable in Italy. In other words, it narrates the story of those who left the country for treatment that year. Turning to the camera at the start of the episode, Franco cites Article 13,3B of Law 40 (2004) of the Italian constitution ("Non si può effettuare alcun tipo di selezione sui gameti maschili e femminili" (No selection of male or female gametes is permissible) and glosses this with, "Ecco perché noi siamo costretti ad andare fino in Spagna" (That's why we have go as far as Spain). Franco's short legal summary refers to the debate and thus, implicitly, to the

---

5   Transsexuals have little on-screen visibility either in this documentary or elsewhere: a transmedial project for RAI, *Transiti: Il mondo sconosciuto dei/delle trans* (2011), and a film for the big screen by Matteo Botrugno and Daniele Coluccini, *Rito di primavera* (2013), are two of the very few sensitive images of this community on Italian television and or in cinema.

position of the Church in Italy, a Church that influences politics and lawmaking and, therefore, ultimately the choices citizens can make (this point is reinforced in the next episode, "Matrimonio," in which a gay couple goes to Spain to have their partnership legally recognized because this cannot be done in Italy). The "Leviathan" position of the Italian race is therefore foregrounded.

"Maternità," like "Matrimonio," which follows it, ostensibly sets a backward Italy against an ultramodern and secular Spain, the liberal Spain of the anticlerical José Luis Rodríguez Zapatero, prime minister from 2004 to 2011. Martin Dines and Sergio Rigoletto (2012) note that the two countries have long had a close and "comforting" relationship, but that there was evidence in television fiction of "what has been described as the 'sorpasso' of Italy by Spain" (42) under Zapatero's socialist government. In *Manuale d'amore 2*, Barcelona is, for Franco and Manuela, a city of chrome, white walls, and glass, complete with a hypermodern minimalist hospital and hotel, both of which resemble science fiction sets.

If there are clear limits to protest in the films dealing with homosexuality in Italy, limits emerge here too. The film looks with some envy at the utopian freedom found in another Catholic country, but it also expresses a distinct uneasiness at its ultrasecular modernity. Asked to produce sperm at the hospital in Barcelona, Franco finds the room assigned to him "un poco frío" (a bit cold), as it is made up of hard surfaces and cool greys. He turns down a porn magazine and settles for the broadsheet *El País*. The only suitable inspiration within is Leonardo da Vinci's enigmatic and fully clothed Mona Lisa. The Mona Lisa, of course, represents the epitome of the Italian Renaissance and is contrasted with the cold, efficient hypermodernity of Spain. Paolo's choice of the iconic Italian portrait implies his sensual reconnection with Italian iconography over the anonymity of a modernity that is revealed as at least in part dystopian behind its sophisticated exterior. The relocation of maternity to the medical sphere removes it not just from Vatican intervention but also from human intervention, and threatens Italian national identity.

So while Paolo and Manuela are impressed and excited by the hard, secular modernity of Barcelona, their dreams remain quintessentially Italian and traditional: Paolo's real fantasy is about playing football with his son; for Manuela, the search for the child's name brings her back to her grandmother, Nonna Lisa – which provides the episode's final punchline ("Mona Lisa") – but also suggests an atavistic urge. Secular Spain provides a practical solution; that country is seen as more advanced, but the comfort afforded by an ahistorical and unchanging *italianità* prevails:

Spain appears repeatedly constructed as Italy's double, as an uncanny projection of a national collective "noi" losing its stability and recognisable contours. Under these terms, Spain emerges as a reflection of what Italy could become, should the country lose sight of its perceived Catholic roots and its family-based moral and legal traditions. (Dines and Rigoletto 2012, 483)

The tension in "Maternità" between the longing for maternity[6] – a maternity rooted in tradition, religion, and nature – and the coldness and alienation of modern medical redefinitions of maternity is a sign of a nostalgia and of a certain discomfort about the medicalization of birth. Italy's failure to resist the power of the Vatican is contested in the episode, yet the replacement of the Catholic Church by science leaves the couple uneasy. This same discomfort is found in other films, such as Paolo Virzì's *Tutti i santi giorni*, which deals with the same theme, and Francesca Comencini's *Lo spazio bianco* (The White Space, 2009), which treats premature birth. That uneasiness arises from the sense that if religion were no longer to exercise control over the human body, its place might be occupied not by an "authentic" human experience but by cold secular science and pornography.

The final issue I explore in this section is euthanasia. The conflict between secular and religious forces has been played out in recent years around a series of high-profile media cases: Piergiorgio Welby (who died 2006), Eluana Englaro (died 2009), and DJ Fabio Antoniani (died 2016). All three cases were debated long in the public sphere and revealed deep fissures between Italy's liberal voices and the Vatican position, which condemns crimes against life, including euthanasia and "willful suicide" (*Gaudium et Spes* no. 27). The Eluana Englaro case, in particular, revealed the power that the Church still held over the state. In 2008, in the wake of a ruling by Milan's Court of Appeal and Italy's Court of Cassation to uphold the wishes of Eluana Englaro's family and allow the suspension of her nutrition and hydration after seventeen years of coma, the Vatican expressed its outrage. It intervened by pressuring the then prime minister, Silvio Berlusconi, to act. Berlusconi attempted to pass an emergency decree that would reverse the ruling and save Eluana; however, the legislation failed to be passed before her death.

In 2012, Marco Bellocchio – a director who, as we have seen earlier in this book, frequently takes an oppositional stance towards the Catholic Church – released *Bella addormentata*. The film narrates the story of Eluana Englaro through news bulletins, interviews, social media, and documentaries on TV

---

6   Maternity is central to Catholicism. Daniela Treveri Gennari (2010, 111) notes that "motherhood is the most popular visual image of femininity in Catholicism" and that "fertility and reproduction define the primary role of Catholic women." The iconization of maternity in Italy, and in the national cinema, means that wherever maternity is consciously resisted, as it is by the lead female character in Marco Bellocchio's *Buongiorno, notte* (2003), the woman is typically branded unnatural, disruptive, and threatening (in this film, as a terrorist, in short). Only in a very few recent films, such as Maria Sole Tognazzi's *Viaggio sola* (2013), is the choice to put maternity aside, while problematized, ultimately cast in a positive light. Even then, the maternal aspect of a female character is displaced. Margherita Buy's character in *Viaggio sola* is reinscribed into a maternal role through her protectiveness and care both of her sister's children and of her ex-partner's unborn child.

and computer screens. Around this absent-present mediatic centre he develops three further stories of "Sleeping Beauties": that of a drug addict (Maya Sansa) determined to kill herself; that of a girl lying in a decorous coma while her mother prays fervently for her awakening; and that of a senator in Berlusconi's political party (Toni Servillo) and his Catholic daughter, Maria (Alba Rohrwacher), who are bound together and torn apart by the assisted suicide of the senator's wife many years previously.

Bellocchio uses the fairy tale of Sleeping Beauty as his mythical frame. From it he drains any Manichaean sense of good and evil. Instead he renders its ethics complex and ambiguous. He deconstructs the image of a peacefully sleeping Botticelli beauty awaiting her prince by means of multiple stories that screen both Italys – the Catholic and the secular – that went head to head in the debate. The multiple stories use two well-respected actresses (Alba Rohrwacher and Isabelle Hupert) to represent the Catholic side of the argument and treats them with some sympathy.[7] However, beneath the apparently magnanimously balanced argument, Bellocchio's protest is clear. An early sign of this is when a distressed man rushes into a hospital ward, pulling the sheets off the beds, uncovering the patients, and claiming to be in search of his loved one who has been admitted to one of the city's hospitals. All he knows is that the hospital is named after a saint. Alarmed by his behaviour, the doctors reel off a long list of hospitals to him. This short scene makes little narrative sense, except when it is read as a satiric attack on the power of the Church over hospitals, each of which bears the name of a Catholic saint. Later in the film, the signs of protest become more explicit: a priest prays for the sedated drug addict while she sleeps and leaves a prayer card before being chased away by the doctor: the praying, while the woman is unable to prevent it, is seen to take advantage of her and is a clear invasion of her privacy. The randomness of these two scenes is only apparent: both take issue with the Church for its insidious inhabitation of Italy's hospitals. The point they are making is that religion insinuates itself into the medical profession and medical ethics, which means that personal choices around life and death cannot be made freely.

---

7   Nonetheless, the senator's Catholic daughter, Maria (Alba Rohrwacher), while constructed in positive terms (she is young, sensitive, strong, and exercises independence, especially from her father), is shown to be misguided. Her attachment to the pro-life argument is rooted in a misunderstanding of her father's place in assisting her mother's death. Moreover, certain scenes belie the manifest construction of her character as positive. For instance, when Maria has sex, she flicks a crucifix to her back so that it does not get in the way. That small flick signifies that she is aware, as is the audience, that the crucifix and the freedom to enjoy her body through extramarital sex do not fit together. Later, her lover's brother calls her "suora," a word that carries a highly negative charge for Bellocchio. It has been borrowed from *Buongiorno, notte,* where it is used of the terrorist Chiara to suggest her frigidity, her inability to love, her lack of sexuality. If intimate sexual love is the highest ideal in Bellocchio's cinema (and it is), the Church still gets in its way.

Ultimately, behind the multiple Sleeping Beauties there is only one protagonist and one antagonist, and it is the conflict between these two that holds the
stories together. The protagonist is freedom of choice; and the antagonist is any
obstacle to that freedom, be it politicians, who endeavour to force a colleague
to vote in a particular way, or the Vatican, which tries to force the parliament's
vote, or the doctor, who chooses to stop the drug addict Maria from killing
herself. At the centre of all this is Bellocchio's call to remove the Vatican and
Catholic-inspired politicians from their positions of power over the end of life
so that Sleeping Beauties can die if they or their loved ones so wish it. This
is the same conclusion as emerges from a documentary made on the Englaro
case – *Love Is All: Piergiorgio Welby: Autoritratto* by Francesco Andreotti and
Livia Giunti (2015) – as well as from Pau's *L'Accabadora* and Golina's *Miele*. In
the latter two films, the Catholic Church is notably absent as two women, both
euthanasians, "Miele" and the "Accabadora," do their work (an *accabadora* is a
woman who, in some areas of Sardinia, quietly put an end to the lives of people
who are suffering from a long illness). Both Golina's and Pau's films implicitly
take the Vatican's position to task. The directors make the case for the positive
effect on society of the women's role and show the sacrifice they must make, as
well as their moral fibre and strength in the face of this complex and harrowing
task. Nevertheless, both directors avoid explicitly framing their films as part of
the contemporary debate. In Pau's film the role of the "Accabadora" is knitted
into the past, an untold and rarely revealed part of Sardinian history. In "Miele,"
a contemporary woman who administers drugs to sick clients to kill them gen-
tly enters a synagogue at the end of the film to pray, a finale that explicitly extri-
cates her from a Catholic ethical frame.

All of these films – on homosexuality, in vitro fertilization, and euthanasia
respectively – draw a line between freedoms and rights seen as belonging to
the personal sphere and Catholic obstacles to those freedoms and rights. What
the films I have investigated in this section all share is that they put the rights
of individuals first. Taken together, they therefore indicate a deeper and wider
clash that inheres between divergent ideologies on the peninsula today. Liberal,
relative, and secular voices supporting civil rights and freedom of choice clash
with official Vatican voices supporting absolute Catholic positions on hetero-
sexuality and the sanctity of all human life, whether that life is embryonic or
suspended between life and death on a life support machine.

Charles Taylor notes how "freedom" and "rights" are "slogan terms" that
repeatedly resurface in Western society and that are used as "argument-stopping
universals" (Taylor 2007, 479). "Bare choice" is a "prime value," argues Taylor,
"irrespective of what the choice is between or in what domain" (478). The priv-
ileging of free choice has its roots in the concept of the authentic self, and the
ethic of the authentic self is, as Taylor (2007) states, one of the most deeply
rooted ideologies in contemporary society, so influential that Taylor assigns to

the period since the 1960s the label "Age of Authenticity" (473). The ethic of authenticity, with its roots in late-eighteenth-century Romanticism, means that "it is important to find and live out one's own [life], as against surrendering to conformity with a model imposed on us from outside, by society, or the previous generation, or religious or political authority" (475). Authenticity presupposes that "lives are devoted to things of intrinsic value," that "'organic' rather than mechanical ties are foremost," and that "creativity, individuality, and imagination are at very core of a flourishing selfhood" (476).

Authenticity is at the heart not just of the films discussed here but of many others I explore in this book: from *Habemus Papam* to *The Young Pope* and *Corpo celeste*, and from *Alla luce del sole* to *Chiamatemi Francesco* and *La buona battaglia: Don Pietro Pappagallo*. Along with the attack on diffuse religion, discussed in the first section, this is the key fault line between secular and religious perspectives, or at least between secular liberal and religious conservative positions in Italy today.

Conclusion: The Shifting Fault Line and the Limits of Protest

At this point, I revisit the question of what is subject to protest and what is not in order better to pinpoint where the line between secular and religious space can be drawn today. In this conclusion, I first explore why the revelation of the corruption and political power of the Catholic Church does not necessarily result in protest against it. Then, taking diachronic and synchronic perspectives in turn, I investigate first whether there are protests previously voiced in Italy that are no longer subject to protest on twenty-first-century screens. Through this, I estimate how far the fault line has shifted since the "Age of Authenticity" came into being in the 1960s. Then I examine the synchronic access and see whether there are issues that Italian filmmakers have not addressed but that have been subject to protest in other Western democracies. Finally, by bringing synchronic and diachronic perspectives together, I hypothesize where the fault line between Italian secular and religious perspectives can now be drawn. This will enable me to identify how protest has been changing and what this may mean for the place of religion in the public sphere today.

In this chapter I have identified two key points of conflict between religious and secular perspectives: the tentacular nature of contemporary "diffuse religion," which threatens a democracy already weakened by the encroachment of economic interests, organized crime, and Masonic lodges (the first section), and the Vatican's intervention in body-centred debates on homosexuality and medical ethics, which pits liberal values of freedom of choice and authenticity against an institution that threatens these (the second section). While in chapter 3 I explored how the Catholic Church was positioned counterculturally on Italian screens, here I have shown how a smaller but not inconsequential range of films challenge this, presenting the Vatican instead as a hierarchical institution capable of influencing Italy's legislation and shaping its political and economic interests. While it may seem contradictory that countercultural and hierarchical positioning coexist, the religious objects of the two positions are usually different: in the first, the focus falls on positive Catholic values and on those who represent them; in the second, the focus falls on the institution of the Vatican and its power as an institutional player. It is the former that has been garnering increasing support on Italian screens, while the latter is seen, on the big screen at least, to be of ever-diminishing consequence.

The first point to make here is that it is still overwhelmingly the Catholic Church that instils protest in Italian filmmakers. While there is deep uneasiness about the minority religions on the peninsula (as I will show in the following chapter), so far this has rarely resulted in protest against them, at least in the filmmaking mainstream. Indeed, the dominant trend, as I will argue, is towards assimilation rather than ejection. The weak foothold that Italy's minority religions have gained in the corridors of power ensures that they are not (yet) seen as influencing the peninsula's policies and legislation, and therefore they are not yet figures of authority against which to rebel.

The second point to make at this stage is that even where anxieties about the power of the Catholic Church emerge, this does not necessarily result in protest. It would be all too easy to conclude that films screening anxieties about the Church's strength and the way it has woven itself into society are mounting an ethical challenge and a call for a change to the status quo. But this is not always the case. The films dealing with body-oriented protest, explored in the preceding section, are the ones that most obviously protest the contemporary situation in Italy. Yet even in these films there is often an attempt to reduce conflict by re-employing Catholic discourses of "family" (*Improvvisamente l'inverno scorso*) and "maternity"("Maternità") to frame and soften their contestation, or to complicate the message by expressing nostalgia for premodern Italy (again "Maternità") or by presenting a multiplicity of viewpoints, including Catholic ones (*Bella addormentata*). Another tactic is simply to remove the Catholic Church – and therefore explicit conflict – entirely from the screen (*L'Accabadora*; *Miele*). Nonetheless, those films that pit Catholic teachings against civil rights, freedom of choice, and authenticity, dealt with in the second section of this chapter, are motivated by protest even where this is softened. The case is much less clear in those films that treat the tentacular workings of the Vatican in politics.

If we return to two of the films dealt with in first section, *Il divo* and *I banchieri di Dio*, for instance, the webs of power they portray are as glamorous as they are enticing. This puts into question these films' capacity for, or intention to, contest those webs. In *I banchieri di Dio*, Roberto Calvi's labyrinthine and zigzagging descent, as he is expelled from the luxurious spaces of power he had inhabited and dragged into ugly, small, dark rooms, is not a path a spectator might be encouraged to follow. In Ferrara's thriller, lack of power is repeatedly painted as dark, dirty, seedy, and wet (the Thames; the damp hotel in London), the antithesis of the fine, airy buildings, golf courses, and yachts to which those in power are accustomed. Whatever message the film attempts to convey about the iniquities of power, the reality of the descent is that the shoddiness into which Calvi is catapulted is much less attractive than either worldly or Vatican riches. The latent message of both this film and *Il divo*, under their bitter unmasking of power, is the unwitting but inevitable *celebration* of power. What one might term a "*Da Vinci Code* wash," in which luxurious Vatican interiors and intrigue are bound together into a lucrative filmic product promising international circulation, has an important role in this. Religious glamour and intrigue, here refracted through an American lens, undermine these films' capacity to mount protest.

Furthermore, *Il divo* and *I banchieri di Dio* owe a great deal to the conspiracy thriller genre, and this in turn undermines their capacity for protest. Citing Karl Popper, Alan O'Leary (2011) observes that conspiracy theories create an all-encompassing, evil divinity whose omnipotence encourages not protest but paranoia, passivity, and inaction. Conspiracy thrillers do not, therefore, encourage reform. Of the three films dealing with the Vatican Bank scandals, in only one – *La verità sta in cielo* – does the revelation of corruption actually reflect genuine protest and desire for reform. Roberto Faenza challenges the silence of the Church, and he had hoped that his film would galvanize protest, compelling the Church to publish the purported dossier on the Emanuela Orlandi case (an objective that failed). Vatican glamour and conspiracy theories are intertwined. Together they halt the formation of protest and protect the status quo in the face of a network of forces in society that threaten Italian democracy. They, along with the softening of conflict found in body protest films, mark the contemporary limit to protest.

A diachronic approach quickly clarifies this limit by sketching out the marked shift in the quality, quantity, and kind of protest found in contemporary Italian cinema relative to Italian mid-century filmmaking. The cinema of the 1960s and early 1970s represents the start of Taylor's "Age of Authenticity" and the apex of political engagement and contestation on screen. It therefore presents a useful paradigm against which to measure the growth and decline in protest. Here, I take the two pressure points discussed in this chapter in turn (diffuse religion, body protest) to demonstrate what kind of shift has taken place.

With regard to the first category – diffuse religion – on-screen portrayals of the corrupt intermingling of politics and religion are nothing new. In *Divorzio all'italiana* (Divorce Italian Style, 1961), for instance, the local priest infamously concludes his sermon by telling the assembled flock that they should vote for "un partito [...] che sia democratico e cristiano" (a party that is democratic and Christian), demonstrating the inextricable link between Italy's main political party at that time and its Catholic support. Luigi Magni's *Nell'anno del Signore* (The Conspirators, 1969) and Damiano Damiani's *Il sorriso del grande tentatore* (The Tempter / The Devil Is a Woman, 1974) make similar kinds of links. In other words, a strong line of continuity can be drawn between mid-century films and contemporary films like *I banchieri di Dio*, *Il divo*, and *La verità sta in cielo* as well as others like *Suburru* and *Corpo celeste*, all of which criticize overly close links between secular and religious power bases. Nonetheless, there is a shift even here. In the twenty-first century, Catholic power has grown diffuse and mobile. The Church is no longer an institution that mobilizes the flock explicitly and from the pulpit and the Vatican balcony. Instead what *Il divo*, *I banchieri di Dio*, and *La verità sta in cielo* demonstrate is that religion spreads through a highly diffuse and subtle network of channels in society.

It is in the second category that the most significant shift can be seen. Protest against the control of the body by the Catholic Church is heavily inscribed onto the history of Italian filmmaking. It can be found in mid-century narrative tropes in which a respectable man is revealed as a hypocrite, as he is in Giorgio Bianchi's *Il moralista* (The Moralist, 1959). It can be found too where a repressed man, hounded by the Catholic teachings of his childhood, slowly shakes off its strictures and indulges his sexual fantasies (Federico Fellini's *8½* (1963), or where a woman is encouraged to do the same, as she is in Fellini's *Giulietta degli spiriti* (Juliet of the Spirits, 1965). Some mid-century narratives revolve around the right of a woman to abort, as we see in Marco Bellocchio's *La Cina è vicina* (China Is Near, 1967), or of a man to divorce, as in *Divorzio all'italiana* (Divorce Italian Style, 1961). Since the late 1950s, in other words, Italian filmmakers have frequently cast the Church as a repressive antagonist in narratives that pit it against "authentic" sexual desire. One might argue that the very "look" of the golden age of Italian cinema was inscribed by the Catholic Church's control over the body. If on-screen nudity was so difficult to get past the censor's scissors, figure-hugging costumes and low décolleté were used in its place, as seen in the attire of actresses such as Gina Lollobrigida, Sophia Loren, Silvana Mangano, and Claudia Cardinale. This clothing then became a hallmark of cinema at that time. The censor's scissors also resulted in metonymic scenes like Silvana Mangano's infamous mambo in Giuseppe De Santis's *Riso amaro* (1949), and Sophia Loren's no-less-famous striptease in Vittorio De Sica's *Ieri, oggi, domani* (Yesterday, Today, and Tomorrow, 1963), as well as in a vast array of beach, bed, and bath scenes. Such metonymies, along with the use of cuts and fades to interrupt voluptuous embraces, are etched into the films of Italy's golden age.

In the twenty-first century, the line between what is protested and what is not has shifted markedly. With the end to censorship and the mainstreaming of sex on screen, it is no longer heterosexual sex that marks the hard-fought boundary between religious and secular spaces. The Italian filmmaking industry has continued to push the boundaries of taste, as demonstrated by two releases from 2015 (Davide Ferrario's documentary, *Sexxx*, and Stefano Sollima's *Suburra*), and Catholic organizations now comment on it only rarely. As a result, the filmmaking industry no longer uses (heterosexual) sex to symbolize rebellion and to goad repressive religious authorities. Although Italian filmmaking remains conservative when compared to other European national cinemas, suppresses queer (as argued in the previous section), and lacks the "graphic and confrontational images" and the interrogation of extreme sex found in the work of European auteurs like Catherine Breillat, Claire Denis, Agnes Varda, Lars Von Triers, and Gaspar Noé (Horeck and Kendall 2011), the differences between Italy and other European countries are no longer so marked.

Moreover, in an extraordinarily rapid shift from mid-century Italian filmmaking, the narrative focus in contemporary films that explore sex is no longer directed towards guilt and hypocrisy or towards private lives overshadowed by anxieties about the punishment meted out by the Church or by a bourgeois society dominated by its mores. We are far from Fellini's protagonists, who struggle with guilt in the face of sexuality. We are far too from Bernardo Bertolucci's guilt-racked protagonist in *Il conformista* (The Conformist, 1970), who struggles to come to terms with his homosexual feelings, and from Pier Paolo Pasolini's cinema, throughout which we find "the trauma of guilt and destructive excess which subtends the presence of the body as a locus of homosexual desire" (Gordon 1996, 166). In almost all contemporary films this guilt has vanished. The Church no longer dominates the personal, inner lives of characters, providing a superego to a guilty ego. It has shifted to an external, public, and political space. In the narrative focus of films treating gay marriage, such as *Improvvisamente l'inverno scorso* and *Il padre delle spose* (2006), and in the episode on gay marriage in Carlo Verdone's *Manuale d'amore 2*, guilt has vanished. The two protagonists of *L'improvvisamente l'inverno scorso*, Gustav and Luca, for instance, are free from any need to hypocritically hide their feelings; instead they must campaign for their civic identities. The replacement of Church as superego with Church as political antagonist is nowhere clearer than in two short sequential scenes in that film. In the first, we see the two young men freely and happily running hand-in-hand across a park, against the scenic backdrop of the Roman Forum. Wide framing, outdoor on-location shooting, and sunshine create a sense of carefree liberty. In the following scene, however, the two men are tightly framed in a narrow corner of their apartment as they watch TV together on the sofa. While they watch, their space, and ultimately their very bodies, are obliterated by the progressive superimposition of twelve television screens. Each contains reports of negative political and religious reaction to the proposed legislation on civil partnerships. One after another, politicians line up alongside the Church's official viewpoint. Gustav and Luca's faces are finally obliterated by the final words of Pope Benedict XVI, who slowly annunciates the words "non posso tacere la mia preoccupazione per la legge sulle coppie di fatto" (I cannot silence my concerns over the law on civil partnerships). In this scene, religion, the media, and politicians conspire to rob two young gay men of their rights. Without this trinity of interlocking forces these two young men would be as carefree as they are running through the field in the previous scene.

As the Church as a private, scolding superego is replaced by the Church as public obstacle and antagonist, motifs of guilt and hypocrisy are replaced by motifs of political struggle and political protest. The focus is no longer on the Church's effect on the private lives of individuals; rather, it is on the Church's effect on their *civic* lives. Their private lives lie beyond its reach. They lie on the other side of fault line. It is the public and political expression of those private lives that is now at stake.

Another important change is that protest against the Church's control of relationships has diminished substantially, retreating into the last bastion of LGBTQ concerns. On-screen attitudes towards "family," which long represented a fault line between secular and religious positions on screen, have changed dramatically. In mid-twentieth-century filmmaking the family was often "an authoritarian structure, repository – especially in its bourgeois form – of hypocrisy, pettiness, and an abuse of power" (Brook 2009, 140). Marco Bellocchio, for instance, in *I pugni in tasca* (Fists in the Pocket, 1965), launches a savage attack on it, portraying the Catholic family structure as empty and decayed: the father is absent; the mother is literally and metaphorically blind. The film's finale sees the youngest son taking it upon himself to clean up the decay by eliminating the family's members one by one. Bellocchio's early nihilistic attack on the family, which tore down one structure without positing an alternative, was, in part at least, a product of the left-wing, anti-authoritarian ideologies of the 1960s and early 1970s, and is reflected in many other films of the time. Bernardo Bertolucci's *Il conformista* (The Conformist, 1970) and *Ultimo tango a Parigi* (Last Tango in Paris, 1972) both present attacks on authority. Pasolini's *Teorema* (Theorem, 1968) viciously attacks the Catholic bourgeois family. Comedies such as Giorgio Bianchi's *Il moralista* (The Moralist, 1959) and many of the subsequent *commedia all'italiana* films, including Pietro Germi's *Divorzio all'italiano* and *Sedotta e abbandonata* (Seduced and Abandoned, 1964) use satire and ideological critique to attack a hypocritical structure bound together by social necessity and custom.

When one turns to twenty-first-century filmmaking what one discovers is that the angry, satirical, and negative attacks on a confining family structure have vanished. These have slowly been replaced with more positive alternatives that presuppose a broader definition of family and that shift the emphasis from a narrower reproductive and religious paradigm to a new frame that foregrounds close interpersonal relationships. As the twenty-first century progresses, there has been a boom in new on-screen models for family life, models that quietly set aside the Catholic paradigm of the nuclear family. In *Viaggio sola* (A Five Star Life, 2013), for instance, a single, childless woman is surrounded by close friends and an extended family. In *Si può fare l'amore vestiti* (Donato Ursitti, 2012), myriad kinds of sexual partnerships are delineated. Then there are the extended friendship groups found in Ferzan Özpetek's films, and the new gay family model introduced in *Improvvisamente l'inverno scorso* and in other films treating gay experiences. These alternative relationship structures provide new, plural conceptions of "family" that contrast with traditional Catholic teaching but that no longer necessarily lead to the contesting of Catholic understandings of family. The Catholic paradigm has become just one of the possible alternatives in a post-secular world: it no longer needs to be contested as it no longer dominates and presents an existential threat to alternative models. For this reason, by and large, it now sits peacefully alongside those alternatives without entering into conflict with them. The contestation of the family, endemic in the 1960s and 1970s, is over.

When one turns to the issue of medical ethics a stronger line of continuity can be drawn. Here, while the objects of discussion have changed, the underlying viewpoints have not. Some of the key flashpoints that had historically generated protest in Italy have been resolved through legislation permitting advertising of contraception (1971) and abortion (1978). Prior to the passing of abortion legislation, religious prohibitions on abortion were the subject of several films, including Marco Bellocchio's satirical *La Cina è vicina* (1967), which cynically revealed the Catholic imperatives and petty hypocrisies behind pro-life positions,[8] and Sergio Nasca's episodic film *Stato interessante* (1977), made in the run-up to the referendum, which tackled the issue head on. A few documentaries have been made that protest attitudes towards abortion in contemporary Italy – Federica Pontremoli's 2002 documentary, *Quore*, for instance, reveals the widespread resistance among doctors in contemporary Italy to performing abortions (Kirchgaessner et al. 2016) – but these are exceptions. Once the conflict between religious and secular positions is resolved through legislation, protest dies down.

Overall, it is clear that anticlericalism on screen has rapidly and radically died down in Italy. The dramatic critique of the Church found in Pier Paolo Pasolini's *I racconti di Canterbury* (The Canterbury Tales, 1972) is unthinkable

---

8 The film presents the ineluctability of Catholic control of a woman's body: in its final scene, Elena, a woman who had wanted to abort, instead completes her prenatal exercises under a large painting of a Madonna and child and reads a book called *Sarò madre* [I will be a mother], which has a Madonna on the cover. The message is clear: women will be mothers, whether or not they want to be. Their being mothers, Bellocchio argues, owes a great deal to the reified position of motherhood in a country that has a mother and child as its central iconography.

now. In Pasolini's film, the Summoner describes how, through his great anus, a giant red devil noisily farts friars out onto the wilderness of hell. Hordes of friars, thus ejected, now inhabit the infernal regions. Pasolini positions the Summoner's story as the final tale, in place of the Parson's pious sermon, which concludes Chaucer's original. In this way he manipulates the narrative structure in order to underscore its scatological eschatology: grim bodily punishment is meted out to greedy clerics who looked to terrestrial rather than celestial gain.[9] Pasolini thus ends his film with the Summoner's gleeful revenge on the greed, lust, and hypocrisy of clerics. Pasolini is channelling a long history of anticlerical, body-centred satire that draws into its fold some of Italy's most illustrious writers: Dante (1265–1321), for instance, lays the accusation of avarice and simony at the feet of clerics, and Boccaccio (1313–1375) merrily pokes fun at lecherous friars. While Facciamo Breccia's life-size transvestite Pope Benedict draws on a venerable history of anticlerical satire, with a few exceptions – such as Ciprì and Maresco's *Totò che visse due volte* (1998) – the filmmaking industry has almost entirely escaped its long anticlerical, body-centred satirical lineage. Something radical has changed.

If we return now to the synchronic axis, we find that it brings to light one final point that helps define the limits to protest in Italy today. In Italy, what is missing, when we compare the country to other Western nations today, is the quintessential anti-Catholic protest of the twenty-first century: paedophilia. The almost total absence of the abuse question in Italian filmmaking will come as a surprise to those familiar with the filmic attacks on priests in the United States and Ireland and elsewhere in Europe. In the UK and Ireland, for a time, the cinema screens were crammed with portraits of priests and nuns who had abused those in their care sexually, physically, or emotionally. These films range from *The Butcher Boy* (Neil Jordan, 1997), *The Magdalene Sisters* (Peter Mullan, 2002), and Aisling Walsh's *Song for a Raggy Boy* (2003), to *Philomena* (Stephen Frears, 2013). In the United States and Canada, the impact of the abuse scandals has been even more pronounced. Films here include *The Boys of St Vincent* (John Smith, 1992), *Our Fathers* (Dan Curtis, 2005), *Deliver Us from Evil* (Amy Berg, 2006), *Doubt* (John Patrick Shanley, 2008), *Mea Maxima Culpa: Silence in the House of God* (Alex Gibney, 2012), and *Spotlight* (Tom McCarthy, 2015).

It is very difficult to understand why paedophilia and other forms of clerical abuse have not attracted denunciation by Italian fiction filmmakers, especially when the filmmaking industry has been quick to convert other scandals, whether political or religious (the Calvi case; Mafia killings; P2; the Aldo Moro case; the G8 in Genoa) into raw material for cinema. Two hypotheses can be

---

9   There is also clearly an emphasis on male homosexual sex in this final tale, which may provide a second explanation for its positioning.

put forward. The first, and most striking, is that there is widespread resistance in powerful political and religious circles to airing controversies around the paedophile priest question in Italy. The proposed screening in Italy of the controversial BBC documentary *Sex Crimes and the Vatican* (O'Gorman, 2006), for instance, resulted in calls by Forza Italia politicians to boycott RAI ([Anon.] 2007). Eventually, an agreement was reached to screen the documentary as part of Michele Santoro's discussion program Anno Zero, provided it was balanced with the opinions of Church representatives. However, despite this agreement, Isabella Bertolini (Forza Italia) still called for a ten-minute boycott of the broadcaster ([Anon.] 2007). *The Magdalene Sisters*, which addressed the abuse of girls in Ireland's Catholic-run laundries, also met with an icy reception in Catholic quarters: it garnered the Vatican's explicit disapproval on the pages of its newspaper, the *Osservatore romano*, and a journalist from *Avvenire* walked out of the screening in protest (O'Toole 2003). Powerful Catholic lobbying within RAI television and in certain parts of the press places pressure on television channels, in particular, to avoid or mitigate screenings of certain films on television.

However, the big screen, as I argue elsewhere in this book, has not been subject to the same control on the part of political and religious players, so the explanation cannot rest solely on the power of politico-religious voices. While the reception of films that tackle abuse has often been negative on television and in certain conservative sections of the press, it is typically more positive in cinema circles. *The Magdalene Sisters* was attacked in parts of the press, for instance, and at the time of writing has yet to be screened on RAI television; even so, it was warmly greeted at the Venice Film Festival, where its denunciation of clerical abuse garnered it the Golden Globe. A second hypothesis, then, that might explain Italy's lack of protest against abuse scandals on film has to do with the lack of attention to home-grown Italian cases. Massimo Introvigne's 2011 article "Preti pedofili: un panico morale," for instance, discusses paedophilia primarily as a foreign problem, despite some high-profile cases in Italy. This lack of attention to home-grown cases has been the subject of several recent sociological and psychological analyses, which posit, for instance, a greater sense of shame on the part of victims in Italy, or the proclivity for "insabbiamento [...] nelle questioni criminali che sfiorano il mondo vaticano" (cover-ups of criminal questions that touch the Vatican world) (Prosperi 2010) – a factor that Federico Tulli refers to as the "omertà delle gerarchie ecclesiastiche" (the code of silence of the ecclesiastical hierarchies) (cited in Prosperi 2010, 11). Tulli's use of the term "omertà," often used with regard to the Mafia, links Vatican silencing tactics to organized crime in Italy. The legal freedoms enjoyed by the Vatican state have meant it has not been obliged to report cases of abuse to the Italian police, and there is still no clear picture of how many clerical abuse cases there are in Italy. The lack of information about cases in Italy, coupled with the public broadcaster's reluctance to address the issue, does not make for an environment in which abuse can easily be exposed. It is hardly surprising, then, that one film that does tackle abuse (albeit before the millennium), Antonio Capuano's *Pianese Nunzio, 14 anni a maggio* (Sacred Silence, 1996), excuses a priest for having sex with a thirteen-year-old by inscribing him onto the "good countercultural priest" mode. Set in the impoverished Sanità district of Naples. Capuano's film portrays a sensitive and caring fictional parish priest, Father Lorenzo Borelli, who heroically stands up to the Camorra, a stand that will cost him his life. Contemporaneously, he establishes a sexual relationship with a thirteen-year-old boy, Nunzio. Given that the film positions the Camorra as Goliath and the priest as a warrior-hero, the only narrative outcome available, once the Camorra uses the priest's relationship with the boy to frame him, is for the film to tolerate paedophilia. Capuano, in fact, takes pains both to show that the boy is fully complicit and to show that paedophilia is not so bad after all: far worse things can happen to a thirteen-year-old outside the walls of the Church than can happen within them. The film's title reveals the peculiarity of the Italian ethical frame that provides its context. The Italian title, *Pianese Nunzio, 14 anni a maggio* emphasizes how close the boy is to being fourteen, the age of consent; the English title, *Sacred Silence*, by contrast, signals the silence of the Church regarding paedophilia and aligns the film with the paedophilia scandal that struck the Catholic Church in the States in the 1990s. Within the Italian filmmaking frame, as I argued in chapter 3, figures constructed as politically and socially committed to the poor and disadvantaged become untouchable. They are the nation's heroes. They escape condemnation, even when a narrative code – the paedophile priest – would, within many other cultural frames, destabilize and overturn their heroism. The moral indignation and bitter condemnation found in American and Irish films is therefore absent from this film. The only other fictional work in contemporary Italy to treat abuse is Paolo Sorrentino's series, *The Young Pope*. This, however, does not tackle or even acknowledge Italian cases. For Sorrentino, abuse is still something that takes place elsewhere.

Given the peculiarly rapid change with regard to a religion-centred protest culture in Italy, and the blind spots that exist in Italy's contemporary protest, bringing the synchronic and diachronic axes together allows certain key points to emerge about the boundaries of protest. The first point to reiterate, of course, is that protest against the Catholic Church has not vanished from twenty-first-century Italy, even if it has diminished. Body-centred protest, underpinned by an "ethic of authenticity," is still alive and well, and continuity with earlier negative attitudes towards the institutional Church can be found in today's filmic attacks on Vatican corruption and its links to the political class (although protest is now limited to a handful of thrillers, which are, as I argued earlier, weak purveyors of protest). The second point to make, however, is that

Italy's contemporary protest is now strictly circumscribed and delimited. It is currently is at its lowest ebb since the 1960s. Vast areas of protest have been withdrawn, or substantially redrawn, since Italy's economic boom, especially those areas of protest centred on the Church's position on sex, divorce, and abortion. Moreover, a comparison of Italy to other Western countries shows that some areas of protest, such as those related to queer sex and abuse at the hands of priests, have not yet emerged on Italian screens or have emerged only in part. Perhaps most noticeable of all is the dramatic decline in anticlerical satire targeting clerical hypocrisy and guilt. As I noted in chapter 3, filmic priests now typically work ethically and counterculturally on the side of the poor and marginalized instead of chasing women, as they did so doggedly in the nunsploitation genre of the 1970s, and in many dramas and comedies of that era and in the following years, in which priests grappled with temptations of the flesh: Pasquale Squatteri's *Io e Dio* (1970), Marco Vicario, *Il prete sposato* (The Married Priest, 1970), Dino Risi's *La moglie del prete* (The Priest's Wife, 1971), and Carlo Mazzacurati's *Il prete bello* (The Handsome Priest, 1989). Carlo Verdone's recent, *Io, loro e Lara* [Me, Them and Lara, 2009], a comedy that deals sympathically with a priest who meets a beautiful girl, is radically distinct from an earlier film by the same director, *Un sacco bello* (Fun is Beautiful, 1979), in which the priest was subjected to far more sustained satire.

The diminishing of protest reveals that Catholicism no longer has the same power to generate public debate as it did sixty years ago. It points to a widespread perception that the Church is a less powerful player in the public sphere and no longer stands as the towering figure of authoritarian discipline on Italian screens. If, as I argued at the start of this chapter, protest is a key driver in the circulation of stories, the diminishing of protest necessarily reduces the circulation of those stories and threatens the visibility of the dominant religious voice in Italy. However, this finding needs to be mitigated in the light of other points that have emerged in this book so far. If protest has diminished on Italian screens, Catholic filmic production (chapter 1) and iconography (chapter 2) have seen something of a Renaissance and these have led to a return to the screens, after the 1990s, of Catholic themes and images. Catholic values have been circulating widely, especially but not exclusively on the small screen. So it appears that the positioning of the Church on Italian screens is more harmonious and that this has less to do with a growing indifference to the Church and its place in the public sphere, and more to do with a growing acceptance of an often-watered down Catholicism as the foundation of Italian identity.

5 Voicing the Religious Other:
Assimilation, Horror, Resolution

Introduction

In Ferzan Özpetek's *Le fate ignoranti* (The Ignorant Fairies, 2001) Antonia (Margherita Buy) finds her maid crying in front of an altar that she has assembled in their home. A Buddhist statue stands upon it. Caught off guard, Antonia blurts out, "ma non eri Cattolica?" (but weren't you a Catholic?). Through her tears, Nora replies, "Non del tutto" (not entirely). This simple phrase, "non del tutto," speaks volumes about the on-screen position of minority faiths in Italy. Nora's is a highly ambiguous response, open to several interpretations. Perhaps the maid does not feel comfortable talking about her faith to the nominal Catholics in whose house she works. In this reading, she is censoring herself to fit in, smoothing down the differences between her religion and that of the majority, "normalizing" her own practices, rendering them unthreatening, and providing the semblance of assimilation. An alternative reading, however, is that, having lived in a country so dominated by a single faith, she has adopted attributes of that faith as part of her multiple identity. Consciously or not, she has layered Catholicism on top of her Buddhism. In the latter case, her words "non del tutto," rather than indicating guardedness or discomfort, would imply a hybrid of diverse religious practices with which she has made her peace.

This chapter explores the position of minority faiths on screen, investigating how these are constructed in contemporary Italian fiction filmmaking and how they emerge in the public sphere. Given the dominance of Catholicism both demographically and in the production and distribution of religiously oriented film (chapter 1), as well as its iconographic and performative dominance (chapter 2) and the centrality of Catholic values, whether these are assimilated (chapter 3) or disputed (chapter 4), we can expect the emergence of Italy's minority faiths on screen to be limited and impeded.

The corpus of films I treat in this chapter is especially wide, reflecting the variety of genres that feature minority religions. This corpus comprises comedies, conspiracy thrillers, horror, *cinema di qualità*, and Lux Vide's miniseries for television. As will become apparent, genre matters. The screening of wild and fearsome religious others in low-budget horror diverges significantly from, for instance, a Lux Vide miniseries, which provides carefully measured portrayals. Given the wide-ranging corpus, I will make the discussion manageable by focusing in the main on films that treat Islam. This is not because I believe Islam represents all minorities. It does not. I choose Islam because it is the second religion today in Italy and because it is the minority religion that stands at the heart of Italy's current debates and controversies about multiculturalism, transnational identities, the integration of ethnic and religious minorities, and the post-secular. Nonetheless, I draw in other minority religions at appropriate times over the course of the chapter.

I argue in this chapter that contemporary Italian cinema typically takes one of two paths towards religious minorities. The first path is Nora's. This one assimilates and hybridizes the religious other, often by obliterating religious difference in the name of shared values. In the first section of this chapter I unpack some of the readings that Nora's ambiguous "non del tutto" response elicits: discomfort, self-censorship, assimilation, threat of elimination, and hybridity. The second path leads in the opposite direction. It exposes the religious other as irretrievably different and unassimilable and thus as profoundly threatening. Typically, the other is obliterated by ejecting it from the screen in what amounts to a purging of the Italian body politic. Contemporary horror movies and a conspiracy thriller by Renzo Martinelli provide illustrations of this approach. Finally, in the conclusion, I investigate films that negotiate an emerging third way, the only way that promises some kind of voice to minority religions in a public sphere already bursting with secular clamour and a Catholic hum. Italian cinema can embark on the third way only when it faces the question of religious difference head on.

The Path of Religious Assimilation

In 2000, the controversial Cardinal of Bologna, Giacomo Biffi, stated the following:

> se volete il vero bene dell'Italia e risparmiare tante sofferenze non potete lasciare entrare tutti gli immigrati. Dovrete privilegiare l'afflusso dei cattolici. [...] I criteri per ammettere gli immigrati non possono essere solo economici e previdenziali. Occorre che ci si preoccupi seriamente di salvare l'identità della nazione. (Smargiassi 2000)

> If you have Italy's best interests at heart and want to save yourself a lot of suffering, you cannot let all the immigrants in. You must privilege the influx of

Catholics ... The criteria for admitting immigrants cannot simply be economic and welfare-oriented. It is necessary to seriously commit to saving the identity of the nation.

The cardinal was speaking before the 9/11 terrorist attack in the United States. Although he does not name Islam directly, Islam is implied, since at that time 33 per cent of recent immigrants were Muslim (indeed, only around 5 per cent of immigrants came from other non-Christian faiths).[1] In 2013, Italian media rhetoric darkened further. Michela Ardizzoni outlines the media's treatment of Islam in Italy in the wake of 9/11, highlighting two particularly significant events that were captured and promulgated by the media: the publication of Oriana Fallaci's best-selling *La rabbia e l'orgoglio* (The Rage and the Pride, 2006), which warned of the dangers of the propagation of Islam on Italian soil; and the conversion to Catholicism of the Muslim Magdi Allam, the influential vice-director of *Corriere della sera*. Magdi Allam claimed that he could no longer practise a religion that was "fisiologicamente violento e storicamente conflittuale" (physiologically violent and historically conflictual) (cited in Ardizzoni 2013, 154). The high-profile rejection of Islam for its purported innate violence by one of its most high-profile Italian practitioners sent shock waves through the Italian press. The concerns about Islam raised by the actions of two such prominent intellectuals were accompanied by growing national concerns about migration from Islamic countries and mounting international concerns about Islamic terror threats. Islam has repeatedly been treated monolithically in the media and subjected to fearful and suspicious responses. It is frequently presented as a threat to Italian values and as fundamentally and irremediably different to "us."

In the face of these anxieties among vast swathes of the press and television, the Italian filmmaking industry treads a rather different path. As is often the case, significant segments of Italian cinema, especially its art-house wing, are independent; they postulate resistant readings to dominant media perspectives and chip away at the Manichaean dichotomy of good and evil,

---

1 According to the Catholic agency Caritas, among immigrants who have not (yet) gained citizenship, Muslims are the most numerous faith group after Catholics (33 per cent of immigrants), followed by Orthodox Christians (20.3 per cent), other Christians (6.6 per cent), Hindus (2.4 per cent), Buddhists (1.9 per cent), and Jews (only 0.3 per cent) (Introvigne and Zoccatelli 2006). These figures are not entirely reliable; nonetheless, they reveal that immigration, rather than conversion, is the single biggest cause of the growth of minority faiths in contemporary Italy. More recent Pew Research Centre figures (Hackett 2017) show that the numbers are constantly increasing and are set to increase more over the coming decades. Hackett says that across Europe, even if migration were to be stopped now, the Muslim population is likely to rise to 7.4 per cent by 2050 due to the youth of the migrants and high fertility rates. If migration continues, the numbers are set to rise to 11.2 per cent by 2050.

providing an alternative narrative. Cinema, in other words, carves out a different ethical space than its mass-media cousins. More surprisingly, perhaps, given the negative television debates, fiction filmmaking for the small screen endeavours to position religious minorities positively. The influence of Lux Vide, which produces films not just for the predominantly Catholic audiences in Italy but also for ecumenical audiences in the United States and elsewhere, can be plainly felt. Lux Vide carves out a positive space for Abrahamic faiths, and followers of these faiths are key consumers of its products such as its Bible series (*La Bibbia*, 1993–2002). Moreover, it consults with a range of religious leaders before filming stories that implicate other religions. Ultimately, most post-9/11 portrayals of Islam in fiction on both big and small screens endeavour to be broadly liberal and sympathetic. Most endeavour to demonstrate that Islam can live side by side with Italian Catholicism on a modernizing and tolerant multi-faith peninsula. As I will show, however, the consequences of this endeavour are not without problems.

In this section I investigate two forms of assimilation: the co-opting of the Islamic migrant on the part of Italian filmmakers, and the blending of Islam and Catholicism on the part of filmmakers from Islamic cultural backgrounds. In this section I first investigate Claudio Cupellini's *Lezioni di cioccolato 1* (Lessons in Chocolate 1, 2007), a comedy made by an Italian director that explores differences between Catholic and Islamic values. In the second part I trace the work of filmmakers working in Italy who were born in Islamic countries, filmmakers like Ferzan Özpetek and Fariborz Kamkari. My aim is, first, to show how constructions of well-integrated migrant experiences often highlight Islam's difference only to subsequently neuter it, subduing conflict and rendering such difference unthreatening. I hypothesize the causes of this narrative pattern and its consequences.

Cuppellini's *Lezioni di cioccolato* is a classic comedy of mistaken identity. It recounts the tale of an unscrupulous Italian entrepreneur, Mattia (Luca Argentero), and his Egyptian worker, Kamal (Hassani Shapi). Mattia has cut corners with his scaffolding, and when Kamal falls off a roof, he exits hospital encased in plaster, and blackmails his boss. To meet the terms of the blackmail, Mattia is forced to assume the Egyptian's identity and enter a chocolate-making competition in Kamal's place. Mattia must now contend with issues affecting migrant integration in addition to learning the Egyptian's culture. And, of course, he exits the competition a better man (the word "lessons" [*Lezioni*] in the title points to the comedy's moralistic undercurrent). Mattia-Kamal's chocolate, which marries the flavours of Umbria and Egypt, wins first prize. In the final scene, a slowly rising crane shot reveals Mattia and his new-found friend Kamal lit by the late-afternoon sunshine and framed against idyllic Umbrian hayfields. They are still teasing each other about their sameness-difference, but with companionable humour and warmth.

Kamal's character in this film is revealing. He provides a comforting portrayal of alterity for an Italian audience. As a consequence, the abject – so often inscribed on Italian films about migrants – is eschewed.[2] Kamal is a well-integrated Egyptian Muslim constructed throughout the film as a positive role model, the antithesis to Mattia. Mattia uncritically embraces late capitalism, and his life revolves around profit and the exploitation of others for personal gain; Kamal, by contrast, works diligently in construction, pursues a career for which he has a genuine passion (chocolate), and is married, with an extended family network. As Mattia says to Kamal, "Perché non sono come te? Tu, tu hai tutti i valori, la famiglia, Dio, i parenti. Sei la perfezione!" (Why am I not like you? You, you have all the values, family, God, relations. You're perfect!). It is to Kamal's Islamic value system that Mattia, on some level at least, begins to aspire.

Kamal's crudely sketched Islamic values – little more than avoidance of pork and alcohol and a warm attachment to an extended family – are not, however, what they seem. The film progressively erases the religious and cultural difference it initially establishes. Ultimately, the Islam represented by Kamal is revealed to have much more to do with a vanished Catholic Italy than with the Koranic faith. An imagined, pre-relativist, pre-multicultural, premodern Italian identity is precisely what – somewhat paradoxically – Kamal comes to inhabit and represent. *Lezioni di cioccolato* is a comic tale that harbours a deeply conservative message: the Muslim other is assimilated and co-opted as a safe, recognizable self, one who shares the "authentic" values of "family, God, the relations." This leaves no space for discussion of the difference between two religious systems or for the possibility that there might be real incompatibilities.

This escapist comedy withdraws from the discomfort of facing the other by repositioning the other within a safe and familiar southern Italian Catholic ethical frame, which here is seen not as abject but as charmingly backward and simple. Hassani Shapiri's Italian is much more grammatical in real life than it is on screen. In Cupellini's film, he is orientalized and constructed as a child, with large, innocent, wide eyes, childish linguistic constructions, and naive value assertions such as, "Uomo e donne uguale figli ... se no che serve tua vita!" (Man and women equal children ... if not what serve your life!). The need to reaffirm the basic values that Italian Catholic children are taught – values that many Italians will abandon as they grow up and face adult complexity – is portrayed by the film as critical. Doing so is the only way to escape the spiritual corruption of a contemporary partly secular, capitalist Italy in which profit has become the central value. This lesson leaves visible marks on Mattia: by the end

---

2 Áine O'Healy (2010, 3), drawing on Julia Kristeva, notes that "[s]outherners are symbolically abjected from the European social body. Italy's new migrants from Africa and other parts of the global south are destined, by implication, to share a similar abjection."

of the film he is hybrid – part Italian (the well-cut designer suit) and part North African (the tan and "Sahara" shade curly hair).

As in many films that deal with minority religions, the conflict that appears initially to exist between Islam and a secularized Catholic Italy does not actually inhere between these two forces. Instead, the real conflict is between individualistic, capitalistic secularization and a liberal Italian value system that, perhaps paradoxically, comes to be represented by an unrecognizably watered-down Islam. In other words, films like *Lezioni di cioccolato* present concerns that are only in small part about the Islamic other. Rather, they indicate a deep-rooted unease in the face of secular modernity. This, while important (and it is after all important for a country to reflect on its relationship with its own religion), has a profoundly negative effect on how far films can go in tackling real difference. Kamal does not merely reveal to Italians what they have become; he also reveals the *Italiani brava gente* (good Italians) they once were. The unspoken paradox of this film is that the nostalgia it voices for a time of absolutes (especially with regard to the family and God) reflects not a gold-tinted, multicultural future but a rose-tinted past: a pre-multicultural Italy in which Catholic values were once – so the myth goes – the norm. This nostalgic backward glance sidesteps contemporary challenges created by the bewilderingly wide array of choices that arise from the multitude of moral and ethical values, lifestyle models, and spiritual directions that are now available. Buried beneath the manifest dream of solidarity with the religious other is the search for a lost and utopian self, a self that existed *prior to* the advent of such a visible other, a self that is incompatible with it. We should not be surprised that the role of abject victim or criminal is not assigned to Kamal. He circumvents the negative attributes so often linked to the migrant since, under his surface appearance, he is the mythical, authentic Catholic through and through.

This obliteration of the other through his or her assimilation into a remembered and nostalgic Catholic past is not unique to *Lezioni di cioccolato*. Luca Miniero's poorly received comedy *Non c'è più religione* (2016) assimilates the Muslim community of a small southern Italian island: the absence of a Catholic baby Jesus for the town's living nativity scene leads to a pregnant Muslim migrant being called upon for the role of Mary. The Muslim is soon replaced by an Buddhist Madonna. The differences between the religions are flattened for the sake of humour, while the nostalgic iconography of Christianity (the nativity scene) continues to dominate visually. Roberto Benigni's comedy *La tigre e la neve* (The Tiger and the Snow, 2005) also flattens difference. Benigni's film shows an Italian poet, Attilio (Roberto Benigni), praying to Allah as a last resort. The woman he loves is dying in a hospital in Baghdad, and he must save her. Attilio directs his eyes heavenwards, or more precisely, towards the ceiling of a hospital basement. He politely speaks to "Allah" to ascertain whether the only prayer he knows ("Our Father") would be acceptable, remarking that "tanto le preghiere sono tutte uguali" (in any case, prayers are all the same). Having heard nothing to the contrary from Allah, the poet then kneels at the woman's bedside, an iconic trope of nineteenth-century pious paintings, and recites a prayer that all Catholics learn as children. Like *Lezioni di cioccolato*, this scene represents a return to a Catholicism learned in infancy. The scene's implicit message is that Islam's God is so like a Christian God that he can receive the same prayers. In the face of a foreign religion, the response here is to radically reduce the specificity of the other's God and religious practices and thus to negate difference.

The path to assimilation is taken not just by Italians but also by migrants from Islamic backgrounds who now work, or have worked, in Italy. An example of this is Iranian-born Fariborz Kamkari's comedy *Pitza e datteri* (2015). In this film, Hassani Shapi, star of *Lezioni di cioccolato*, plays another comic role. This time he is Karim, the head of a small, peaceful Muslim community in Venice. He is forced to find a solution when his makeshift mosque is bought by a seductive and liberal French Muslim, Zara (Maud Buquet), and transformed into a beauty parlour. Shapi's Karim is once again charming, but this time he is distinctly more grammatical and rather less infantile. He plays a liberal and well-integrated Western Muslim. Unlike the films discussed above, in this film made by an Iranian, "Muslim" is, unsurprisingly, not synonymous with "premodern Catholic."

Pitza e datteri presents a successful multi-ethnic, multi-faith community in Venice, a city that for centuries was the crossroads between East and West. While the film references Western stereotypes of Islamic terrorism and violence against women, these are repeatedly de-dramatized, rendered comic, and presented as ridiculously ineffective: the foreign *imam* sent to lead the charge against Zara and take back the mosque employs violent words and ideas but is feminine and sensitive and faints at the slightest emotion; a boat filled with rocks in preparation for stoning Zara sinks; a suicide bomb in an Italian convert's life vest fizzles out and fails to detonate. Thus, while extremist Islamic violence is acknowledged throughout the film, it is repeatedly disavowed. Islam presents no threat: its violence is bluster, and its community is tiny, amounting to a mere twenty souls. The newly arrived foreign imam tries to impose stricter rules, but the Islam he finds in Italy, a hybrid form that has absorbed local characteristics, is far too easy-going and liberal to accommodate him: the Muslim men in Venice have wives who are independent and strong-willed; Zara dresses and acts provocatively, hires a camp gay man to work for her, and runs a unisex beauty parlour. The film's message is distinctly assimilationist, portraying Islam as diverse but primarily moderate and liberal (albeit with a wild, if ineffective, fringe represented by the Afghan imam and the offbeat Italian Muslim, Bepi). It also presents the practice of Islam as perfectly coherent with a range of national and local identities, from Afghan to French Moroccan to Venetian.

Bepi (Giuseppe Battison), an Italian convert to Islam, still converses colourfully in Veneto dialect and retains his strong regional identity despite his conversion. The film's denouement is also distinctly integrationist: the Jewish community donates its synagogue to the Muslims for use as their new mosque, and the mosque is blessed by the Italian mayor. In this utopian finale, the Abrahamic religions learn to get on with one another; Islam successfully negotiates secular civic society and accepts its contemporary secular rules, especially regarding women's rights; and all live happily ever after.

While *Pitza e datteri* exhibits religious difference only to later deny it in favour of interfaith harmony and assimilation, it does present significant differences from *Lezioni di cioccolato*. Kamkari's film does not look backwards towards an ideal rose-tinted, pre-multicultural past in which Catholic values and traditional family relations dominate. Instead it looks forward to an ideal multicultural and multi-religious future of interfaith harmony based on the expulsion of extremism and the post-secular embrace of, and cooperation between, liberal religious groups.

Fariborz Kamkari is a Kurdish Iranian, and *Pitza e datteri*, his first film made in Italy, reflects the path towards assimilation also seen in the films of Ferzan Özpetek (Turkey) and Mohsen Melliti (Tunisia) – directors who came to Italy from Islamic countries in the 1970s and 1980s respectively. All three directors are witness to the importance of assimilation in finding an audience for their films in Italy. Özpetek, a Turkish national who moved from a primarily Muslim country to Rome in 1976, took Italian citizenship and successfully carved out a space for himself within the Italian film industry. He has increasingly and visibly absorbed aspects of the religious and socio-political matrix in which he works. His first two films, *Il bagno turco* (1997) and *Harem suare* (1999), worked with an exoticized, remembered, Oriental matrix blended with Western values. However, *Cuore sacro* (Sacred Heart, 2005), released six years later and set entirely in Rome, explicitly references Catholic iconography in the sacred heart of its title and in a visual reference to Michelangelo's *Pietà* in one of its scenes. It also employs a conversion narrative familiar to Catholicism: a spoiled business tycoon (Barbara Bobulova) befriends a destitute little girl and, through her friendship with the girl and a cleric, finds redemption and dedicates her life to helping the poor. The film highlights the importance of assisting the needy through a narrative that embraces that peculiarly Italian fusion of *giustizia* (justice), *pietà* (mercy), and opposition discussed in chapter 3. Catholic social teaching is blended with left-wing thought – a combination that, as I argue elsewhere, dominates a great deal of Italian *cinema d'impegno* (committed cinema) (Brook 2017). Over time, then, Ferzan Özpetek erased his "accent" and embraced a Catholic-imbued world view; the result here is a recognizable RAI Cinema production (Grassilli 2008), with fewer references to Turkish culture.

Mohsen Melliti a writer and filmmaker who moved to Italy in 1989 as a political exile and took citizenship in 2010 before moving to Los Angeles, demonstrates similar assimilation. His only feature film, *Io l'altro* (2007), deliberately erases religious difference. Melliti's main characters – Yosef and Giuseppe – work together on a fishing boat. When the two find a dead Somali woman in the sea, Giuseppe remarks how similar the hand of Fatima is to the Christian cross, and each man prays to his own God for her in their different yet analogous ways. The southern Italian and the Tunisian share cultural variants of the same name (Yosef/Giuseppe), and are "brothers." Their different religious customs are underpinned by a shared set of values. Their relationship is soured not by friction between them but by attitudes towards Muslims in the media: a radio broadcast brings news of an Islamic terrorist on the loose with the same name as Yosef, and with this broadcast suspicion enters their fishing boat.

Mohsen Melliti, Fariborz Kamkari, and Ferzan Özpetek illustrate how the path of religious assimilation has been travelled by several directors born into Islamic religious contexts. The attainment of *italianità* affects whether or not cinematic voices from minority religions can enter a national industry that has such a well-defined Catholic iconography and such a strong sense of ethical-political identity. Assimilation is therefore crucial to their career trajectory. The path of religious assimilation is taken not only by Italians keen to find solutions for the problem of the "other," but also by directors who have settled in Italy from countries dominated by Islam. The outcomes for the two groups are far from identical. Cupellini and Benigni reveal a vague, monolithic, and stereotyped vision of Islam that is quickly brushed aside once assimilated. Muslims are accepted provided they conform to a nostalgic ideal of Catholicism; their God is acceptable only if he answers to the Lord's Prayer. Ultimately, these films are not about integrating Islam. Instead, they often betray their nostalgia for a Catholicism under threat on all sides from secularism, neoliberal capitalism, and multiculturalism. By contrast, films made by directors from Islamic cultural backgrounds present a distinctly more nuanced vision of religions outside Catholicism. Moreover, Melliti and Kamkari broach the need for interfaith dialogue, a need that is absent from Benigni and Cupellini's vision. What Özpetek, Melliti, and Kamkari *do* share with their Italian colleagues is a longing to smooth out the differences between religions, to make the case for the similarity of different religious beliefs, focusing attention on communal belonging and shared values: family, charity, and love for the other. These films posit a generic religion, shorn of specificity, as a source of good.

The zeroing of intrinsic religious difference pertains especially to Islam, as this section makes abundantly clear. "Muslim" and "migrant" have become synonymous, and this has resulted in well-meaning efforts to integrate the migrant and his or her value system by making them "just like us" – by overstating sameness and flattening difference. On-screen portrayals of other minority religions have been less quick to follow the path of assimilation. As I argue in the conclusion to this chapter, interpretations of Judaism receive more subtle and reflective attention. It appears less difficult to face – and accept – Jewish difference, and many films dealing with Judaism thus embark on the third way. Other religions, on the other hand, especially Buddhism and Hare Krishna, are reserved only short, exotic cameo roles, as discussed in chapter 2, and are typically not assimilated.

The path to assimilation is problematic. Hamid Naficy (2001, 210), discussing transnational film from an American perspective, notes how "capitalism continually reterritorializes its liminars and transnationals through strategies of assimilation and co-optation, transforming them into ethnic subjects and productive citizens." Italian cinema and television, be it home-grown or transnational, is highly complicit with the process outlined by Naficy. Moreover, there is a notable absence on Italian screens of Naficy's "liminars," those who "reterritorialize themselves as exiles, as refusniks" (211). The co-opting of a rather generic and inoffensive religious value system as a mark of Italian assimilation may look on the surface like a post-conciliar opening towards a religious other, but in fact what it signals is anxiety about the religious difference that the other represents, a difference that must be repeatedly neutralized in order to be accepted. In other words, the films I have addressed here, however well-meaning, point to an inability to face difference head on. They welcome the other only when neutralized.

The Path to the Horrific Religious Other

Art-house and mainstream Italian comedies and dramas typically assimilate the religious other, especially the Islamic other, by rendering difference invisible. However, some films move in the opposite direction and make spectacularly visible the differences in religious values and symbolism. They then use this visibility to establish this faith as unacceptable. In mainstream filmmaking, the most obvious examples are Renzo Martinelli's controversial conspiracy thrillers, *Il mercante di pietre* (The Stone Merchant, 2006) and *11 settembre 1683* (Day of Siege, 2012). I focus on the first of these at the beginning of this section. Outside the mainstream, it is the horror genre that most often screens anxiety about the faith of others, and this provides the focus of the second part of this section. Martinelli's conspiracy thrillers and horror movies both construct religious difference as spectacular and frightening and abort spectator identification with the other. Both prove difficult to market in Italy's mainstream. They either circulate underground (the horror genre) or are rejected by most of Italy's cinema critics (Martinelli's films). What I examine in this section might well be described, in other words, as that upon which the public sphere cannot look.

Martinelli's *Il mercante di pietre* should have been a sensational hit. It is based on Italy's most-read novel of 1999, Corrado Calabrò's *Ricorda di dimenticarla*, and it follows the formula of the international blockbuster thriller, complete with high-profile American actors like Harvey Keitel and F. Murray Abraham. It updates the socio-political milieu of Calabrò's book, replacing his references to the Italian political terrorism of the 1970s with twenty-first-century Islamic terrorism. It constructs Islam as a threat to the very heart of the contemporary Western world.

The film tells the story of Alceo (Jordi Mollà) and his pretty wife, Leda (Jane March), two Italians who are victims of multiple Islamic terrorist plots. Alceo is a university lecturer who lost both legs in the terrorist bombing of the US embassy in Nairobi and now authors Islamaphobic books. His wife is caught up in a fictional terrorist attack at Fiumicino airport at the start of the film and is then targeted by another Islamist – a stone merchant (Harvey Keitel) – while the couple are recovering on holiday in Turkey. An Italian convert to Islam, the stone merchant has links to a radical mosque in Turin. He seduces Leda and makes her his "dove": an innocent woman used as a vehicle for a terrorist attack. The woman is enlisted to drive her car, packed with explosives, onto a ferry bound for Dover. She dies in the ensuing explosion. The shocked and repentant Italian stone merchant is shot in the back by his fellow terrorists while he kneels in sorrow and prays to Allah.

The film bears all the signs of an international co-production, with international stars and high production values. Martinelli claims a "based on fact" truth-status for it, asserting that every word spoken by the film's imam is grounded in a speech given by the imam of the Roman mosque in 2003 (Giulidori 2006). He claims truth-status too for the strategy of the dove, which, he says, was used in the Lockerbie bombing. However, this film, like his problematic earlier thriller *Piazza delle cinque lune* (2003), is played out not within any realist frame, but within the conspiracy thriller genre. It posits Islam as an imminent and real threat, a religion too dangerous to reside safely in Europe, and one that Europe has seriously underestimated. The film's *incipit* presents the argument *in nuce*. As the opening titles roll, an immense mosque is captured in aerial camerawork by a circling helicopter, accompanied on the soundtrack by evocative Arabic music. Given the exotic aural and visual cues, the words "Roma, Italia" (Rome, Italy) projected at the bottom of the screen are meant to shock. It looks like a movie set in some distant, perhaps apocalyptic, future, in which the mosque – the really existent mosque on the outskirts of the capital – has become the symbol of Rome, displacing Rome's cultural and religious history and encapsulating the victory of Islam over the Christian West. The subsequent aerial shots of the Vatican re-establish the centrality of the Catholic Church and reassure the spectator that Christianity is still standing, even while the continuing Arabic music on the soundtrack threatens it.

With this opening scene, the idea that Catholicism's authority in Italy could be displaced has already been sown.

The film employs Alceo, the university lecturer and protagonist, to voice the message that the Islamic menace is at hand and has been misrecognized and underestimated by the mainstream media. The film plays on the idea that Alceo's anti-Islamic arguments may be the sublimated castration complex of a man who has lost his legs in a bombing and is about to lose his wife. This provides a comfortable ideological viewing perspective for a sceptical spectator throughout much of the film. The final apocalyptic scene, however, in which the ferry explodes in the port of Dover, functions as incontrovertible proof of the veracity of Alceo's theories and strives to convert the sceptic. As the ferry blows up, the liberal public sphere is proved blind and fatally misguided.

In this film, Islam's variety is compressed into a single, bloody Saudi Arabian Wahhabism, and more moderate varieties of Islam are abandoned (except for an orientalized Sufi dance in the Turkish section of the film). *Il mercante di pietre* presents Islam as a dire threat to Italy's identity and to the safety of the entire West. The assimilation lauded in the films discussed in the previous section is revealed as deadly, since it is precisely because Islamists are "confusi tra noi" (mixed up with us), to cite Alceo, that there is a problem. These Muslims only *appear* to be assimilated, living unobserved within European society; that assimilation is in fact a ruse, one that enables them to materialize unannounced all over the world: at Calais or Fiumicino airport; in Tunis or Cappadocia; on a ferry to Dover. Indeed, they possess uncanny, superhuman mobility – much like Martinelli's alarming camera zooms – as evidenced when Leda discovers a letter from the stone merchant *inside* her locked car in Italy. They also possess superhuman invisibility, deliberately and mysteriously erasing photographic images of their presence from the Italian couple's camera. They are like the cells of a spreading cancer within the body politic: invisibly spreading, their deadly consequences discovered too late.

Il mercante di pietre adopts the contemporary language of white masculinity in crisis (see Robinson 2000; Carroll 2011; O'Rawe 2014) to make its point. For Martinelli, the process of assimilating Muslims leads to reverse discrimination: while Muslim men are protected as minorities by the nations that host them, white European males are left powerless and open to attack. Alceo, whose legs were amputated after a terrorist attack, is referred to several times as "half a man." His castration stands for the castration of *all* men, who are powerless to halt an Islamic threat that seduces their wives and threatens their country. The stone merchant too – an Italian, not an Arab – is a victim of Islam. At the end of the film he falls to his knees in the rain, praying to Allah for forgiveness as he is shot in the head by his Arabic terrorist counterparts, who, unlike him, show no mercy or remorse. In fact, in its apportioning of blame, this film recalls Roberto Rossellini's *Roma città aperta* (Rome, Open

City 1945), which spared Italian fascists much of the responsibility for the destruction of the country, the weight of blame falling instead on their foreign Nazi German counterparts. In *Il mercante di pietre*, two white Italian males are literally brought to their knees by Islam. They become abject victims rather than perpetrators, while the woman who unites them gets her just reward for her betrayal of a good but "castrated" white man (the same role assigned to the conspiratorial Italian women in Rossellini's film). Europeans are either too weak (Alceo), too blind (journalists), or too easily corrupted (Leda) to reject the Islamic other and thereby survive a toxic and deadly post-secular society. For Martinelli, this multi-faith, post-secular society is not tolerant and open, as posited in *Pitza e datteri* and *Lezioni di cioccolato*. Moreover, while *Il mercante di pietre* implicates the media in the narrative spun around Muslims, it also reverses the outcome seen earlier in Melliti's *Io l'altro*. It is not that Islamophobia is amplified and circulated through the media, as Melliti's film argues, but rather that the media conspire to silence and suppress Alceo's "unacceptable" Islamophobic views. These two films thus present conflicting views of the media's role in the circulation of Islamophobia; in Melliti's they facilitate it, in Martinelli's, they silence it. Despite the opposing outcomes, both films assign to the media significant powers in the construction of Italian attitudes towards the Islamic other.

The reception of this blockbuster-turned-flop is indicative of contemporary positions held by the cinema industry towards minority religions. It thus provides insight into the position of Islam's visibility in the public sphere. Mainstream Italian film journalism, dominated by the left and centre-left, rejected the film. It achieved only limited circulation in Italian cinemas and suffered a substantial loss (its takings amounted to little more than 853,000 euros, a fraction of its ten million euro budget). The support it did find came, predictably enough, from the political right. The Lega Nord (Northern League) praised it in an article on its website titled "Sveglia, Occidente L'Islam ti assedia" (Wake up, Western World: Islam is Besieging You), which explicitly references Oriana Fallaci's call for Europe to wake up and recognize that moderate Islam does not exist. Many members of the conservative Alleanza nazionale (AN, National Alliance) also expressed enthusiasm for a film that, according to one AN member, "racconta la realtà" (recounts reality), although AN's leader, Gianfranco Fini, distanced himself from the film, calling it "spazzatura" (rubbish) and "propaganda" (Bei 2006). Viewer comments registered at the time of the film's release on sites like www.davinotti.com describe the film "ideologicamente forzato, per non dire falso e in malafede," "allarmista," "ignobile," "pagliaccesco," and "privo di nesso logico" (ideologically forced, false, and in bad faith; alarmist; ignoble; clownish; lacking a logical nexus). It is worth noting, however, that some years later, in the wake of a run of terrorist attacks across Europe in 2015–16, comments on YouTube were considerably more inclined to interpret the film's narrative as realistic, the implication being that its message might be better received today. Nonetheless, the widespread condemnation of the film at the time of its release across a wide range of public sources (from party leaders to film critics, commentators, and the general public) suggests that, as far as mainstream cinema and its reception in the public sphere is concerned, the simplistic, Manichaean Islamophobia offered up by *Il mercante di pietre* cannot gain traction.[3]

So deprived of room to thrive in the cinematic space, fear is driven underground and resurfaces in the horror genre. Given the tiny budgets involved and the genre's niche circulation, most such films are released to minimal media attention. Moreover, the national and international importance of Italy's horror genre has lessened markedly since the millennium, with only a handful of low-profile films released each year. Given their limited impact on the public sphere, in terms of both number of spectators and level of debate, the films I consider here, while fascinating in terms of their exposure of the peninsula's deeply repressed fears, must nonetheless be interpreted as a marginal phenomenon.

In horror filmmaking, other cultures' sacred spaces are framed to provoke fear. Horror, writes Douglas E. Cowen (2008), is the "horror of those that are not us." In the horror genre, foreign religious and spiritual practices are highly charged, and the narrative plunges the spectator into Charles Taylor's premodern "enchanted world" (2007). Italy's contemporary horror films come face to face with the religious other in three key ways. First, through tales of the deadly rebirth of buried religions, which enable the resurfacing of beliefs that Christianity has long laid to rest. This first category includes the religion of the Maya in David Hunt's *La tomba* (The Tomb, 2004),[4] of the Etruscans in Ted Nicolaou's *La maschera etrusca* (The Etruscan Mask, 2007), and of pre-Christian demons in Alessio Nencioni's *Possessione demonica* (Demonic Possession, 2015) and Diego Carli's *Il caso Anna Mancini* (The Anna Mancini Case, 2016). Each of these films hypothesizes what lurks beneath the surface of the civilized world and beyond the grasp of orderly, mainstream Catholicism. In an archaeologically rich peninsula like Italy, these barely submerged worlds are particularly strongly felt: the presence of past civilizations and their arcane religious beliefs is still heavily inscribed on Italy's landscape and ancient ruins and can easily be drawn upon and reactivated.

---

3   While the attitudes towards Islam expressed by *Il mercante di pietre* were found unacceptable at the time by the mainstream media, this did not create insurmountable obstacles for the production of further films of this nature. In 2012, Martinelli released a second film on the clash between Islam and Christian civilization: *11 settembre 1683*, a film that implicitly links the halting of the spread of Islam in Europe in 1683 with the terrorist attack on the Twin Towers in 2001 and again creates a warring binary between Christianity and Islam.

4   In horror, as in other international genres such as the so-called "spaghetti westerns" and "sword-and-sandal films," Italian directors have often assumed American-sounding names. David Hunt is the pseudonym for Italian director Bruno Mattei.

The second category of horror includes films that screen religions and spiritual or magical practices engaged in by contemporary ethnic others. This is the case in vintage horror director Dario Argento's *La terza madre* (2007). In this film, an excavation at Viterbo brings to light an urn containing a medieval tunic, which awakens a witch (the third witch in Argento's *Three Mothers* trilogy). Mater Lacrimarum's awakening draws to Rome a vast horde of foreign witches, who launch a wave of violence: rapes, murders, suicides, obscene rituals, desecration, and vandalism. The witches are disruptive and wild; they silently glare, laugh, or gibber incomprehensible foreign words. In other words, they have no will to dialogue with the city into which they pour, and which they treat with disdain. With their extreme sexual preferences, their obscene rituals, and their lack of communication or engagement with their Italian hosts, these witches carry enormous energy and excitement. They quickly infiltrate the host society, bringing about the collapse of its social, sexual, and moral order. The fear of the religious (and ethnic) other, an other interpreted as the cause of societal collapse in Argento's film, mirrors the outcomes of Martinelli's two thrillers. Religious others carry profound threats to the very fabric of Italian society.

Third and finally, horror "others" religion through non-Christian Italian practices. Films of this sort remind us that the religious other and the ethnic other are not always identical. By relegating these alternative religious practices to Italy's rural spaces, it signals Max Weber's claim that Christianity was from the very start an urban religion and that the city, rather than the countryside, is regarded by Christianity as the site of piety (1922). A handful of contemporary Italian horror films, including *Custodes bestiae* (Lorenzo Bianchini, 2004) and the Lovecraftian *Road to L* (Federico Greco and Roberto Leggo, 2005), posit isolated rural communities, cut off from urban influences, trapped within non-canonical religious practices. To some extent these films share characteristics with American hillbilly horrors like *Cabin Fever* (2002), which depict rural places in which a "half-civilized mongrel race" lives, and in which is acted out the "archaic disorder, savagery and pantheistic paganism of the American other" (Blake 2008, 128). They are also clearly shaped by the highly influential *Blair Witch Project* by Daniel Myrick and Eduardo Sánchez (1999). However, one cannot draw the Italian and American genres together too closely – Italian rural horror is of a different order.[5] There is, for instance, far greater anthropological veracity in the Italian horror films discussed here than is found in either hillybilly horrors or *Blair Witch*. Local, non-professional actors from Friuli (*Custodes*

---

5   There are a few examples, nonetheless, that are closer in form to the subgenre of Hillybilly horror. Edo Tagliarini's splatter, *Bloodline* (2005), narrates the tale of a film troupe staying in a cabin in a dark forest inhabited by zombies.

bestiae, 2004) and the Po delta (*Road to L*, 2005) provide realistic local colour, and their dialects are faithfully represented. It is evident, in other words, that even while they belong to the horror genre, these films draw upon the Italian realist tradition and legacy. The scene in *Road to L* in which the old people of the Po recount their local tales in a fire-lit cave is closer to the transcendent realism of Ermanno Olmi's *L'albero degli zoccoli* (The Tree of Wooden Clogs, 1978) than it is to horror. *Custodes bestiae* and *Road to L* both excavate supposed Northern Italian folk practices and dig out uncharted villages lost to contemporary urban life. They narrate invented or embellished rural religious systems, which, although sinister, are also intriguing. These films are far from the splatter and gore of the first two horror categories outlined here. Instead, they narrate an intriguing and mysterious "enchanted" natural world that is too deeply isolated and rural for Catholicism to have successfully penetrated. Significantly less fear is directed towards alternative indigenous religious practices today than towards practices that are buried in time or ethnically distant. From this, one can hypothesize that the most deep-rooted fears arise when race and religion are intertwined. In this twofold entwining lies a double unknown.

A curiosity of the horror genre is that until very recently it was one of the few filmic spaces in Italy in which alternative religious faiths were foregrounded. That the horror genre is one of the few cinematic spaces in which non-Catholic religions are screened is patently problematic. Horror marks the religious other as radically different. It shows that other as uncontrollable, sexually deviant, and savage. It has no respect for the rules of the world it enters, and it repeatedly threatens that world's very existence. Horror, in other words, proposes a radical disjuncture between the religious other and the host society. While the host society is modern, rational, civilized, and sexually conservative, the horrific religious other is premodern, irrational, uncivilized, and lacking any kind of moral regulation.

What is striking about contemporary Italian horror is that Catholicism is never abject or monstrous. This distinguishes Italian horror from a series of recent American horrors and thrillers in which the Vatican provides the source of arcane and scheming evil (Mark Neveldine's *The Vatican Tapes* [2015]; Ron Howard's *The Da Vinci Code* [2006] and *Angels and Demons* [2009]; the American series *American Horror Story* [2011]). It also distinguishes twenty-first-century horrors from Italy's horrors of the past, such as Michele Soave's *La chiesa* (The Church, 1989), for instance, in which the buried history of massacres perpetrated by Christian crusaders during the Middle Ages spawns a demonic twentieth-century killing spree. In contemporary Italian horrors, while Catholicism is not always effective in warding off evil, it is at least rational and engaged on the side of the good. In other words, whenever desperate characters turn to priests for advice, as protagonists do in *La terza madre* and *La maschera etrusca*, they receive good council. By contrast, the gods of the religious other are dictatorial and enslaving. They have no inter-est in council; they simply issue orders, imperatives, and punishments. The di-chotomy between the peninsula's official religion and the religious other thus curiously mirrors the opposition between democratic society (voluntary, ra-tional, non-coercive) and totalitarianism (direct domination). The aligning of Catholicism with rationality and democracy is important, for it implies that however powerful the Vatican is today, it is no longer perceived as a lethal pres-ence on the peninsula. It is the religion of *others* that is posited as dangerous – as stronger than the indigenous one, as well as contagious, quickly infecting and converting others. Alarmingly, faith's capacity to infect does not follow the lines of race, so anyone can be converted: from bored young Italians looking for thrills through a seemingly innocent dose of Satanism in *DeKronos – Il demone del tempo* by Rachel Bryceson Griffiths (2005), to soldiers contaminated by a sickening Islam in Ivan Zuccon's *L'altrove* (The Darkness Beyond, 2000). In a gross misrepresentation, the religion of others repeatedly appears as an ex-treme, highly contagious, and utterly enslaving fanatical horror.

In many ways, it is unsurprising that Martinelli's thrillers and so many horrors reveal foreign faith as fearful. These films have been released during a period of extreme and intensifying religious Manichaeanism. Mainstream media report-ing in Italy often divides the world into rational Westerners going about their business, on the one hand, and fearsome religious fanatics in the East, on the other. The latter burn American flags, behead journalists, and mow down inno-cent people on European sidewalks. Footage of moderate Muslims going about their lives and engaged in their secular and religious routines has been much rarer. Media images of an other seemingly enslaved to an incomprehensible, irrational, and extreme set of religious beliefs have generated fears that appear to have been channelled through the horror and conspiracy thriller genres in Italy. Martinelli's thrillers and the religiously oriented horrors considered here represent only a small part of Italian twenty-first-century filmmaking; even so, they need to be integrated into discussions of religion in the public sphere, for they reveal the hysterical underbelly of the official cinematic discourse of assimilation. Moreover, they reveal how Italy's cinema industry works to prevent these discourses from reaching the mainstream.

Casatielli Halal: A Multi-Faith, Post-Secular Italy Emerges?

My analysis in the two preceding sections suggests that two models for handling the religious other operate in Italy: the assimilationist model, which thrives on the surface of Italian cinema, and the conflictual horror model, which lurks underfoot, leaking out in the "dark" genres of the conspiracy thriller and horror. The first of these models reveals that, in negotiating the shift from a primarily mono-religious to an increasingly multi-religious, post-secular landscape, the

Italian filmmaking industry is making a sustained effort to accept those of other faiths. However, as both models show, acceptance is still uncomfortable, partial, and circumscribed. In other words, while in large part the contemporary Italian film industry is successfully confronting ethnic and racial difference, there is still a widespread failure to confront *religious* difference. This has led to disavowals and repression, which together drive fears underground.

What has emerged so far from this analysis is that Italian filmic fiction rarely seriously engages with the religious other. Its easy assimilation or demonization of the other rests on facile stereotypes through which minority religions are rendered exotic and spectacular. Metonymies used to denote religious others, such as the call to prayer and the robed and exotic believer, are frequent. Muslims are almost always portrayed as young North Africans who have recently made the journey across the Mediterranean and are inscribed on a migration narrative in which they face being racially othered, as in Mohsen Melliti's *Io l'altro* (2007), Carlo Mazzacurati's *La giusta distanza* (The Right Distance, 2007), Laura Muscardin's *Billo: Il grand Dakhaar* (2007), and *Non c'è più religione* (2017). Their presence acts as a metonymy for twenty-first-century Italian modernity. Jews are still cast primarily as victims of the Shoah, especially in movies and miniseries made for television: Alberto Negrin's *Perlasca – un eroe italiano* (The Courage of a Just Man, 2002); Leone Pompucci's *La fuga degli innocenti* (Hidden Children, 2004); Alberto Negrin's *Il cuore nel pozzo* (The Heart in the Well, 2005); Carlo Carlei's *Fuga per la libertà –L'aviatore* (The Pilot, 2007); Pasquale Squitieri's *Il giorno della Shoah* (2010); Christian Duguay's *Sotto il cielo di Roma* (Pius XII: Under the Roman Sky, 2010). Unlike Muslims, who denote Italy's present, Jews belong to the country's past. Where they inhabit Italy's present, they are most often lonely, elderly figures haunting the contemporary world, characters who exist principally to remind Italians of the horrors of the Holocaust. From Ferzan Özpetek's *La finestra di fronte* (Facing Windows, 2003) to Ermanno Olmi's *Il villaggio di cartone* (The Cardboard Village, 2011) and Paolo Sorrentino's *This Must Be the Place* (2011), Jewish characters reveal their abject past, or that of their fathers, in concentration camps. They are identified not as Sephardi or as Ashkenazi, or as conservative, liberal, or orthodox, but in terms of their identities as survivors of the camps. Nor is it just Judaism or Islam that is stereotyped in this way. Hare Krishna is a source of dismissive on-screen ridicule and spectacle. The Hare Krishna monks who make fleeting appearances in Moretti's *La stanza del figlio* (The Son's Room, 2001) and in Kamkari's *Pitza e datteri* are inserted for purely scenographic and comedic reasons: their stylized shaved heads and orange robes are colourful, and their chanting, as Moretti's character acknowledges as he hums along, is catchy. In *Pitza e datteri*, Bepi, an Italian convert to Islam, appears in the film's finale as a Hare Krishna monk, a conversion designed only for its comic potential. What is immediately noticeable about these stereotypes – whether of Jews, Muslims, or followers of Hare Krisha – is that most commonly their spiritual and ethical content is erased.

Tim Jon Semmerling (2006), citing Gordon W. Allport, notes that religious stereotypes are a way of "imposing order where there is none, a lifeline to tried-and-tested habits when new solutions are called for, and an opportunity to 'latch onto what is familiar, safe, simple, definite.'" (Semmerling 2006, 6). The desire for safety and familiarity in a contemporary Italy undergoing rapid change is understandable. However, the repeated deployment of a simplistic iconography, of consolation narratives that underplay religious difference, as well as the driving underground of the fear of difference, blocks the filmmaking industry – including its art-house wing – from using the screen to imagine real solutions that might create a successful multi-religious, post-secular society.

There are now signs of change in contemporary Italy, nonetheless. Several Italian filmmakers are engaging with minority religions, especially Judaism and Islam, as spiritual and ethical practices worthy of serious attention. This does not necessarily result in a questioning and deconstruction of the "us"; even so, it marks an effort to understand different religious perspectives. There are several important examples of this "third way." The first of these was broadcast on television between 1994 and 2002 and is indicative of nascent attempts at modernization by the national broadcaster. Lux Vide's *Progetto Bibbia*, made for RAI and for European and American television stations, screened nine stories from the Old Testament Bible during this period. Especially noteworthy here is how the research for the series was carried out. The producer, Ettore Bernabei, instead of relying solely on Catholic experts, consulted authorities from Protestant, Jewish, and Orthodox faiths (Rusconi 2011). Representatives from Islam were initially excluded; however, once filming began in Morocco, Bernabei requested an expert on Islam (a request that was initially turned down, given Islamic concerns about images of the prophets) (Rusconi 2011). The turn to Islamic expertise for a Catholic-made project is significant even if the delay in contacting the Islamic expert points to the distance and diffidence that inheres between the two religions. Nonetheless, Bernabei's ecumenical approach was not aimed at overturning the power hierarchy that located Catholicism at its apex. The production process clearly prioritized Catholicism. Bernabei delib- erately selected technicians who were Catholic and who possessed, he declared, "obbedienza cieca e assoluta" (blind and absolute obedience) (Rusconi 2011). That the Catholic vision was made to dominate other faiths is not to deny that Bernabei's efforts were an important step forward that would have been unthinkable even twenty years earlier.[6] Italy, for the first time, was conceiving

---

6 This relationship had been revolutionized in the 1960s by the Second Vatican Council's revised teachings on ecumenism. No longer was it forbidden to attend the ecumenical meetings of non-Catholics. Instead, there was a recognition of the "imperfect" communion with other Christians through baptism (*Unitatis redintegratio*, 1964), as well as a recognition of the right to religious freedom (*Dignitatis humanae*, 1965). However, the Catholic church retained the belief that Catholicism was the most perfect route to God.

of an American-style, televised Bible series that could be watched by all those of the Abrahamic faith, not just Catholics. Given that this was an international production and that the United States required ecumenical, pan-religious products for its market, Bernabei's opening to the other may have been driven primarily by market forces. Even so, it was a significant move on the part of one of the most important players in Italian television production.

A second critical step was taken on the big screen during the same period. Just on the cusp of the new millennium, Alessandro D'Alatri made *I giardini dell'Eden* (The Garden of Eden, 1998). While the film is undoubtedly flawed, it nonetheless marks a significant step on the road to understanding the faiths of others, and it is poles apart from the clumsy, heavily orientalized, spectacular, and improbable explanation of another faith seen in Bernardo Bertolucci's *Piccolo Buddha* (Little Buddha) just five years previously.[7] For *I giardini dell'Eden*, which narrates the early years of the historical Christ, D'Alatri enlisted a Jewish writer, Miro Silvera, to work with him on the screenplay. The ensuing film draws on the Gospels but is sensitive to Jewish culture and beliefs. It also focuses attention on Christianity's rootedness in other faiths. The film sets out to reconstruct the lost years in the story of Christ: the years before he took up the teaching mission recounted in the Gospels. D'Alatri's Jesus, who is given his Jewish name Joshua, is shown travelling among zealots, spending time among the Essenes sect at the Qumran settlement, witnessing other faiths, and absorbing their ideas. The film rewrites Jesus for a post-secular age of postmodern relativity and of multiple religious viewpoints. Its approach is explicitly voiced in the film: "Dio si manifesta agli uomini sotto svariate forme ma la sua essenza è sempre la stessa sotto ogni cielo" (God reveals himself to men in myriad forms but under every sky his essence remains the same).

While D'Alatri's attempt to relocate Christianity in a multi-faith world was condemned by some critics as New Age approximation (Baugh 2007; Nepoti 1998), the director was clearly attempting to face the challenge of relating monotheistic Catholicism to other faiths. His proposed solution is to have Jesus crystallize a variety of religions. This does not exactly resolve the problem, as Christianity becomes a distillation of the best of other religions, having removed the worst of their faults – such as selling blind girls for sex or stoning prostitutes. Nonetheless, it does portray Christianity as a melting pot of Arabic, Jewish, and Buddhist faiths and sects. The film faces the spiritual and ethical substance of a range of religions and makes the case for a world in which all

---

7   Liliana Cavani's *Milarepa* (1974) and Bernardo Bertolucci's *Little Buddha* (1993) both treat influential Buddhist spiritual leaders. However, these hail not a heterogeneous religious audience, but an audience with a Catholic background, who need to be informed about the foreign religious history. Treatments of Padre Pio or Jesus do not show the same didactic need to inform, and presuppose their audience's familiarity with the story.

religions live in harmony together in a Garden of Eden in which an exceed-
ingly liberal Christ states, "C'è posto per tutti" (There's room for everyone). The
importance of D'Alatri's attempt to develop a solution to modern multi-faith
society was overlooked by many critics at the time.

Since the millennium a greater number of films have gone beyond narratives
of assimilation or conflict in order better to understand the faiths of others.
Treading this middle path is uncomfortable. It means demonstrating difference without erasing it either by flattening it through easy platitudes (which
D'Alatri's film risks) or by revealing it as so different as to be incompatible. It
means finding a way to face religious difference. This has proved easiest for
Judaism, an Abrahamic religion with which Catholicism shares narratives, out-
looks, and values. Television directors Pasquale Squitieri (*Il giorno della Shoah*)
and Carlo Carlei (*Fuga per la libertà – L'aviatore*) have succeeded in giving
equal weight to Judaism and Catholicism in a way that distinguishes their films
from pre-twenty-first-century portrayals (Gaetani 2013). The contemporary
focus on the Shoah nonetheless risks rendering Jews irrelevant to contemporary post-secular debates except as reminders of the horrors of the past and as
enablers of the myth of good Italians ("Italiani brava gente" [Gaetani 2013]), a
myth that circulates in part thanks to the stories of heroic Italians saving Jews.

The equal treatment of Islam is proving more challenging. Films that try to
deal with Islam in this third way include Vittorio De Seta's *Lettere dal Sahara*
(2006), Vittorio Moroni's *Le ferie di Licu* (2006), Laura Muscardin's *Billo: Il grand
Dakhaar* (2007), and Ernesto Pagano's documentary *NapolIslam*. Muscadin's
Billo: Il grand Dakhaar is a particularly interesting case. An Italian-Senegalese
co-production, it narrates the tale of a young Muslim who arrives in Italy from
Senegal. It does so without reinforcing essentialist views of Italian identity or
drawing a clean separation between Italian Catholics and immigrant Muslims.
The conflict between value systems is foregrounded through a narrative climax
that sees Billo becoming a father in Italy at the same time he is undertaking
an arranged marriage back in Senegal. It thus brings to the fore the issue of
polygamy, a practice not easily assimilated into the Italian moral code. The film
negotiates this frankly in several ways. It deconstructs the Italian Catholic family by introducing a gay couple into its heart and positing the relationship an
Italian mother has with her unfaithful husband as polygamous in practice. Billo,
the main character, provides the audience with a character with whom to identify who expresses different religious values about an issue essential to Italian
identity construction: the family. While the film is not without its weaknesses,
this co-production is a rare film, one that presents a way for Italy to accept the
religious other *as* other, without attempting to convert him, and that challenges
Catholic family values in order to support a liberal and inclusive perspective.

To return to the discussion of liminar people: Billo, to some extent at least,
succeeds in becoming a liminar. He is "neither the society's other against

whom its overarching identity could be formed nor its full citizen who could be pressed into servicing its values" (Wilson and Dissanayake 1996). This is not "passive alienation" but rather "proactive psychic denial and social refusal" (Wilson and Dissanayake 1996). This social refusal emerges even more forcefully in the recent ethnographic documentary *NapolIslam*, in which ordinary Neapolitans who have converted to Islam defend their decision and are seen going about their daily routines. They provide examples of an interestingly blended post-secular identity. As its director, Ernesto Pagano, explains, "Naples is a city where everything mixes up and where you can see the (local deserts) *sfogliatelle* and *casatielli halal*" (Bellino 2015).

Conclusion: Seeing Is Believing – Italian Filmmaking Looks Post-Secularism in the Eye

Introduction

In this conclusion I explore several recent works that deliberately and knowingly foreground the place of religion in a post-secular world, questioning it and positing it as the object of debate. These films appear to recognize that changes are afoot in one of Italy's most important power bases, and they highlight and chronicle those changes, adopting self-conscious and reflective post-secular attitudes towards the religions on the peninsula. I focus in this concluding chapter on two big-budget auteur works, Nanni Moretti's *Habemus Papam* (2011) and Paolo Sorrentino's ten-part series *The Young Pope* (2017),[1] as well as Alice Rohrwacher's low-budget auteurial debut, *Corpo celeste* (Heavenly Body, 2011) and the comedy *Pitza e datteri* (2015) which shines the spotlight on Islam. Their self-conscious reflections on religion in the public sphere provide this book with some tentative conclusions.

Post-Secular Public Space: The Italian Square and the Virtual Piazza

Scholars of religion, media, and the post-secular – religious and secular alike – have expressed concern about the exclusion of religion from the public sphere, what Christoph Baumgartner, following Habermas, describes as its "communicative disablement" (2014, 91). Baumgartner claims that only "a specific form of religion and religious subjectivity" allows the religious subject to participate in society. This creates an "informal but powerful discrimination and exclusion" (91). My aim in this conclusion is to consider whether religion is "communicatively disabled" in three films that represent the highest-profile

---

1 *The Young Pope* was aired as a five-part, ten-hour series in Italy and as a ten-part, ten-hour series on Sky Atlantic.

vehicles for the discussion of the place of the Catholic church in Italian society today: *Habemus Papam* (2011), *Corpo celeste* (2011), and *The Young Pope* (2017). I also look at Fariborz Kamkari's *Pitza e datteri* (2015), which treats Islam's liminar occupation of real and virtual space in Italy. While these works are as distinct as their directors, they all share a preoccupation with religion's occupation of public space and the communication channels religion is afforded. The films typically foreground two public sites for communication *par excellence*: the piazza and the media (the latter a kind of virtual piazza, a deterritorialized and contemporary cousin of the Tannoy broadcast). I examine each film in turn to investigate how they position religion in public space through their construction of the piazza – emblematic of Italian public and political life – and the "virtual piazza" (the public space of the media); from these positionings I draw conclusions about how those filmmakers who have most consciously contributed to the public debate on religion see the place of religion in twenty-first-century Italy.

Habemus Papam's positioning of the Catholic Church in public space provides an intriguing insight into contemporary cinema's understanding of religion in Italian society. St Peter's Square, the strikingly theatrical and monumental piazza in front of the Vatican, becomes the film's symbol of public urban space. The Italian piazza has long been a symbol of the *polis* (Caniffe 2016), as well as a visible sign of the elements that Susan Fainstein (2010) lists as belonging to the just city: diversity, democracy, and equity. It can be a significant site of political demonstration in Italy, so much so, indeed, that it has been read as a "synecdoche for protest" (Brook and Ross 2009): a space in which social movements and political parties hold rallies and political gatherings, as seen in *Improvvisamente l'inverno scorso*'s use of the piazza for Family Day and No-Vat events.

The construction of St Peter's Square in *Habemus Papam* appears to show that the Church has not been marginalized from public space and that it maintains successful communication with its people. Through its soundscape (the hum of a huge crowd, the pulsing blades of a helicopter) and in its magnificent visual impact, the square reinforces the sense of a vast public ritual and display through which is sketched out a sense of community and common purpose. The filming emphasizes dialogue between two players. Parallel editing and action/reaction shots establish a strong communicative channel between two interlocutors: the world within the walls of the Vatican (which communicates with smoke and multilingual speeches from the balcony), and the world of anxious Catholics waiting in the square outside (which responds with flags and cheers).

However, St Peter's Square, while reflecting many elements of the socio-political uses to which Italian piazzas are put, and apparently establishing successful communication within its colonades, nevertheless is a more anachronistic and fragile seat of communication than it at first glance seems. In this age of "participatory culture" (Jenkins 2006), the footage of St Peter's Square in *Habemus Papam* firmly separates the Church leaders from those who are led, the institution from those it serves, the Catholic hierarchy from the ordinary people (both religious and lay), and seals the religious into one space, raising questions about how the Church talks to those *outside* the square. This all puts into question the function of this piazza with regard to the "diversity, democracy, and equity" outlined by Fainstein (2010).

The film's opening scenes, which sew together documentary footage from the funeral of John Paul II and use multiple high-angle shots to capture the vast, crowded piazza, clearly mark the distinction between the "stage" – the part of the piazza that is cordoned off, set above the piazza, and occupied by the Church (and state) hierarchy – and the "stalls," where the vast audience is positioned. This is a stage setting of nineteenth-century formation, where the fourth wall between actor and audience is unbroken and carefully policed, and participation on the part of the audience is limited to watching a spectacle that has been organized and choreographed by the hierarchy prior to its unfolding. There is no reciprocal interaction by means of which the audience in the stalls and the institution portrayed on stage work together to modify the narrative of the funeral, reciprocally altering events – a feature that Jenkins cites as a key aspect of contemporary participatory culture in *Convergence Culture* (2006). The structure of communication between the institutional Church and its flock, as presented through the establishing footage of the piazza, is one of nineteenth-century separation, hierarchy, and passive consumption in place of twenty-first-century participation, inclusion, and democracy whereby audiences become producers and consumers of culture (Jenkins 2006). My references to staging, audiences, and fourth walls here are not casual: as I mentioned earlier in this book, *Habemus Papam* spins its discourse on the place of the Catholic Church in contemporary public space around the central axis of the metaphor of theatre. While the Church is shown to have supreme control over the use of a key public space (the vast piazza that stretches in front of it), which it stage-directs and organizes on its own terms, its pre-participatory use of that space for its communicative needs puts into question the relevance of that control in a changing communicative environment. It quietly raises the question of whether the Church is really ready for a participatory twenty-first century public debate.

The media – the "virtual piazza" – constitute the second aspect of public space that *Habemus Papam* treats. The film's relationship with this second space again initially appears well-grounded. A series of short scenes inserted into the film's narrative emphasize the pervasive omnipresence of the story of a vanishing pope across a range of terrestrial media: radio, television, and newspapers. The story is debated on the car radio as neo-Pope Melville leaves the Vatican to attend an appointment with one of the city's psychoanalysts. In his hotel room, after his escape, Melville flicks between television channels and finds no escape from it. Later, as he approaches a newsagent's kiosk, the camera zooms in on, and then pans across, a well-filled rack of multilingual newspapers, all of which carry the story of the missing pope on their front pages. Through these scenes, the film emphasizes the terrestrial media's fascination with the story, and therefore the continuing importance of religiously oriented stories in the public sphere. On the surface, at least, the terrestrial media do not seem to disable religious communication, but instead give it prime-time, front-page space. Moreover, the media's reporting throughout the film expresses widespread concern about and benevolence towards the Church rather than hostility.

A closer analysis, however, of the way the media deal with the Vatican tells a more complex story and puts into question the Catholic Church's capacity for managing twenty-first-century communication. Throughout the film, the media are satirized as trivial, pushy, shallow, and ill-informed – satire that recalls Federico Fellini's *La dolce vita* (1960). They seem to misconstrue and mistranslate the signs and are capable of misreading the most elementary of the Vatican's visual signals, even the white smoke that signifies the election of a new pope. This reveals that, ultimately, media and religion do not share the same sign system. It is only in the physical piazza that religion and audience (i.e., the believers who share its sign system) work together. The *translation* from religious to secular discourse, which journalists facilitate, is flawed, for the translators do not grasp the language they must translate. Habermas views this process of translation as fundamental if religion is to contribute to debate in the public sphere. In Habermas's normative account, the public sphere must be "epistemically adjusted" to the continued existence of religious communities, and religious and secular citizens must equally collaborate in the translation of religious language (Habermas 2006). This collaboration is clearly not functioning in *Habemus Papam*.

Instead, *Habemus Papam* can be interpreted as carrying forward Fellini's exploration of the mediatization of society and the earlier director's establishment of a link between desacralization and mediatization, in which the religious event, rather than being faithfully translated, is transformed into media spectacle (Bertetto 2010). In his article on Fellini's cinema, Paolo Bertetto claims that religion is crushed "dentro la logica dello spettacolo e diventa uno dei modi forti attraverso cui il visibile sociale viene trasformato in scena" (into the logic of the spectacle; it becomes one of the key ways in which the visible social sphere is transformed on stage). While this does not annul religion, it does reduce it to an "esperienza riservata, ricondotta alla dimensione dell'interiorità dell'uomo" (unsharable experience, which can be traced back to man's interiority) (11). Bertetto's analysis of Fellini's films suggests that the interdependence of mediatization and the Catholic Church leads inevitably to desacralization and the removal of all genuine religious experience from the public sphere. This view is commonly held: Michael L. Budde (1998, 82) notes that when the news media do cover religion, they "usually focus on controversy, scandal, the unusual or freakish," and that such coverage does not "nurtur[e] an adult understanding of faith." This interpretation of the relation between the media and religion is pessimistic about the media's ability to communicate religion, and Moretti's film supports it.

A second point needs be made here. When Melville looks at the newspaper titles at the news stand, all of which spell out the story of the missing pope, the camera pans over one of the newspapers on the rack (*Il Secolo XIX*), exposing three further titles on its front page, all of which announce developments in digital media. *Il Secolo XIX* is at the centre of the camera's focus throughout the scene, and its subtitles are the only ones on the newspaper display that are clearly visible. If situating references to digital media on a paper titled *The Nineteenth Century* is a visual joke, this would indicate that Moretti is aware of his own film's focus on old media, and even that he has made this choice knowingly. Given the place of new media in "expressing individualistic perspectives on spirituality and carv[ing] out new identities and cultures" (Gilmore 2011), the decoupling of the representation of the contemporary Catholic Church from new media in *Habemus Papam* positions the Church outside the major trends in contemporary communication. If it is not part of these trends, then the apocalyptic fate that the film's ending heralds for the Church may yet come to pass.

If the piazza as public theatre for a public religion is a key visual trope in Moretti's film, in *Corpo celeste* this is replaced by a dry riverbed, the epitome of the anti-spectacular, which, together with Rohrwacher's gritty cinematography and her meta-theatrical focus on the props of religious ceremony, sucks drama out of the Catholic spectacle besides radically reducing the separation of Church hierarchy and audience. If this is Catholicism as theatre, then it is twenty-first-century theatre in which an amateur troupe reclaims an abandoned urban space, reconfigures it into a pop-up, and, by leaving the props in full sight, ensures that the audience will not forget it is a play. True to the form of modern theatre, the opening scene breaks the fourth wall that *Habemus Papam* had so rigidly retained: at the end of the scene, the long-awaited bishop drives slowly through the audience in his car – an entrance through the aisles, so to speak, rather than through the official stage door. This is not to say, however, that the Church has taken on all aspects of modern theatre: the cloak of participatory culture has not been put on here any more than it is in *Habemus Papam*. Rather, perhaps ironically, the on-screen spectators participate far less in this contemporary anti-spectacle than Moretti's audience does: there is no cheering; instead people look distracted and disengaged.

In this scene the Church's claim to public space is limited to a peripheral, off-centre, marginal space, a space that is not designated for public use and is otherwise abandoned. This appears to signal not a powerful religion cherished by the state and the *polis*, but one that has been pushed towards the margins of society and divested of its terrestrial trappings, the *chiesa della minoranza* (see chapter 3). It is a Church whose voice appears to be drowned out even for its own parishioners, not to speak of its relations with the rest of the city. Yet as the film develops, this displaced picture of the Church is not exactly what emerges. Rohrwacher instead constructs Catholicism as a pervasive aspect of the community dynamics of the south, whether in the spheres of education, politics, or community ritual. Religion is embedded in the community's annual events, punctuating the year with the pilgrimage and religious festival led by the parish priest that opens the film. The rite of passage from childhood to adulthood is marked by the sacrament of confirmation, and this sacrament, as the catechist states, acts as a gatekeeper into the other significant rites of passage in life: marriage and the entrance into heaven after death. Catholicism filters through into the language of the everyday, in the "Maria santissima!" (Most holy Mary!) and "Maria Vergine!" (Virgin Mary!), expressed by Marta's Calabrian aunt, and it is visible in the crosses worn by Marta's uncle and sitting prominently in a television presenter's cleavage. The Church is also embedded in both the local economy and its politics: it collects rent from parishioners, a sign of its property-owning status, and it supports named local politicians, successfully manipulating its parishioners to vote for them. Giovanni Cogliandro (2011) acknowledges that Marta, as an external observer, is struck by the extent to which the parish is "un forte centro di vita sociale, in controtendenza con la disgregazione degli spazi pubblici e dei luoghi di incontro in città sempre più grandi e spersonalizzanti" (a strong centre of social life, bucking the trend of the disintegration of public spaces and meeting spaces in cities that are ever larger and more depersonalizing). This is the case despite, as one of the frustrated Church organizers blurts out, there being only children, women, and old people in the church, "gente che non ha un'accidente da fare!" (people who don't have a damn thing to do!).

However pervasive the Catholicism that Rohrwacher describes, it lacks depth, spirit, and charisma. The contrasting on-screen audiences for the religious events in *Corpo celeste* and in *Habemus Papam* signal the difference: In *Habemus Papam*, St Peter's Square is filled with people who are caught in reaction shots, responding emotionally to every word uttered from the papal balcony. In *Corpo celeste*, the response is almost always impassivity, as if people attend events but the Church fails to touch them. Behind *Corpo celeste*'s representation is a Church that, while still playing a part in the daily lives of the people, has lost the power to affect them.

The film's relationship with the media is also revealing. Rohrwacher represents a Church that has become a passive consumer of contemporary media and society, imitating its impoverished televisual language in a clumsy and ultimately unsuccessful attempt to gain acceptance from a contemporary young audience. During the catechism class, the children are quizzed on Church history through the format of the "Who Wants to Be a Millionaire?" television quiz show, a scene that Rohrwacher portrays satirically. The parish's "piccole vergini" (little virgins) dance provocatively for the parishioners in a way that is absolutely coherent with the sexualized *veline* (showgirls) on Berlusconi's television channels. In showing the Church's relationship with the media as one of passive consumption rather than active influence and participation, Rohwacher's vision diverges from both Moretti's and Sorrentino's. This flattening of Catholicism's rich heritage by its aping of superficial and Americanized/Berlusconian television production is worsened by the constant interruption by mobile phones throughout: there is no stillness in this religion. It is filled with the noise, distraction, and interruption of contemporary culture. It is completely porous to the secular world around it, and it appears to accept that to combat rising secularism one must adopt its methods. Stewart Hoover's discussions of the intertwining of religion and media in *Religion in the Media Age* (2006) seem particularly appropriate here. The two elements are not separate for Hoover; rather, they converge. For Rohrwacher, commodification of the religious marketplace is inevitable.

This banal, mediatized, and distracted religion is contrasted with an older version of religion that Marta uncovers towards the end of the film. The parish priest (Don Mario) and Marta go in search of a figurative cross, which his parishioners want in place of their contemporary neon one. Don Mario and Marta travel along a winding country road that brings them into the first sunshine of the film: the houses fade away behind them and green hills appear. Inside an old abandoned church, where the dusty cross lies, the sacred still exists. As Don Mario attempts to remove the cross from the church, an old priest unexpectedly materializes and tries to wrest it from him. The sequence is startling. The old priest evokes a gritty passion and sense of fear that Don Mario, in his bored, careerist impassivity, does not. The Christianity found here is dusty, but fiery. The old priest turns to Marta and explains to her a phrase that she had learned by heart in the catechism class and has carried with her like a talisman without understanding it: "eli eli lama sabachthani." He tells her that this is the cry of Christ on the cross. He takes her image of a good, smiling, blue-eyed Christ and replaces it with a Jesus who is angry and anti-conformist, who is followed about by ignorant disciples who fail to understand him and who are scandalized by him. In a yellowing copy of the Bible, he shows her Mark 3:22, where Christ, says the priest, is described as being "fuori di sé" (beside himself with rage). He then leaves Marta alone. Marta slowly blows the dust off the cross and runs her fingers over the figure of Christ, exploring him with sensual, curious fingers, as if, in this relic, she was discovering man, or God, anew. Her wonder creates out of the statue one of the film's many *corpi celesti* (celestial bodies). The figurative cross implies that somewhere there exists a Catholicism that is fiery rather than banal, mediatized, and conformist. However, on the way back to the city, the cross, which has been strapped to the car's roof, falls from it, and in a scene of tragicomedy, tumbles down a cliff into the sea below. There can be no triumphant return to an angry anti-conformist Christ. Marta will quit the Church. She will discover that the miracle glimpsed in the "croce figurativa" is what her own defamiliarizing eye can see when she looks for celestial bodies in ordinary things.

If Moretti's construction of the supreme public space of the piazza facilitates direct and unambiguous communication between the pope and Catholics (albeit not fit for twenty-first-century use), Rohrwacher desacralizes this communication, exposing the mundanity of its communicators and the inadequacy of its channels (which are repeatedly interrupted by mobile phones and by the meta-theatre of the wires, microphones, and paraphernalia of the stage). She exposes too the mediocrity of the message, whereby the sacred has been hybridized with the grammar of television. And, finally, she shows the unreceptiveness of the public. While an older form of fiery, pure Catholicism seems to provide a momentary answer, the figurative cross that represents it cannot be brought back to the city: in a postmodern world it is too late for the grand narratives and great but dusty symbols of the past. With Catholicism's ability to communicate effectively disabled, the only answer is for the sacred to retreat into private space, where Marta's personal openness can allow simple things to tell their sacredness to her directly. In *Corpo celeste*, the "heavenly body," even where it is represented by a public religious icon like the cross or a verbal talisman like "eli eli lama sabachthani," sits firmly in the private sphere.

Made seven years later, *The Young Pope* again questions how religion sits in the public sphere. This series defies expectations and radically deconstructs, interrupts, and reconfigures religious communication channels in a knowingly post-secular vein. Pius XIII is a pope reluctant to appear. He refuses to put his image before either the piazza or the mediasphere. He does not show himself. He does not believe in exhibition. His face will not be photographed, printed on a plate, circulated as marketing merchandise. He will not step onto the balcony of St Peter's Square and speak to the faithful. When finally he does appear, at the end of Episode 2, he is silhouetted so that his face cannot be seen.

Lenny's is a radical distancing of religion from the public sphere, from both the media circus and the faithful in the piazza below. It is a deliberate questioning, and overturning, of the warm, media-friendly papacies that proceeded him, especially that of John Paul II. He refuses to adopt the correct communicative language for the papacy, the banalized language through which much contemporary religion circulates, including that revealed in *Corpo celeste* and in *Habemus Papam*'s media circus. In Episode 2, Lenny has an audience with the Vatican's marketing and communication campaign manager, Sofia Dubois

(Cécile de France). During their conversation, she takes out an iPad and shows him the handcrafted Italian plates onto which his photograph can be printed. He leaves the room. Returning with a blank plate, he tells her that this is the sort of merchandise he is prepared to authorize. He will become "as unreachable as a rock star." He will appear only as a blank plate, a shadow or silhouette before the faithful.

The de-facing of the pope is not without its cinematic precedents (notably in *I banchieri di Dio*, *Suburra*, and Ermanno Olmi's *E venne un uomo* [And There Came a Man], 1965),[2] but it is radical nonetheless. The absence of a speaking face during Lenny's first address in St Peter's Square leads to the voice appearing only semi-synced, as if it emanated from somewhere beyond him, rather than from his mouth; this defamiliarizes and abstracts him (Campan 1999). The lack of the face, in other words, de-anchors and partly dislocates the voice, ensuring that he is isolated from all other characters on screen, rendering him barely human, a category apart. Michel Chion's *La voix au cinema* (1999) theorizes the relation between voice and power regarding what he calls the "acousmatique" (an off-screen voice), which, in a Foucaultian reading of cinematic sound, Chion identifies with power as panoptic and all-knowing. The uncanny effect of the off-screen and semi-off-screen voice constructs the pope as "other," providing him with a superhuman mantle of all-knowing power and removing him from his worldly context. The non-representational techniques forge a sacred *noli me tangere* motif around a pope who, to cite Jean-Luc Nancy (2005) is then "here but not here."

The communicative tactics Lenny adopts are therefore radical – or better perhaps, radically conservative. Sorrentino's use of *noli me tangere* diverges markedly from *Corpo celeste*'s hypothesis, which portrays the Church as passively adopting the media-dominated language of the public sphere, having lost its guiding foothold there. In *The Young Pope*, by contrast, Lenny (through his

---

2   In *I banchieri di Dio*, we are told that the pope's face will not be displayed onscreen "per doveroso rispetto" (out of respect). Nor is Pope Benedict XVI's face shown in *Suburra*. In *La verità sta in cielo*, Pope John Paul II is not re-enacted, nor is Pope Francis: public footage of them is used instead. This reticence towards re-enactment is long-standing. Thus in *E venne un uomo*, a biopic of Pope John XXIII, the actor Rod Steiger "mediates" the story, telling it in the first person but without impersonating the pope, and in the only film critical of Pius XII, George Pan Cosmatos's *Rappresaglia* (Massacre in Rome, 1973), the pope is not visible. It appears that the Italian cinema industry is willing to show an on-screen pope in the hagiopic genre (a genre in which he shares the prestigious company of saints, prophets, and Jesus Christ), but is uneasy about portraying him in films where clerical corruption is portrayed. The erasing of the pope's face in films that treat corruption in the Vatican hierarchy shows a deep reverence for the papal presence and distances the pope from representations of the curia and other sections of the church hierarchy. It also serves to remove him from full accountability.

author, Sorrentino) has the Church actively run its own marketing campaign, on its own terms and in its own language: in the grammar of *noli me tangere*, of the sacred as other and untouchable. As the series develops, the displaying of miracles-as-miracles (without couching them in the language of Todorovian hesitation preferred by the secular media) reflects the confidence the pope has in an alternative language, a language of authority and mystery, of the "enchanted world," that is quite foreign to twenty-first-century sensibilities. He rejects a banalized mass-media language that might reach the vast majority of people but that in so doing would contaminate and so destroy the message. Belardo, however, as he reveals in his first audience with Sophia, sees the marketing potential of this. He recognizes that the tiny Vatican state cannot possibly compete with mass marketing tactics on their own terms, by adopting their strategies (a tactic that fails in *Corpo celeste*). To succeed, Belardo believes, the Vatican needs to adopt the opposite strategy to theirs: an authoritarian, pre-participatory grammar of separation and mystery. This is a radical proposal, which of course ultimately proves impossible. The piazzas empty out, a sign that radical "communicative disablement" has occurred. The nineteenth-century grammar cannot be translated for twenty-first-century audiences that have been nourished on participatory talk-back and that dare shout back up to the balcony, "we want to see your face."

Belardo's anachronistic focus on nineteenth-century communication is impossible in a hybrid, participatory modernity. From the film's outset, Sorrentino's complex sound world hints at this impossibility. Media interruptions and overlappings are a defining feature of the series. In the opening scene of the first episode, the pope wakes from a dream to the secular ringtone of a mobile phone; this is immediately followed by, and juxtaposed with, a radio alarm clock playing Gabriele Faure's *Requiem*. Within seconds, the requiem is itself interrupted by radio interference, which then merges with a mash-up of opera singer Sumi Jo and the contemporary electronic beats of a track from Labradford. Slowly we discover that this is another dream. Later, one of *The Young Pope*'s most iconic scenes, discussed earlier in this book, juxtaposes the donning of medieval papal vestments with the contemporary track "Sexy and I Know It." The sound world of Sorrentino's film, in other words, is hybrid, contradictory, and postmodern: sacred music and gritty contemporary pop interact and overlap. Whatever Lenny may believe, the complex and contradictory sound world in which he moves means that his drive for unabashed purity will fail.

The paradox that underlies *The Young Pope*, of couse, is that Sorrentino's pope is radically averse to appearing in the piazza and allowing himself to be projected virtually through the media, but Sorrentino's film is not. The opening credits capture this paradox in one visual nutshell. As Lenny Belardo strolls along the gallery of paintings, he looks straight ahead as if his spectators were not there: we see only his profile, which breaks identification and communication.

Gabriele Prosperi (2016) explains that the side of his face that is lit is the left side of his profile, the part we cannot see, the part that faces the wall, thus confirming his role within the institution. The right side of his face, that which he offers to us as viewer, remains in darkness. Yet with his deliberate wink to the camera at the end of the sequence, Lenny not only recognizes his viewers but also instigates complicity with them. In other words, from the outset *The Young Pope* is aware that Lenny's attempts to remain out of the public eye and interrupt communication with the faithful are impossible. He has, and knows he has, a vast public who are watching him not from the piazza below but on myriad television and computer screens around the globe. Unlike Melville, Lenny is perfectly aware of his new-media circus.

Sorrentino's series is consciously aimed at the same contemporary audience from which his protagonist attempts to shelter. Prosperi observes that the series is posited as a "tentativo di ricerca di un nuovo spazio di incontro tra 'pubblico e privato'" (an attempt to find a new meeting space between "public and private"), noting how it attracted widespread attention on social media, "grazie alla sua adattabilità a forme di riutilizzo e risemantizzazione tipiche del read-write, paradigma contemporaneo basato sullo sfruttamento di opere per fini citazionistici o comunicativi" (as a result of its adaptability through reuse and re-semanticization that characterizes the "read-write," a contemporary paradigm based on the tapping of works for citational or communicative aims). Prosperi (2016) notes how Twitter and Facebook were alive with GIFs from the series. The spreadability of the series enabled it substantially to increase its audience share. Ironically, but not entirely surprisingly, the seemingly most unparticipatory of popes has facilitated the most participatory of products.

The three films discussed here adopt three different approaches to the public sphere. Moretti's *Habemus Papam* places its faith in a nineteenth-century communicative model. The director establishes a pre-participatory but nonetheless direct communicative model between the pope and the faithful and pushes to one side the twitterings of the media, which misunderstand and miscommunicate. This model is threatened, however, by the Age of Authenticity (discussed earlier in this book), which encourages Melville to privilege his authentic self above his sense of civic duty. It is threatened too by the failure to take new media into account as a means of communication for the contemporary sacred, as well as by the overreliance on old media, which mistranslate religion, rendering it banal and misunderstanding it. All of this lands the Church in crisis. In *Corpo celeste* the banal workings of the channels of media communication, the mediatized hybridity of the message, and the disinterestedness of the audience combine to weaken the power of religion in the public sphere. Religion relies too heavily on media, and this drags it down to the level of American quiz shows and Berlusconi's television channels, hybridizing it so that its voice can be fully understood but it has little left to say. Faced with this, and with the impossibility of a return to the grand narrative of a pre-conciliar religion, the only solution is for religion to take its place within the private sphere, where it mingles with other forms of the sacred but where its mystery is still safe. In *The Young Pope* Lenny Belardo takes back control of the media, defying media channels of communication and refusing to allow his image to be used. He knowingly embraces the anachronistic mystery of the *noli me tangere* motif. His communication becomes radically othered in the contemporary world. All three films struggle with problem of how Catholicism communicates in post-secular Italy today. They provide diverse readings and diverse, and not wholly satisfactory solutions.

To these readings, I add one final one, that provided by Kamkari's *Pitza e datteri*, a film that puts a minority religion – Islam – centre stage. *Pitza e datteri* narrates the story of an Islamic community thrown into crisis when their prayer house is shut down by a Muslim woman who converts the space into a unisex hairdressing salon. The film's plot then centres on the tiny and marginalized Islamic community in Venice and its quest for space in which to pray. The prayer-house/hair salon highlights the two sides of Islam portrayed in the film: a hybrid, secularized, and liberal Islam represented by the people (mainly women) who attend the salon; a fundamentalist Islam represented by Bepi (Giuseppe Battiston), an Italian convert to Islam, and the Afghan imam (who is, however, converted to a more liberal style after his Italian experience). The spaces occupied by the Islamic faith comically bear testimony to the difficulty of occupying a public sphere that, as we have seen, is far more welcoming to Catholicism. In *Pitza e datteri*, the dozen faithful are forced to pray in the corner of bookshops, in boatyards, graveyards, in abandoned spaces, but they cannot occupy an Italian square unless they are consuming pizza there. The imam's call to prayer comes not from a minaret but from a docklands crane. The imam's audience, rather than responding with reverence, involvement, and prayer, as seen in *Habemus Papam* and in many of the *The Young Pope*'s papal balcony scenes, shouts at him, begging him to descend. Occupying such lofty aerial space is impossible for Islam; the Muslim community itself censors the ascension of its members into that space for fear of damaging the harmony of their relations with the host community. Hiding from the Italian authorities is a repeated trope in the film. When compared to the papal balcony scenes found in Sorrentino's and Moretti's films, the vastly different positioning afforded to different religions in Italy is clear. The imam's call to prayer takes place not in a huge central Roman piazza but in a Venetian dockland dominated by empty warehouses and empty quays, liminal, marginal spaces, abandoned places of transcience and transition. In the film's happy ending, when the Islamic community finally finds a space to worship, it is a Jewish synagogue. In other words, while Islam does find a legitimate religious space in the end, it is borrowed and shared with a rival minority religion; it is therefore still transcient and unstable.

Moreover, Islam's presence in the synagogue is never fully legitimized by the Italian burocratic infrastructure, which pays it little more than lip service: the Italian mayor leaves hurriedly before cutting the sash that would announce the building's official opening. If *Corpo celeste* shows the Catholic Church occupying liminal spaces in contemporary society, it nonetheless balances this by showing how Catholicism is still knitted into regional Italy through local politics, language, and custom. Islam has none of these entry points. Instead, it exists on the very edge geographically, politically and legally: in the finale the imam is removed from Italy by Italy's border police and the Italian convert Bepi is sentenced to jail for attempting to blow up the hair salon. The radical fringes of Islam are thus expelled; the faith occupies a place in Italy only insofar as it keeps away from minarets and from fundamentalism, maintains a low profile, and embraces the liberal, secularized and hybrid form symbolized by the Muslim community of the hairdressing salon.

Kamkari's film also shows Islam's exclusion from Italy's mediasphere. The tiny Muslim community in Venice is shown to be knitted into a larger virtual and international Islamic community, as signified in an early scene in which an Egyptian imam leads their worship via Skype from Cairo. This scene firmly displaces Islamic spiritual leadership from Venice, relocating it firmly beyond Italy. This signals the community's attention to a global mediasphere over a local Italian one, and draws their attention away from active involvement in Italian media. As the end titles roll, the full extent of Islam's communicative disablement in the Italian mediasphere is clear: we hear the voice of an Italian newsreader reporting the story of the trial of the convert Bepi. The tale of the Islamic community's attempt to occupy religious space in Venice becomes the story of a minor breach of public order. The public discussion of the event, an event that up till then had been shown only through the point of view of the Islamic community in Venice, is presented to the wider world exclusively through the eyes of the Italian media, effectively dismantling the Muslim community's public voice.

These four films all approach their subject matter from a knowing and post-secular perspective, but proffer differing conclusions. They refute the dialectic approach to religion that dominated filmic responses to the Catholic Church in Italy in the mid-twentieth century. Until recently, critical positions marked by dialectic thinking had forced films either to align with the Catholic Church or to align against it, thus flattening complexity. Pierpaolo Antonello and Rosa Barotsi (2009) have described Moretti's position prior to *Habemus Papam* as "perplexed, self-doubting and contingent." Catherine Wheatley's analysis (2014) goes a step further. She claims that in *Habemus Papam*, Nanni Moretti is "withholding critique" and presenting a "confused and confusing" approach to his material that she claims provides a key to the ambiguity, complexity, and post-secular positioning with which the film engages. Moretti undoubtedly critiques the Church in his film. He criticizes a system of thought that roots its meaning in externally given answers and that will not face the "nessun senso" and "nessuna consolazione" (no sense and no consolation) of life. This renders the faith infantile.[3] However, Moretti balances this critique by making the cardinals objects of contemplation and indulgence rather than judgment (Wheatley 2015). That they are portrayed as childish makes them all the more sweet and endearing. To the surprise of international critics, who are used to Moretti's harsh attacks on institutions, the Vatican is not subject to attack in this film. It is precisely the "withheld critique," the "self-doubting," and the "confusion" that position this film as post-secular: it eschews the dialectic approach to Catholicism and instead, within a single form, presents a kaleidoscope of observations on the conflicted position of Catholicism in Italy's public space.

This "confused and confusing" approach dominates the four films I have discussed in this section. In *Pitza e datteri*, Catholicism is not an antagonist as it is almost eradicated from the screen; it is irrelevant to the Muslim community. The film treats Islam with humour and indulgence. A secularized and liberal Islam, one that can share space with Judaism and allow women to hold power, is embraced. Only radical Islam is expelled. Rohrwacher too approaches her material with an open, post-secular eye in *Corpo celeste*. She is more curious than hostile. While painting the Church in drab, washed-out colours, she does not lightly dismiss its place in society. Marta, the film's focalizer, adopts a sceptical, open approach to religion. She does not rebel against the strictures of religion, like the young Guido in Federico Fellini's *8½* (1963) or Angelo in Bellocchio's *Nel nome del padre* (In the Name of the Father, 1972), nor does she conform to it like some of her classmates. She is not indifferent, as are so many of the jaded characters in the film. Rohrwacher creates a very particular position for her protagonist: that of interested, even curious, open-eyed autonomy. Marta watches everything: the catechist, the priest, her degraded environment with its knots of traffic-filled roads, the dry riverbed below her, the unattainable sea in the background. She tries to learn the words from the catechism she is taught. What is so peculiar about her, especially in the Italian national context,

---

3   The film emphasizes the childishness of the cardinals' behaviour: they copy like schoolboys during the conclave, are childishly greedy for cakes, do jigsaw puzzles in their rooms at night, are easily tricked by Brezzi-Moretti during a card game, and tell tales on one another when Brezzi-Moretti asks them which medicines they are taking. The allegory the film develops around parenting shows that even those in the highest position in the Church are children looking for a parental figure to tell them how to act and how to anchor meaning. The apocalyptic finale places these child-men in front of their worst nightmare: the parental figure on whom they rely stands down and refuses to fill the role. The cardinals' visible collapse, mirrored by that of the audience in the *piazza*, is the collapse of those who have not faced the "nessun senso" and "nessuna consolazione" of life. They do not look to themselves as the answer.

is that she seems to be free of a preordained, prescribed approach to religion. She is free especially of the conformist/rebel binaries so beloved of Italian auteur cinema. Marta occupies an open, anti-ideological, and perhaps uniquely post-secular position. Her religion is her sense of the sacred, in which beauty and otherness can be seen in everything, be it urban or rural, secular or religious, her own body or the body of Christ. The sacred is secular and the secular sacred, and both – in *Corpo celeste*, as in *Habemus Papam* – can exist beyond, but also *within*, the Church's structures.

The Young Pope also deliberately and explicitly eschews dialectics. While audiences and critics struggled to understand whether Lenny Belardo was a saint or a demon, the series set him up as contradictory and non-binary. He is both malicious and scheming *and* beautiful and good. He is both a saint capable of miracles *and* a lost child. He is able to stroll along a row of paintings without catching the audience's eye as the credits roll, and to turn deliberately to the camera and wink. The series highlights the shattering of binaries as its key message. In the final homily with which he addresses the crowd in Venice, Bellardo cites the Blesséd Juana's response to the question "Who is God?" with the enigmatic, "God is a line that opens." Bellardi then presents the children's questions to the dying Juana, each of which presents a binary: "Are we dead or are we alive?," "Are we tired or are we vigorous?," "Are we healthy or are we sick?" Juana's response to this is, "It doesn't matter." *The Young Pope*'s dismantling of binaries allows a space for an "enchanted world" within a mashed-up media world. Secular rationality must prevail, but miracles are unavoidable. The time of neat distinctions between the secular and the religious is over. We have entered post-secular territory.

Conclusion

Habemus Papam, *Corpo celeste*, *The Young Pope*, and *Pitza e datteri* demonstrate and make explicit many of the findings that I have drawn out in this book. Even the film providing the least spectacular portrayal of religion, *Corpo celeste*, reveals the enduring fascination that Catholic iconography holds for Italian filmmaking: Marta's young fingers, and the camera, linger sensually over the figure of Christ on the cross. Sorrentino's camera cannot but frame Lenny Belardo against the backdrop of the maternal paradigm found in Michaelangelo's beautiful sculpture, *La pietà*. Neither Moretti nor Sorrentino can quite resist the juxtaposition of the worldly politics (and games) of present-day cardinals and the soaring art of the Sistine Chapel. *Pitza e datteri* is excluded from this iconic world and in turn excludes it, replacing it with robed imams and worshippers that help forge alternative iconographies. Each film meditates too on religious ethics, on values and what the place of these are in a contemporary world in which Catholicism's foothold is less assured and Islam's not (yet) established. These religious figures, ethics, and symbols have been remediated, decontextualized, recontextualized, and sometimes challenged. Catholic and secular mash-ups in which religion is hybridized are evident throughout. Catholicism is bound up with a neoliberal mediasphere in which it cannot be free of marketing publicity or social media and televisual distraction. Any return to a pure, pre-conciliar version of Catholicism, briefly entertained in *Corpo celeste* and embraced in *The Young Pope*, is revealed as anachronistic. There is no way of separating out post-secular contradictions into neat threads. Religion follows the path of contradiction, paradox, and blending.

The great crowds captured in St Peter's and St Mark's squares in *Habemus Papam* and *The Young Pope* are as fascinating as they are revealing. In the final scene of Sorrentino's series, as Belardo comes to a verbal full stop, the crowd cheers in a single, unnaturally choreographed roar. In *Habemus Papam*, banners and heads sink together as one when the crowd hears the news from the balcony that Melville will not lead them. These crowds represent the contemporary audience for Catholicism in the public sphere. They are diverse, multicultural, international, fervent, emotional, united, and converging. The differences between their members are masked by a "semblance of agreement and convergence generated by shared communal symbols, and participation in a common symbolic discourse of community membership" (Jenkins 2008). In other words, they *belong*. They share a grammar of Catholicism in which they participate dialogically. This grammar continues to define the discourse possible in the public sphere in Italy. It pushes to the edge any believer who does not converge on the piazza to cheer or to lower a flag, including – as I have shown – Italy's religious others. While Islam occupies Italy's liminal docklands – a place of transition from which it may still definitively depart – Catholicism still provides a framework for interpretation and a profound sense of belonging ... even where there is no believing.

References

Abbiezzi, Paola, and Giorgio Simonelli. 2006. "Agiografia e costruzione della memoria nazionale nella fiction televisiva." In *Attraverso lo schermo: Cinema e cultura cattolica in Italia: Dagli anni Settanta ai nostri giorni*, ed. Dario E. Viganò and Ruggero Eugeni, 131–41. Rome: Ente dello spettacolo.

Ahmad, Ali Nobil, ed. 2015. *Cinema in Muslim Societies*. London: Routledge.

Allum, Percy A. 1990. "Uniformity Undone: Aspects of Catholic Culture in Post-War Italy." In *Culture and Conflict in Post-War Italy: Essays on Mass and Popular Culture*, ed. Zygmunt G. Baranski and Robert Lumley, 79–97. Basingstoke: Macmillan.

Andall, Jacqueline, and Derek Duncan, eds. 2005. *Italian Colonialism: Legacy and Memory*. Oxford: Peter Lang.

[Anon.]. 2007. "Italy Screens Controversial Pedophile Documentary." *Sydney Morning Herald*, 1 June. http://www.smh.com.au/news/world/italy-screens-controversial -pedophile-documentary/2007/06/01/1180205462935.html

Antonello, Pierpaolo, and Rosa Barotsi. 2009. "The Personal and the Political: The Cinema of Nanni Moretti." In *Postmodern Impegno: Ethics and Commitment in Contemporary Italian Culture*, ed. Florian Mussgnug and Pierpaolo Antonello, 189–212. Oxford: Peter Lang.

Antonello, Pierpaolo, and Florian Mussgnug, eds. 2009. *Postmodern Impegno: Ethics and Commitment in Contemporary Italian Culture*. Oxford: Peter Lang.

Applebaum, Patricia. 2015. *St Francis of America: How a Thirteenth-Century Friar Became America's Most Popular Saint*. Chapel Hill: University of North Carolina Press.

Arasa, Daniel. 2009. "Il Magistero della Chiesa Cattolica sulla comunicazione." In *Introduzione alla Comunicazione Istituzionale della Chiesa*, ed. José María La Porte, 11–40. Rome: EDUSC.

Arasa, Daniel, Lorenzo Catoni, and Lucio Adrián Ruiz, eds. 2010. *Religious Internet Communication: Facts, Experiences, and Trends in the Catholic Church*. Rome: EDUSC.

Ardizzoni, Michela. 2013. "Nuove narrative sull'Altro: Arabi e musulmani nel cinema italiano contemporaneo." In *A New Italian Political Cinema? Emerging Themes*, ed. William Hope, Luciana d'Arcangeli, and Fabiana Stefanoni, 152–62. Leicester: Troubador.

Armstrong, E.A. 1973. *Saint Francis: Nature Mystic – The Derivation and Significance of the Nature Stories in the Franciscan Legend*. Berkeley: University of California Press.

Bailey, Tom, and Michael Driessen. 2016. "Mapping Contemporary Catholic Politics in Italy." *Journal of Modern Italian Studies* 21.3: 419–25. https://doi.org/10.1080/1354571X.2016.1169885.

Bandy, Mary Lee, and Antonio Monda, eds. 2004. *The Hidden God: Cinema e spiritualità*. Milan: Edizioni Olivares.

Barker, Philip W. 2009. *Religious Nationalism in Modern Europe: If God Be for Us*. London: Routledge.

Bartoli, Clelia. 2012. *Razzisti per legge. L'Italia che discrimina*. Rome and Bari: Laterza.

Baugh, Lloyd, SJ. 2007. *Imaging Jesus in Film: Sources and Influences, Limits and Possibilities*. Regina: Campion College.

Baumgartner, Christoph. 2014. "Re-examining an Ethics of Citizenship in Postsecular Societies." In *Transformations of Religion and the Public Sphere: Postsecular Publics*, ed. Rosi Braidotti, Bolette Blaagaard, Tobijn de Graauw, and Eva Midden, 77–96. Basingstoke: Palgrave Macmillan.

Beermann, Bernd, Thomas Dienberg, and Markus Warode. 2017. "Integral Ecology from a Franciscan Perspective." In *Integral Ecology and Sustainable Business (Contributions to Conflict Management, Peace Economics and Development*, vol. 26), pp. 89–100. Bingley: Emerald.

Bei, Francesco. 2006. "E Fini stronca 'Il mercante di pietre.' Film anti Islam, propaganda becera." *La repubblica*, 19 October. http://www.repubblica.it/2006/10/sezioni/politica/fini-martinelli/fini-martinelli/fini-martinelli.html. Accessed 15 March 2013.

Bellino, Francesca. 2015. "The Islamisation of Naples in a Documentary." *ANSAmed*, 8 June. http://www.ansamed.info/ansamed/en/news/nations/italy/2015/06/08/cinema-the-islamization-of-naples-in-a-documentary_64f7f3b4-8ee1-408b-a1ed-d219878d51ec.html. Accessed 5 May 2016.

Ben-Ghiat, Ruth, and Stephanie Malia Hom, eds. 2016. *Italian Mobilities*. London: Routledge.

Benjamin, Walter. 1936; 2008. *The Work of Art in the Age of Mechanical Reproduction*, trans. J.A. Underwood. London: Penguin.

Benshoff, Harry M., and Sean Griffin, eds. 2004. *Queer Cinema: The Film Reader*. London: Routledge.

Berger, Peter L. 1969. *The Sacred Canopy: Elements of a Sociological Theory of Religion*. Garden City: Doubleday.

Bergoglio, Jose. 2013. "Audience to Representatives of the Communications Media: Address of the Holy Father Pope Francis," 16 March. http://w2.vatican.va/content/francesco/en/speeches/2013/march/documents/papa-francesco_20130316_rappresentanti-media.html.

– 2015. "Laudato si': On Care for Our Common Home." http://w2.vatican.va
/content/francesco/en/encyclicals/documents/papa-francesco_20150524_enciclica
-laudato-si.html.

Bertetto, Paolo. 2010. "Fellini, la religione, lo spettacolo." In *Cinema e religioni*, ed.
Sergio Botta and Emanuela Prinzivalli, 99–112. Rome: Carocci.

Bettetini, Gianfranco. 2006. "Chiesa cattolica e cinema: Dal sessantotto a oggi."
In *Attraverso lo schermo: Cinema e cultura cattolica in Italia: Dagli anni Settanta
ai nostri giorni*, vol 3, ed. Dario E. Viganò and Eugeni Ruggero, 71–102.
Rome: Ente dello spettacolo.

Biltereyst, Daniel. 2006. "'Down with French *Vaudevilles!*' The Catholic Film
Movement's Resistance and Boycott of French Cinema in the 1930s." *Studies in
French Cinema* 6: 29–42. https://doi.org/10.1386/sfci.6.1.29_2.

Biltereyst, Daniel, and Daniela Treveri Gennari, eds. 2015. *Moralizing Cinema: Film,
Catholicism, and Power*. London: Routledge.

Blake, Linnie. 2008. *The Wounds of Nations: Horror Cinema, Historical Trauma, and
National Identity*. Manchester: Manchester University Press.

Blake, Richard Aloysius. 2000. *AfterImage: The Indelible Catholic Imagination of Six
American Filmmakers*. Chicago: Loyola Press.

Boffi, Dino. 2007. "La religione nei media cattolici." In *Direzione strategica della
comunicazione della Chiesa*, ed. Marc Carroggio, Diego Contreras, and Juan Manuel
Mora, 177–87. Rome: EDUSC.

Botta, Sergio, and Emanuela Prinzivalli, eds. 2010. *Cinema e religioni*. Rome: Carocci.

Bottum, Joseph, and David G. Dalin, eds. 2004. *The Pius War: Responses to the Critics
of Pius XII*. Boulder: Lexington Books.

Bourdieu, Pierre, and Richard Nice (trans). 1980. "The Production of Belief:
Contribution to an Economy of Symbolic Goods." *Media, Culture and Society* 2:
261–93. https://doi.org/10.1177/016344378000200305.

Bourlot, Alberto. 2006. "Filmare la Bibbia: La produzione cinematografica e televisiva
(dal 1968 ad oggi)." In *Attraverso lo schermo: Cinema e cultura cattolica in Italia:
Dagli anni Settanta ai nostri giorni*, vol. 3, ed. Dario E Viganò and Ruggero Eugeni.
143–65. Rome: Ente dello spettacolo.

Bradatan, Costica, and Camil Ungureanu. 2015. *Religion in Contemporary European
Cinema: The Postsecular Constellation*. London: Routledge.

Braidotti, Rosi. 2012. *Nomadic Theory: The Portable Rosi Braidotti*, New York:
Columbia University Press.

Braidotti, Rosi, Bolette Blaagaard, Tobijn de Graauw, and Eva Midden. 2014.
"Introductory Notes." In *Transformations of Religion and the Public Sphere:
Postsecular Publics*, ed. Rosi Braidotti, Bolette Blaagaard, Tobijn de Graauw, and Eva
Midden, 1–13. Basingstoke: Palgrave Macmillan.

Brent Plate, S. 2008. *Religion and Film: Cinema and the Re-creation of the World*.
London: Wallflower.

Brook, Clodagh. 2009. "The Cinema of Resistance: Nanni Moretti's *Il caimano* and the
Italian Film Industry." In *Resisting the Tide: Cultures of Opposition under Berlusconi*

(2001–2006), ed. Daniele Albertazzi, Clodagh Brook, Charlotte Ross, and Nina Rothenberg, 110–24. New York: Continuum.

– 2017. "Post-Secular Identity in Contemporary Italian Cinema: Catholic 'Cement,' the Suppression of History, and the Lost Islamic Other." *Modern Italy* 22.2: 197–211. https://doi.org/10.1017/mit.2017.17.

Brook, Clodagh, and Charlotte Ross. 2009. "Conclusions: Splinters of Resistance." In *Resisting the Tide: Cultures of Opposition under Berlusconi (2001–2006)*, ed. Daniele Albertazzi, Clodagh Brook, Charlotte Ross, and Nina Rothenberg, 231–40. New York: Continuum.

Bruce, Steve. 1999. *Religion and Choice*. Oxford: Oxford University Press.

Budde, Michael L. 1998. "Embracing Pop Culture: The Catholic Church in the World Market." *World Policy Journal* 15.1: 77–87. https://www.jstor.org/stable/40209572.

Burns, Jennifer. 2001. *Fragments of Impegno: Interpretations of Commitment in Contemporary Italian Literature: 1980–2000*. Leeds: Northern Universities Press.

Butler, Judith, Cornel West, Jürgen Habermas, Jonathan VanAntwerpen, Charles Taylor, Eduardo Mendieta, and Craig Calhoun. 2011. *The Power of Religion in the Public Sphere*. New York: Columbia University Press.

Butt, Riazat. 2009. "Jewish Anger as Pope Benedict Moves Pius XII Closer to Sainthood." *The Guardian*, 21 December. http://www.theguardian.com/world/2009 /dec/21/pope-benedict-moves-pius-closer-sainthood. Accessed 1 October 2015.

Califfe, Eamonn. 2016. *The Politics of the Piazza: The History and Meaning of the Italian Square*. London: Routledge.

Campan, Véronique. 1999. *L'écoute filmique: écho du son en image*. Saint-Denis: Presses Universitaires de Vincennes.

Campani, Ermelinda M. 2010. "Forme del sacro al cinema." In *Cinema e religioni*, ed. Sergio Botta and Emanuela Prinzivalli, 51–64. Rome: Carocci.

Carroll, Hamilton. 2011. *Affirmative Reaction: New Formations of White Masculinity*. Durham: Duke University Press.

Castellani, Leandro. 1994. *Temi e figure del film religioso*. Turin: Elle Di Ci.

Catoni, Lorenzo. 2010. "Internet and the Catholic Church: A Map and a Research Area." In *Religious Internet Communication*, ed. Daniel Arasa, Lorenzo Catoni, and Lucio Adrián Ruiz, 15–42. Rome: EDUSC.

Cavani, Liliana. 2014. "Ecco il mio terzo 'Francesco,' figlio della crisi e fratello di Bergoglio." *Adnkronos*. 4 December. http://www.adnkronos.com/intrattenimento /spettacolo/2014/12/04/liliana-cavani-ecco-mio-terzo-francesco-figlio-della-crisi -fratello-bergoglio_OXhh7NldkvyYJTpsjAJC7M.html. Accessed 21 October 2017.

Ceruso, Vincenzo. 2007. *La chiesa e la mafia: Viaggio dentro le sagrestie di Cosa nostra*. Rome: Newton Compton.

Chiani, Marco. 2013. "Francesco d'Assisi. Per Liliana Cavani simbolo del rifiuto all'omologazione." *Il fatto quotidiano*. 1 March. https://www.ilfattoquotidiano .it/2013/03/01/francesco-dassisi-per-liliana-cavani-e-simbolo-del-rifiuto -allomologazione/516694/. Accessed 21 October 2017.

Chillura, Angelo. 1990. *Coscienza di chiesa e fenomeno mafia: Analisi degli interventi delle chiese di Sicilia sulla mafia.* Palermo: Edizioni Augustinus.

Chinnici, Giuseppe. 2003. *Cinema, chiesa e movimento cattolico italiano.* Rome: Aracne.

Chion, Michel. 1999. *The Voice in Cinema*, trans. Claudia Gorbman. New York: Colombia University Press.

Cogliandro, Giovanni. 2011. "Corpo celeste, inferno terrestre? Critica del film *Corpo celeste* di Alice Rohrwacher." *Avvenire di Calabria*, 11 July 2011.

Condor Administrator. 2015. "The Controversy of Pius XII in *Shades of Truth*." https://www.condor-pictures.com/comimageshow/pressarticles/62-pasot/104-the-controversy-of-pope-pius-xii-in-shades-of-truth. Accessed 20 January 2017.

Convents, Guido, and Tom Van Beeck. 2009. "Documenting Catholic Media Activities All over the World: The Signis, Ocic, and Unda Archives." *Historical Journal of Film, Radio and Television* 29.1: 113–21. https://doi.org/10.1080/01439680902722600.

Cornwell, John. 2000. *Hitler's Pope: The Secret History of Pius XII.* London: Penguin.

Cornwell, Rupert. 1983. *God's Banker: An Account of the Life and Death of Roberto Calvi.* London: Victor Gollancz.

Cortellazzo, Sara, and Massimo Quaglia, eds. 2008. *Cinema e religione: Forme della spiritualità e della fede.* Turin: Celid.

Cousin, Bruno, and Tommaso Vitale. 2012. "Italian Intellectuals and the Promotion of Islamophobia after 9/11." In *Muslims and Moral Panic in the West*, ed. George Morgan and Scott Poynting, 47–66. Farnham: Ashgate.

Cowen, Douglas E. 2008. *Sacred Terror: Religion and Horror on the Silver Screen.* Waco: Baylor University Press.

– 2009. "Horror and the Demonic." In *The Routledge Companion to Religion and Film*, ed. John Lyndon, 401–18. London: Routledge.

Crittenden, Paul. 1990. *Learning to Be Moral: Philosophical Thoughts about Moral Development.* Atlantic Highlands: Humanities Press.

Cruciani, Mariella. 2003. "Diventare uomini e donne: Il cinema di Marco Bellocchio." *Cinecritica* 30–1: 16–19.

Cuciniello, Antonio. 2013. "Islam italiano sul web." *Arab Media Report*, 4 November. http://arabmediareport.it/lislam-italiano-sul-web. Accessed 15 June 2016.

Dalin, David G. 2005. *The Myth of Hitler's Pope: How Pope Pius XII Rescued Jews from the Nazis.* Washington: Regnery Publishing.

Davie, Grace. 1990. "Believing without Belonging: Is This the Future of Religion in Britain?" *Social Compass* 37.4: 455–69. https://doi.org/10.1177/003776890037004004.

De Groot, Joanna, and Sue Morgan. 2014. "Introduction: Beyond the 'Religious Turn'?: Past, Present, and Future Perspectives in Gender History." In *Sex, Gender, and the Sacred: Reconfiguring Religion in Gender History*, ed. Joanna de Groot and Sue Morgan, 1–30. Chichester: Wiley Blackwell.

Deacy, Christopher. 2001. *Screen Christologies: Redemption and the Medium of Film.* Cardiff: University of Wales Press.

Deacy, Christopher, and Gaye Williams Ortiz. 2008. *Theology and Film: Challenging the Sacred/Secular Divide.* Oxford: Blackwell.

Derrida, Jacques. 1996. "Faith and Knowledge: The Two Sources of 'Religion at the Limits of Reason Alone.'" In *Religion,* ed. Jacques Derrida and Gianni Vattimo, 1–78. Cambridge: Polity Press.

Detweiler, Craig. 2008. *Into the Dark: Seeing the Sacred in the Top Films of the 21st Century.* Grand Rapids: Baker Academic.

Di Donato, Mauro. 2010. "L'evocazione del trascendente nel cinema." In *Cinema e religioni,* ed. Sergio Botta and Emanuela Prinzivalli, 25–49. Rome: Carocci.

Di Marco, Erica. 2009. "The Tides of Vatican Influence in Italian Reproductive Matters: From Abortion to Assisted Reproduction." *Rutgers Journal of Law and Religion* 10.1: 1–30. https://lawandreligion.com/sites/law-religion/files/Tides-Vatican-DiMarco .pdf. Accessed 5 May 2016.

Dines, Martin, and Sergio Rigoletto. 2012. "Country Cousins: Europeanness, Sexuality, and Locality in Contemporary Italian Television." *Modern Italy* 17.4: 479–91. https:// doi.org/10.1080/13532944.2012.706999.

Dino, Alessandra. 2008. *La mafia devota: Chiesa, religione, Cosa Nostra.* Rome: Laterza.

Diotallevi, Luca. 2002. "International Competition in a National Religious Monopoly: The Catholic Effect and the Italian Case." *Sociology of Religion* 63.2: 137–55. https:// doi.org/10.2307/3712562.

Dönmez-Colin, Gönül. 2014. *Women, Islam, and Cinema.* London: Reaktion Books.

Duggan, Lisa. 2002. "The New Homonormativity: The Sexual Politics of Neoliberalism." In *Materializing Democracy: Toward a Revitalised Cultural Politics,* ed. Russ Castronovo and Dana D. Nelson, 175–94. Durham, NC: Duke University Press.

Duncan, Derek. 2008. "Italy's Postcolonial Cinema and Its Histories of Representation." *Italian Studies* 63.2: 195–211. https://doi.org/10.1179/007516308x344351.

Dupont, Natalie. 2015. "Pleasure, Spectacle, Religion: Cinema and Christianity in America." In *The Pleasures of the Spectacle,* ed. Phillip Drummond, 401–12. London: London Symposium.

Dyer, Richard. 1993. *The Matter of Images: Essays on Representations.* London: Routledge.

– 1997. *White: Essays on Race and Culture.* London: Routledge.

Editors of *Marketing Journal.* 2011. "*Avvenire* continua a crescere: risultati positivi." *Marketing journal: Club del marketing e della comunicazione.* http://www .marketingjournal.it/avvenire-continua-crescere-diffusione-risultati-positivi -raccolta-pubblicitaria. Accessed 15 January 2011.

Eisenlohr, Patrick. 2014. "Religious Aspirations, Public Religion, and the Secularity of Pluralism." In *Transformations of Religion and the Public Sphere: Postsecular Publics,* ed. Rosi Braidotti, Bolette Blaagaard, Tobijn de Graauw, and Eva Midden, 195–209. Basingstoke: Palgrave Macmillan.

Elkins, James. 2004. *On the Strange Place of Religion in Contemporary Art.* London: Routledge.

Elvy, Peter. 1990. *Future of Christian Broadcasting in Europe*. Great Wakering: McCrimmon for the Jerusalem Trust.

European Union Agency for Fundamental Human Rights (EUFRA). "EU-Midis Data in Focus Report 2: Muslims." http://fra.europa.eu/en/publication/2010/eu-midis-data-focus-report-2-muslims. Accessed 20 May 2016.

Fainstein, Susan S. 2010. *The Just City*. Ithaca: Cornell University Press.

Ferrero-Regis, Tiziana. 2009. *Recent Italian Cinema: Spaces, Contexts, Experiences*. Leicester: Troubador.

Fondazione ISMU. 2017. *Ventitreesimo rapporto sulle migrazioni 2017*. Milan: Francoangeli.

Fontanarosa, Aldo. 2016. "Fiction Rai, i nuovi Big. In calo Lux Vide, accelera Cattleya. Stabile Palomar di Montalbano." *La Repubblica*, 7 October. https://www.repubblica.it/economia/2016/10/07/news/i_big_della_fiction_rai_in_calo_la_lux_vide_accelera_cattleya_stabile_la_palomar_di_montalbano-149248978/. Accessed 28 July 2017.

Fox, Jonathan. 2008. *A World Survey of Religion and the State*. Cambridge: Cambridge University Press.

Fraser, Peter. 1998. *Images of the Passion: The Sacramental Mode in Film*. Westport: Praeger.

Gaetani, Claudio. 2013. "'This Must Be the Memory: Venti'anni di sguardi di cinema italiano sulla Shoah." In *La shoah nel cinema italiano*, ed. Andrea Minuz, Guido Vitiello, 103–16. Soveria Mannelli: Rubbettino.

Gamson, William A., and David S. Meyer. 1996. "Framing Political Opportunity in Comparative Perspectives on Social Movements." In *Political Opportunities, Mobilizing Structures, and Cultural Framings*, ed. Doug McAdam, John D. McCarthy, and Mayer N. Zald, 273–90. New York: Cambridge University Press.

Gamson, William A., and Gadi Wolfsfeld. 1993. "Movements and Media as Interacting Systems." *Annals of the American Academy of Political and Social Science*, 528: 114–25. https://doi.org/10.1177/0002716293528001009.

Garelli, Franco. 2014. *Religion Italian Style: Continuities and Changes in a Catholic Country*. London: Routledge.

Getsy, David J. 2014. "Acts of Stillness: Statues, Performativity, and Passive Resistance." *Criticism* 56.1: 1–20. https://doi.org/10.13110/criticism.56.1.0001.

Gilmore, Lee. 2011. "DIY Spiritual Community: From Individualism to Participatory Culture." In *Media, Spiritualities, and Social Change*, ed. Stewart M. Hoover and Monica Emerich, 37–46. London: Continuum.

Giovagnoli, Agostino. 2006. "Cattolici e società italiana dal 1968 ad oggi." In *Attraverso lo schermo: Cinema e cultura cattolica in Italia: Dagli anni Settanta ai giorni nostri*, vol. 3, ed. Dario E Viganò and Ruggero Eugeni, 11–34. Rome: Ente dello spettacolo.

Giovanetti, Francesco. 2016. "Giubileo, Benigni: 'Con la Misericordia il Papa tira tutta la Chiesa verso il Cristianesimo.'" *La Repubblica*, 12 January. http://video.repubblica.it/vaticano/giubileo-benigni-con-la-misericordia-il-papa-tira-tutta-la-chiesa-verso-il-cristianesimo/224666?video. Accessed 12 January 2016.

Girlanda, Elio, and Carlo Tagliabue, eds. 1988. *Cinema Anno Mille: Il sacro nel cinema europeo contemporaneo*. Rome: Centro Studi Cinematografici.

Giulidori, Elisa. 2006. "*Il mercante di pietre*: Intervista al regista." FilmUp.com. http://filmup.leonardo.it/speciale/ilmercantedipietre/int01.htm.

Gordon, Robert, S.C. 1996. *Pasolini: Forms of Subjectivity*. Oxford: Clarendon Press.

Grace, Pamela. 2009. *The Religious Film: Christianity and the Hagiopic*. Chichester: Wiley-Blackwell.

Grassilli, Mariagiulia. 2008. "Migrant Cinema: Transnational and Guerrilla Practices of Film Production and Representation." *Journal of Ethnic and Migration Studies* 34.8: 1237–55. https://doi.org/10.1080/13691830802364825.

Grasso, Aldo. 2014. "L'ossessione di Liliana Cavani e il terzo Francesco esoterico." *Corriere della sera*, 10 December. http://www.corriere.it/spettacoli/14_dicembre_10/ossessione-liliana-cavani-terzo-francesco-esoterico-81213e6e-804a-11e4-bf7c-95a1b87351f5.shtml. Accessed 21 October 2017.

Greeley, Andrew. 2011. "Unsecular Europe: The Persistence of Religion." In *The Role of Religion in Modern Societies*, ed. Detlef Pollack and Daniel Olson, 141–62. London: Routledge.

Grzymala-Busse, Anna. 2015. *Nations under God: How Churches Use Moral Authority to Influence Policy*. Princeton: Princeton University Press.

Gurwin, Larry. 1983. *The Calvi Affair: Death of a Banker*. London: Macmillan.

Habermas, Jürgen. 1962. *The Structural Transformation of the Public Sphere: Inquiry into a Category of Bourgeois Society*. Cambridge: Polity Press.

– 2006. "Religion in the Public Sphere." *European Journal of Philosophy* 14.1: 1–25. https://doi.org/10.1111/j.1468-0378.2006.00241.x.

Habermas, Jürgen, and Joseph Ratzinger. 2005. *Dialektik der Säkularisierung: Über Vernunft und Religion*. Freiburg im Breisgau: Herder Verlag.

Hackett, Conrad. 2017. "5 Facts about the Muslim Population in Europe." *Pew Research Centre*. http://www.pewresearch.org/fact-tank/2017/11/29/5-facts-about-the-muslim-population-in-europe. Accessed 15 December 2017.

Halman, Loek, and Ole Riis, eds. 2003. "Contemporary Religious Discourses on Religion and Morality." In *Religion in Secularizing Society: The Europeans' Religion at the End of the Twentieth Century*, 1–21. Leiden: Brill Academic.

Healy, Stephen. 2016. "Saint Francis in Climate-Changing Times: Form of Life, the Highest Poverty, and Postcapitalist Politics." *Rethinking Marxism* 28.3–4: 367–84. https://doi.org/10.1080/08935696.2016.1243422.

Heywood, Paolo. 2015. "Agreeing to Disagree: LGBTQ Activism and the Church in Italy." *HAU Journal of Ethnographic Theory* 5.2: 325–44.

Hjarvard, Stig. 2011. "The Mediatisation of Religion: Theorising Religion, Media, and Social Change." *Culture and Religion: An Interdisciplinary Journal* 12.2: 119–35. https://doi.org/10.1080/14755610.2011.579719.

Hooper, John. 2013. "'Pope Francis Effect' Credited with Boosting Italian Congregations." *The Guardian*, 10 November. https://www.theguardian.com/world/2013/nov/10/pope-francis-effect-italy-catholicism. Accessed 29 June 2016.

Hoover, Stewart M. 2006. *Religion in the Media Age*. London: Routledge.

Horeck, Tanya, and Tina Kendall. 2011. *New Extremism in Cinema: From France to Europe*. Edinburgh: Edinburgh University Press.

Hussain, Amir. 2010. "Islam." In *The Routledge Companion to Religion and Film*, ed. John London, 131–40. London: Routledge.

Iannotta, Antonio. 2016. "Le immagini del potere. Note sull'identità italiana nel cinema di Paolo Sorrentino." *California Italian Studies* 6.2: 1–17. https://escholarship.org/uc /item/69z1s71b.

Innocenti, Orsetta. 2009. "La trasformazione dell'intimità: Anthony Giddens e il *romance* dell'impegno." In *Postmodern* Impegno: *Ethics and Commitment in Contemporary Italian Culture*, ed. Florian Mussgnug and Pierpaolo Antonello, 121–46. Oxford: Peter Lang.

Introvigne, Massimo. 2011. "Preti pedofili: un panico morale." *CENSUR*. https://www .cesnur.org/2010/mi_preti_pedofili.html.

Introvigne, Massimo, and PierLuigi Zoccatelli. 2006. *Le religioni in Italia*. Turin: Elle Di Ci.

ISTAT. 2017. *Statische culturali*. https://www.istat.it/it/archivio/195678.

Jacobsen, Janet R., and Ann Pellegrini. 2008. *Secularisms*. Durham, NC: Duke University Press.

Jameson, Fredric. 1981. *The Political Unconscious: Narrative as a Socially Symbolic Act*. Ithaca: Cornell University Press.

Janni, Paolo, and George F. McLean, eds. 2003. *The Essence of Italian Culture and the Challenge of a Global Age*. Washington, DC: Council for Research in Values and Philosophy.

Jenkins, Richard. 2006. *Convergence Culture: Where Old and New Media Collide*. New York: NYU Press.

– 2008. *Social Identity*. London: Routledge.

Johnson, William Bruce. 2008. *Miracles and Sacrilege: Roberto Rossellini, the Church, and Film Censorship in Hollywood*. Toronto: University of Toronto Press.

Johnston, Robert K., ed. 2007. *Reframing Theology and Film*. Grand Rapids: Baker Academic.

Juurikkala, Oskari. 2015. "Virtuous Poverty, Christian Liberty: A Free-Market Appreciation of Pope Francis." *Journal of Markets and Morality* 18.2: 257–77. https:// www.marketsandmorality.com/index.php/mandm/article/view/1094.

Kabakebbji, Abdallah. 2010. "Uso del corpo nelle arti figurative: Un'opinione musulmana." In *Islam e cinema*, ed. Giulio Martini, 35–44. Milan: Centro Ambrosiano.

Kemp, Martin. 2011. *From Christ to Coke: How Image Becomes Icon*. Oxford: Oxford University Press.

Kershaw, Baz. 2003. "Curiosity or Contempt: On Spectacle, the Human, and Activism." *Theatre Journal* 55.4: 591–611. https://doi.org/10.1353/tj.2003.0170.

King, Geoff. 2000. *Spectacular Narratives: Contemporary Hollywood and Frontier Mythology*. London: I.B. Tauris.

Kirchgaessner, Stephanie, Pamela Duncan, Alberto Nardelli, and Delphine Robineau. 2016. "Seven in 10 Italian Gynecologists Refuse to Carry Out Abortions." *The Guardian*, 11 March. https://www.theguardian.com/world/2016/mar/11/italian -gynaecologists-refuse-abortions-miscarriages. Accessed 20 May 2016.

Lipsky, Michael. 1969. "Protest as a Political Resource." *American Political Science Review* 62.4: 1144–58. https://doi.org/10.2307/1953909.

Lodato, Saverio. 1994. *Dall'altare contro la mafia.* Milan: Rizzoli.

Lövheim, Mia, and Gordon Lynch. 2011. "The Mediatisation of Religion Debate: An Introduction." *Culture and Religion: An Interdisciplinary Journal* 12.2: 111–17. https://doi.org/10.1080/14755610.2011.579715.

Lux Vide. 2010. *Pressbook: Pius XII: Sotto il cielo di Roma.* http://www.luxvide.it /uploads/produzioni/allegati/38.pdf. Accessed 10 October 2015.

Lyden, John, ed. 2010. *The Routledge Companion to Religion and Film.* London: Routledge.

Malone, Peter. 2009. "The Roman Catholic Church and Cinema (1967 to the Present)." In *The Routledge Companion to Religion and Film*, ed. John Lyden, 52–71. London: Routledge.

Malraux, André. 2004. "Esquisse d'une psychologie du cinéma." In *Écrits sur l'art, Oeuvres complètes*, ed. André Malraux, vol. IV, 1–16. Paris: Gallimard.

Martini, Giulio. 2010. "Immagini e Islam: Il cinema e la TV." In *Islam e Cinema*, ed. Giulio Martini, 67–190. Milan: Centro Ambrosiano.

Mathewes, Charles T. 2006. "An Interview with Peter Berger." *Hedgehog Review: Critical Reflections on Contemporary Culture* 8.1–2: 152–61.

Meneghetti, Carlo. 2015. *Elementi di teologia della comunicazione: Un percorso tra etica e religione.* Padua: libreriauniversitaria.it.

Minuz, Andrea. 2014. *Quando c'eravamo noi: Nostalgia e crisi della sinistra nel cinema italiano da Berlinguer a Checco Zalone.* Soveria Mannelli: Rubbettino.

Minuz, Andrea, and Guido Vitiello, eds. 2013. *La Shoah nel cinema italiano.* Soveria Mannelli: Rubbettino.

Modood, Tariq. 2014. "Is There a Crisis of 'Postsecularism' in Western Europe?" In *Transformations of Religion and the Public Sphere: Postsecular Publics*, ed. Rosi Braidotti, Bolette Blaagaard, Tobijn de Graauw, and Eva Midden, 14–34. Basingstoke: Palgrave Macmillan.

Moore, Ellen E. 2017. "The Gospel of Tom (Hanks): American Churches and *The Da Vinci Code*." In *Exploring Religion and the Sacred in a Media Age*, ed. Elisabeth Arweck and Christopher Deacy, 123–40. London: Routledge.

Murphy, Charles. 2014. *Reclaiming Francis: How the Saint and the Pope Are Renewing the Church.* Notre Dame: Ave Maria Press.

Naficy, Hamid. 2001. *An Accented Cinema: Exilic and Diasporic Filmmaking.* Princeton: Princeton University Press.

– 2003. "Phobic Spaces and Liminal Panics: Independent Transnational Film Genre." In *Multiculturalism, Postcoloniality, and Transnational Media*, ed. Ella Shohat and Robert Stam, 203–26. New Brunswick: Rutgers University Press.

Nancy, Jean-Luc. 2005. *Noli me tangere: Saggio sul levarsi del corpo.* Turin: Bollati Boringhieri.

Neale, Stephen. 1981. "Art Cinema as Institution." *Screen* 22.1: 11–39. https://doi .org/10.1093/screen/22.1.11.

Nepoti, Roberto. 1998. "L'ecologia pacifista di Gesù adolescente." *La Repubblica*, 5 October. http://www.repubblica.it/online/cinema/eden/eden/eden.html.

Noam, Eli M. 2016. *Who Owns the World's Media? Media Concentration and the Ownership around the World.* Oxford: Oxford University Press.

O'Healy, Áine. 2009. "'[Non] è una somala': Deconstructing African Femininity in Italian Film." *The Italianist* 29.2: 175–98. https://doi.org/10.1179/0261434 09x12488561926306.

‒ 2010. "Mediterranean Passages: Abjection and Belonging in Contemporary Italian Cinema." *California Italian Studies* 1.1. http://escholarship.org/uc/item/2qh5d59c. Accessed 9 November 2016.

‒ 2012. "Screening Intimacy and Racial Difference in Postcolonial Italy." In *Postcolonial Italy: Challenging National Homogeneity*, ed. Cristina Lombardi-Diop and Caterina Romeo, 203–18. New York: Palgrave.

‒ 2014. "Postcolonial Theory and Italy's 'Multicultural' Cinema." In *The Italian Cinema Book*, ed. Peter Bondanella, 295–302. Basingstoke: Palgrave.

‒ 2015. "Witnessing History, Recounting Suffering: Andrea Segre's Documentary Project." In *Destination Italy: Representing Migration in Contemporary Media and Narrative*, ed. Emma Bond, Guido Bonsaver, and Federico Faloppa, 415–30. Oxford: Peter Lang.

‒ 2016. "Bound to Care: Gender, Affect, and Immigrant Labor." In *Italian Political Cinema: Public Life, Imaginary, and Identity in Contemporary Italian Film*, ed. Giancarlo Lombardi and Christian Uva, 56–67. Oxford: Peter Lang.

O'Leary, Alan. 2011. "Moro, Brescia, conspiracy. Lo stile paranoico nel cinema italiano." In *Strane storie: Il cinema e i misteri d'Italia*, ed. Christian Uva, 63–78. Soveria Mannelli: Rubbettino.

Oliver, Pamela E., and Daniel J. Myers. 1999. "How Events Enter the Public Sphere: Conflict, Location, and Sponsorship in Local Newspaper Coverage of Public Events." *American Journal of Sociology* 105.1: 38–87. https://doi.org/10.1086/210267.

Olivieri, Marco. 2016. "'Le confessioni' come grido dell'anima." In *Le confessioni*, ed. Roberto Andò and Angelo Pasquini, 119–29. Milan: Skira.

O'Rawe, Catherine. 2014. *Stars and Masculinities in Contemporary Italian Cinema.* New York: Palgrave Macmillan.

O'Toole, Fintan. 2003. "The Sisters of No Mercy." *The Guardian*, 16 February. http:// www.theguardian.com/film/2003/feb/16/features.review1. Accessed 15 October 2014.

Pak-Shiraz, Nacim. 2011. *Shi'i Islam in Iranian Cinema: Religion and Spirituality in Film.* London: I.B. Tauris.

Pallavicini, Yahya, and Abd al-Karim Turnley. 2010. "Immagini e simboli della civiltà islamica." In *Islam and Cinema*, ed. Giulio Martini, 19–34. Milan: Centro Ambrosiano.

Paoluzi, Angelo. 2009. "Stampa e giornali cattolici nel mondo." In *Editoria, media e religione*, ed. Giuseppe Costa, 149–70. Città del Vaticano: Libreria Editrice Vaticana.

Parati, Graziella. 2005. *Migration Italy: The Art of Talking Back in a Destination Culture.* Toronto: University of Toronto Press.

Pasolini, Pier Paolo. 1975. "Lo storico discorsetto di Castelgandolfo." In *Scritti corsari*, ed. Pier Paolo Pasolini, 66–9. Milan: Garzanti.

Pasquini, Angelo. 2016. "Il gioco illusionistico del potere." In *Le confessioni*, ed. Roberto Andò and Angelo Pasquini, 143–5. Milan: Skira.

Perugini, Sergio. 2011. *Testimoni di fede, trionfatori di audience: La fiction religiosa italiana anni Novanta e Duemila: Storie di santi, papi e preti esemplari.* Cantalupa: Effatà.

Pew Research Center. 2014. "Pope Francis' Image Positive in Much of World." http://www.pewglobal.org/2014/12/11/pope-francis-image-positive-in-much-of-world/. Accessed 1 June 2016.

Piana, Giannino. 2010. *Omosessualità: Una proposta etica.* Cittadella: Assisi.

Pinchiorri, Simone. 2011. "*Habemus Papam* di Nanni Moretti subito primo negli incassi." *Cinemaitaliano.info.* http://www.cinemaitaliano.info/news/07529/habemus-papam-di-nanni-moretti-subito-primo.html. Accessed 25 August 2015.

Polchi, Vladimiro. 2015. "Alfano convoca i leader islamici 'Rinasce la consulta.'" *La Repubblica*, 24 February. http://ricerca.repubblica.it/repubblica/archivio/repubblica/2015/02/24/alfano-convoca-i-leader-islamici-rinasce-la-consulta18.html. Accessed 2 April 2016.

Pollard, John. 2008. *Catholicism in Modern Italy: Religion, Society, and Politics since 1861.* London: Routledge.

Posner, Gerald. 2014. *God's Bankers: A History of Money and Power at the Vatican.* New York: Simon and Schuster.

Prosperi, Adriano. 2010. "Prefazione." In *Chiesa e pedofilia: Non lasciate che i pargoli vadano a loro*, ed. Federico Tullio, 7–10. Rome: L'asino d'oro.

Prosperi, Gabriele. 2016. "Tra TV e GIF quality: *The Young Pope* come esempio di complessità televisiva." *Annali Online Università degli Studi di Ferrara* 11.2. http://annali.unife.it/lettere/article/viewFile/1404/1192. Accessed 12 December 2017.

Quicke, Andrew. 2010. "The Era of Censorship (1930–1967)." In *The Routledge Companion to Religion and Film*, ed. John Lyden, 32–51. London: Routledge.

Quinzio, Sergio. 1993. "La Chiesa al giro di boa." *Corriere della sera*, 9 May.

Reno, R.R. 2015. "St Francis and Pope Francis." *Nova et Vetera* 13.1: 29–37. https://stpaulcenter.com/03-nv-13-1-reno.

Robinson, Sally. 2000. *Marked Men: White Masculinity in Crisis.* New York: Columbia University Press.

Rumble, Patrick. 1996. *Allegories of Contamination: Pier Paolo Pasolini's Trilogy of Life.* Toronto: University of Toronto Press.

Rusconi, Giuseppe. "Intervista a Ettore Bernabei." *Rossoporpora.* https://www.rossoporpora.org/rubriche/cultura/93-intervista-a-ettore-bernabei.html.

Russo Bullaro, Grace. 2010. *From Terrone to Extracomunitario: New Manifestations of Racism in Contemporary Italian Cinema.* Leicester: Troubador.

Saint-Blancat, Chantal, and Ottavia Schmidt di Friedberg. 2005. "Why Are Mosques a Problem? Local Politics and Fear of Islam in Northern Italy." *Journal of Ethnic and Migration Studies* 31.6: 1083–104. https://doi.org/10.1080/13691830500282881.

Schrader, Paul. 1972. *Transcendental Style in Film: Ozu, Bresson, Dreyer.* Berkeley: University of California Press.

Semmerling, Tim Jon. 2006. *"Evil" Arabs in American Popular Film: Orientalist Fear.* Austin: University of Texas Press.

Siniscalchi, Claudio, ed. 2001. *Giovanni Paolo II e il cinema: Un itinerario di fede e cultura, arte e comunicazione.* Rome: Ente dello Spettacolo.

Smargiassi, Michele. 2000. "BOLOGNA – Biffi: Niente visto d'ingresso ai musulmani." http://www.corsodireligione.it/attualita/biffi.htm. Accessed 1 May 2016.

Sontag, Susan. 1964. "Spiritual Style in the Films of Robert Bresson." In *Robert Bresson*, ed. James Quandt. Toronto: Cinematheque Ontario.

Sorlin, Pierre. 2005. "Cinéma et religion dans l'Europe du XXe siècle." *Journal of Modern European History* 3.2: 183–204. https://doi.org/10.17104/1611-8944 _2005_2_183.

Stabile, Francesco Michele. 1996. "Cattolicesimo siciliano e mafia." *Synaxis* 14.1: 13–55. https://terradinessuno.wordpress.com/biblioteca-di-terra-di-nessuno/francesco -michele-stabile-cattolicesimo-siciliano-e-mafia/. Accessed 1 September 2017.

Stark, Rodney. 1999. "Secularisation RIP." *Sociology of Religion* 60.3: 249–73. https:// doi.org/10.2307/3711936.

Stellardi, Giuseppe. 2009. "*Pensiero Debole*, Nihilism, and Ethics, or How Strong Is Weakness?" In *Postmodern* Impegno: *Ethics and Commitment in Contemporary Italian Culture*, ed. Florian Mussgnug and Pierpaolo Antonello, 83–98. Oxford: Peter Lang.

Szczepanik, Petr, and Patrick Vonderau. 2013. *Behind the Screen: Inside European Production Cultures.* New York: Palgrave Macmillan.

Taylor, Charles. 2007. *A Secular Age.* Cambridge, MA: Harvard University Press.

Toronto, James A. 2008. "Islam Italiano: Prospects for Integration of Muslims in Italy's Religious Landscape." *Journal of Muslim Minority Affairs* 28.1: 61–82. https://doi .org/10.1080/13602000802011069.

Treveri Gennari, Daniela. 2010. "Forbidden Pleasures: Voyeurism, Showgirls, and Catholicism in Postwar Cinema in Italy." In *Italy on Screen: National Identity and Italian Imaginary*, ed. Lucy Bolton and Christina Siggers Mason, 101–14. Oxford: Peter Lang.

– 2011. *Post-War Italian Cinema: American Intervention, Vatican Interests.* London: Routledge.

Tulli, Federico. 2010. *Chiesa e pedofilia: Non lasciate che i pargoli vadano a loro.* Rome: L'asino d'oro.

Turone, Fabio. 2005. "Italians Fail to Overturn Restrictive Reproduction Law." *The British Medical Journal* 330.7505: 1405. https://www.ncbi.nlm.nih.gov/pmc/articles /PMC558364. Accessed 20 December 2017.

Uva, Christian. 2011. "I misteri d'Italia nel cinema. Strategie narrative e trame estetiche tra documento e finzione." In *Strane storie: Il cinema e i misteri d'Italia*, ed. Christian Uva, 9–34. Soveria Mannelli: Rubbettino.

Valli, Bernardo. 1999. *Il film ideale: I cattolici, il cinema e le comunicazioni sociali*. Milan: Franco Angeli.

Viganò, Dario Edoardo. 2002. *Cinema e Chiesa*. Turin: Effatà.

– 2010. *Il prete di celluloide: Nove sguardi d'autore*. Assisi: Cittadella Editrice.

Viganò, Dario Eduardo, and Ruggero Eugeni, eds. 2006. *Attraverso lo schermo: Cinema e cultura cattolica in Italia: Dagli anni Settanta ai nostri giorni*, vol. 3. Rome: Ente dello spettacolo.

– 2006. "Introduzione." In *Attraverso lo schermo: Cinema e cultura cattolica in Italia: Dalle origini agli anni Venti*, vol. 1, ed. Dario Eduardo Viganò and Eugeni Ruggero, 9–14. Rome: Ente dello spettacolo.

Viviers, Hendrik. 2014. "The Second Christ, Saint Francis of Assisi, and Ecological Consciousness." *Verbum et Ecclesia* 35.1, Art. 1310. http://dx.doi.org/10.4102 /ve.v35i1.1310.

Weber, Max. [1922]1978. *Economy and Society: An Outline of Interpretative Sociology*, 2 vols., trans. Ephraim Fischoff et al., ed. Guenther Roth and Claus Wittich. Berkeley: University of California Press.

Wheatley, Catherine. 2014. "Deconstructing Christianity in Contemporary European Cinema: Nanni Moretti's *Habemus Papam* and Jean-Luc Nancy's *Dis-Enclosure*." In *European Cinema: The Postsecular Constellation*, ed. Costica Bradatan and Camil Ungureanu, 11–26. London: Routledge.

White, Lynn. 1967. "The Historical Roots of Our Ecologic Crisis." *Science* 155.3767: 1203–7. https://doi.org/10.1126/science.155.3767.1203.

Wilinsky, Barbara. 2001. *Sure Seaters: The Emergence of Art House Cinema*. Minneapolis: University of Minnesota Press.

Willan, Phillip. 2007. *The Last Supper: The Mafia, the Mason, and the Killing of Roberto Calvi*. London: Robinson.

Williams, Raymond. 1973. "Base and Superstructure in Marxist Cultural Theory." *New Left Review* 1.82: 3–16.

Williams Ortiz, Gaye. 2003. "The Catholic Church and Its Attitude to Film as an Arbiter of Cultural Meaning." In *Mediating Religion: Conversations in Media, Religion, and Culture*, ed. Jolyon P. Mitchell and Sophia Marriage, 179–88. London: T&T Clark.

– 2010. "Feminism." In *The Routledge Companion to Religion and Film*, ed. John Lyden, 237–54. London: Routledge.

Wilson, Rob, and Wimal Dissanayake. 1996. *Cultural Production and the Transnational Imagination*. Durham: Duke University Press.

Zald, Mayer N. 1996. "Culture, Ideology, and Strategic Framing." In *Comparative Perspectives on Social Movements: Political Opportunities, Mobilizing Structures, and Cultural Framings*, ed. Doug McAdam, John D. McCarthy, and Mayer N. Zald, 261–74. New York: Cambridge University Press.

Zhang, Xue Jiao. 2016. "How St Francis Influenced Pope Francis' Laudato si'." *Cross Currents* 66.1: 42–56. https://doi.org/10.1111/cros.12170.

Zizola, Giancarlo. 1996. *La Chiesa nei media*. Turin: SEI.

Zucherman, Ester. 2017. "Designing the Costumes That Made *The Young Pope* Sexy and Know It." *The A.V. Club*, 30 January. http://www.avclub.com/article/designing -costumes-made-young-pope-sexyand-know-it-249351?permalink=true. Accessed 21 July 2017.

Filmography

Official English-language titles are provided in brackets. Where English titles are not provided, films do not, or do not yet, have international titles.

Albano, Gianfranco, *Brancaccio* [TV miniseries, 2001]

Albano, Gianfranco, *La buona battaglia: Don Pietro Pappagallo* [TV miniseries, 2006]

Almodóvar, Pedro, *La mala educación* [Bad Education, 2004]

Andò, Roberto, *Le confessioni* [The Confessions, 2016]

Andreotti, Francesco, and Livia Giunti, *Love Is All: Piergiorgio Welby: Autoritratto* [2015]

Argento, Dario, *La terza madre* [Mother of Tears, 2007]

Battiato, Giacomo, *Karol, Un Papa rimasto uomo* [Karol: The Pope, The Man, TV miniseries, 2006]

Battiato, Giacomo, *Karol: Un uomo diventato Papa* [Karol: A Man Who Became Pope, TV miniseries, 2005]

Bellocchio, Marco, *Bella addormentata* [Dormant Beauty, 2012]

Bellocchio, Marco, *Buongiorno, notte* [Good Morning, Night, 2003]

Bellocchio, Marco, *La Cina è vicina* [China Is Near, 1967]

Bellocchio, Marco, *Fai bei sogni* [Sweet Dreams, 2016]

Bellocchio, Marco, *Nel nome del padre* [In the Name of the Father, 1972]

Bellocchio, Marco, *Lora di religione: Il sorriso di mia mamma* [My Mother's Smile, 2002]

Bellocchio, Marco, *I pugni in tasca* [Fists in the Pocket, 1965]

Bellocchio, Marco, *Il regista di matrimoni* [The Wedding Director, 2006]

Bencivenni, Alessandro, Domenico Saverni, and Alessandra Caneva, *Don Matteo* [TV series, 2000–]

Benigni, Roberto, *La tigre e la neve* [The Tiger and the Snow, 2005]

Berg, Amy, *Deliver Us from Evil* [2006]

Bertolucci, Bernardo, *Il conformista* [The Conformist, 1970]

Bertolucci, Bernardo, *Piccolo Buddha* [Little Buddha, 1993]

Bertolucci, Bernardo, *Ultimo tango a Parigi* [Last Tango in Paris, 1972]

Bianchi, Giorgio, *Il moralista* [The Moralist, 1959]

Bianchini, Lorenzo, *Custodes bestiae* [2004]

Bird, Antonia, *Priest* [1994]

Botrugno, Matteo, and Daniele Coluccini, *Rito di primavera* [2017]

Bryceson Griffiths, Rachel, *DeKronos – Il demone del tempo* [2005]

Calderone, Gianluigi, *Don Zeno – L'uomo di Nomadelfia* [TV miniseries, 2008]

Capitani, Giorgio, *Papa Giovanni* [Pope John XXIII, TV miniseries, 2002]

Capitani, Giorgio, *Papa Luciani. Il sorriso di Dio* [Pope John Paul I: The Smile of God, TV miniseries, 2006]

Capuano, Antonio, *Pianese Nunzio, 14 anni a maggio* [Sacred Silence, 1996]

Carlei, Carlo, *Fuga per la libertà – L'aviatore* [The Pilot, TV movie, 2007]

Carlei, Carlo, *Padre Pio* [TV miniseries, 2000]

Carli, Diego, *Il caso Anna Mancini* [The Anna Mancini Case, 2016]

Castellani, Leandro, *Don Bosco* [1988]

Cavani, Liliana, *Francesco* [St Francis of Assisi, 1989]

Cavani, Liliana, *Francesco* [TV miniseries, 2014]

Cavani, Liliana, *Francesco D'Assisi* [TV miniseries, Francis of Assisi, 1966]

Cavani, Liliana, *Milarepa* [1974]

Chahine, Youssef, *The Emigrant* [1994]

Ciprì, Daniele, e Franco Maresco, *Totò che visse due volte* [Toto Who Lived Twice, 1998]

Columbu, Giovanni, *Su re* [The King, 2012]

Comencini, Francesca, *Lo spazio bianco* [The White Space, 2009]

Coppola, Francis Ford, *Godfather I* [1972]; *Godfather II* [1974]; and *Godfather III* [1990]

Cosmatos, George Pan, *Rappresaglia* [Massacre in Rome, 1973]

Costa, Fabrizio, *Chiara e Francesco* [TV miniseries, 2007]

Costa, Fabrizio, *Madre Teresa* [TV miniseries, 2003]

Costa, Fabrizio, *Paolo VI: Il Papa nella tempesta* [Paolo VI: The Pope in the Tempest, TV miniseries, 2008]

Costa-Gavras, *Amen* [2002]

Costanzo, Saverio, *In memoria di me* [In Memory of Me, 2007]

Cupellini, Claudio, *Lezioni di cioccolato* [Lessons in Chocolate, 2007]

Cupellini, Claudio, *Lezioni di cioccolato 2* [Lessons in Chocolate 2, 2011]

Curtis, Dan, *Our Fathers* [TV movie, 2005]

Curtiz, Michael, *Angels with Dirty Faces* [1938]

D'Alatri, Alessandro, *I giardini dell'Eden* [The Garden of Eden, 1998]

Damiani, Damiano, *Il sorriso del grande tentatore* [The Tempter / The Devil Is a Woman, 1974]

De Santis, Giuseppe, *Riso amaro* [Bitter Rice, 1949]

De Sica, Vittorio, *Ieri, oggi, domani* [Yesterday, Today, and Tomorrow, 1963]

De Seta, Vittorio, *Lettere dal Sahara* [Letters from the Sahara, 2006]

Di Robilant, Alessandro, *L'uomo della carità: Don Luigi Di Liegro* [The Charity Man, TV miniseries, 2007]

Diritti, Giorgio, *Un giorno devi andare* [There Will Come a Day, 2013]

Diritti, Giorgio, *L'uomo che verrà* [The Man Who Will Come, 2009]

Diritti, Giorgio, *Il vento fa il suo giro* [The Wind Blows Round, 2005]

Duguay, Christian, *Sotto il cielo di Roma* [Pius XII: Under the Roman Sky, 2010]

Faenza, Roberto, *Alla luce del sole* [Come into the Light, 2005]

Faenza, Roberto, *La verità sta in cielo* [2016]

Falchuk, Brad, and Ryan Murphy, *American Horror Story* (American TV series, 2011–)

Farina, Giorgia, *Amiche da morire* [2013]

Fellini, Federico, *8½* [1963]

Fellini, Federico, *La dolce vita* [1960]

Fellini, Federico, *Giulietta degli spiriti* [Juliet of the Spirits, 1965]

Fellini, Federico, *Roma* [1972]

Ferrante, Rosalinda, *L'ultimo sorriso* [2017]

Ferrara, Giuseppe, *I banchieri di Dio: Il caso Calvi* [The God's Bankers, 2002]

Ferrario, Davide, *Sexxx* [2015]

Frears, Stephen, *Philomena* [2013]

Gasparini, Lodovico, *Don Bosco* [TV miniseries, 2004]

Gasparini, Lodovico, *Il padre delle spose* [TV movie, 2006]

Germi, Pietro, *Divorzio all'italiana* [Divorce Italian Style, 1961]

Germi, Pietro, *Sedotta e abbandonata* [Seduced and Abandoned, 1964]

Gibney, Alex, *Mea Maxima Culpa: Silence in the House of God* [2012]

Gibson, Mel, *The Passion of the Christ* [2004]

Giordano, Marco Tullio, *I cento passi* [One Hundred Steps, 2000]

Golina, Valeria, *Miele* [Honey, 2013]

Greco, Federico and Roberto Leggo, *Road to L* [2005]

Guazzoni, Enrico, *Il poverello d'Assisi* [short, 1911]

Gyllenhaal, Stephen, *Promised a Miracle* [1988]

Harrison, J.K., *Giovanni Paolo II* [Pope John Paul II, TV miniseries, 2005]

Hausner, Jessica, *Lourdes* [2009]

Hofer, Gustav, and Ragazzi, Luca, *Improvvisamente l'inverno scorso* [Suddenly, Last Winter, 2008]

Howard, Ron, *Angels and Demons* [2009]

Howard, Ron, *The Da Vinci Code* [2006]

Hunt, David (Bruno Mattei), *La tomba* [The Tomb, video, 2004]

Jordan, Neil, *The Butcher Boy* [1997]

Kamkari, Fariborz, *Pitza e datteri* [2015]

Luchetti, Daniele, *Chiamatemi Francesco: Il papa della gente* [Call Me Francesco, 2015]

Luchetti, Daniele, *Chiamatemi Francesco: Il papa della gente* [TV miniseries, 2016]

Luchetti, Daniele, *Mio fratello è figlio unico* [My Brother Is an Only child, 2007]

Luchetti, Daniele, *Il portaborse* [The Yes Man, 1991]

Magni, Luigi, *Nell'anno del Signore* [The Conspirators, 1969]

Marabini, Liana, *Shades of Truth* [2015]

Marra, Vincenzo, *L'equilibrio* [Equilibrium, 2017]

Martinelli, Renzo, *11 settembre 1683* [Day of Siege, 2012]

Martinelli, Renzo, *Il mercante di pietre* [The Stone Merchant, 2006]

Martinelli, Renzo, *Piazza delle cinque lune* [Piazza of the Five Moons, 2003]

Mazzacurati, Carlo, *La giusta distanza* [The Right Distance, 2007]

Mazzacurati, Carlo, *La lingua del santo* [Holy Tongue, 2000]

Mazzacurati, Carlo, *Il prete bello* [The Handsome Priest, 1989]

McCarey, Leo, *The Bells of Saint Mary's* [1945]

McCarey, Leo, *Going My Way* [1944]

McCarthy, Tom, *Spotlight* [2015]

Melliti, Mohsen, *Io, l'altro* [2007]

Miniero, Luca, *Non c'è più religione* [2016]

Moretti, Nanni, *Habemus Papam* [We Have a Pope, 2011]

Moretti, Nanni, *La stanza del figlio* [The Son's Room, 2001]

Moroni, Vittorio, *Le ferie di Licu* [2006]

Mortelletti, Rocco, *La scomparsa di Patò* [The Vanishing of Patò, 2010]

Mullan, Peter, *The Magdalene Sisters* [2002]

Muraca, Fernando, *La terra dei santi* [Land of Saints, 2012]

Muscardin, Laura, *Billo: Il grand Dakhaar* [2007]

Myrick, Daniel, and Eduardo Sánchez, *The Blair Witch Project* [1999]

Nasca, Sergio, *Stato interessante* [1977]

Negrin, Alberto, *Il cuore nel pozzo* [The Heart in the Well, TV movie, 2005]

Negrin, Alberto, *Perlasca – un eroe italiano* [Perlasca – The Courage of a Just Man, TV miniseries, 2002]

Nencioni, Alessio, *Possessione demonica* [Demonic Possession, 2015]

Neveldine, Mark, *The Vatican Tapes* [2015]

Nicolaou, Ted, *La maschera etrusca* [The Etruscan Mask, 2007]

O'Gorman, Colm, *Sex Crimes and the Vatican* [TV documentary, 2006]

Olmi, Ermanno, *E venne un uomo* [And There Came a Man, 1965]

Olmi, Ermanno, *L'albero degli zoccoli* [The Tree of Wooden Clogs, 1978]

Olmi, Ermanno, *Il villaggio di cartone* [The Cardboard Village, 2011]

Özpetek, Ferzan, *Il bagno turco (Hamam)* [The Turkish Bath (Hamam), 1997]

Özpetek, Ferzan, *Cuore sacro* [Sacred Heart, 2005]

Özpetek, Ferzan, *Le fate ignoranti* [The Ignorant Fairies, 2001]

Özpetek, Ferzan, *La finestra di fronte* [Facing Windows, 2003]

Özpetek, Ferzan, *Harem suare* [1999]

Pagano, Ernesto, *NapolIslam* [2015]

Pau, Enrico, *L'Accabadora* [2015]

Parenti, Neri, *Colpi di fulmine* [Lightning Strike, 2012]

Pasolini, Pier Paolo, *I racconti di Canterbury* [The Canterbury Tales, 1972]

Pasolini, Pier Paolo, "La ricotta," in *Ro.Go.Pa.G* [1963]

Pasolini, Pier Paolo, *Mamma Roma* [1962]

Pasolini, Pier Paolo, *Teorema* [Theorem, 1968]

Pearce, Richard, *Leap of Faith* [1992]

Perry, Frank, *Monsignor* [1982]

Piccioni, Giuseppe, *Fuori dal mondo* [Not of This World, 1999]

Placido, Michele, *Un eroe borghese* [Ordinary Hero, 1995]

Pompucci, Leone, *La fuga degli innocenti* [Hidden Children, TV miniseries, 2004]

Pontremoli, Federica, *Quore* [2002]

Richardson, Peter, *The Pope Must Die* [1991]

Risi, Dino, *La moglie del prete* [The Priest's Wife, 1970]

Rohrwacher, Alice, *Corpo celeste* [Heavenly Body, 2011],

Rossellini, Roberto, *Francesco, giullare di Dio* [TV movie, The Flowers of Saint Francis, 1950]

Rossellini, Roberto, *Roma città aperta* [Rome, Open City, 1945]

Roth, Eli, *Cabin Fever* [2002]

Schlesinger, John, *Midnight Cowboy* [1969]

Scorsese, Martin, *The Last Temptation of Christ* [1988]

Shanley, John Patrick, *Doubt* [2008]

Siani, Alessandro, *Si accettano miracoli* [2015]

Smith, John N., *The Boys of St Vincent* [1992]

Soavi, Michele, *Francesco* [TV miniseries, 2002]

Sollima, Stefano, *Suburra* [2015]

Sorrentino, Paolo, *Il divo: La spettacolare vita di Giulio Andreotti* [Il Divo, 2008]

Sorrentino, Paolo, *Il giovane Papa* [TV miniseries, The Young Pope, 2016]

Sorrentino, Paolo, *This Must Be the Place* [2011]

Squitieri, Pasquale, *Il giorno della Shoah* [2010]

Squitieri, Pasquale, *Io e Dio* [1970]

Tagliarini, Edo, *Bloodline* [2005]

Taurog, Norman, *Boys Town* [1938]

Taurog, Norman, *Men of Boys Town* [1941]

Tognazzi, Maria Sole, *Io e Lei* [2015]

Tognazzi, Maria Sole, *Viaggio sola* [A Five Star Life, 2013]

Tognazzi, Ricky, *Il Papa buono* [The Good Pope: Pope John XXIII, TV miniseries, 2003]

Torrini, Cinzia TH, *Don Gnocchi: L'angelo dei bambini* [TV miniseries, 2004]

Tosco, Davide, *Transiti: Il mondo sconosciuto dei/delle trans* [TV documentary, radio series and web miniseries, 2011]

Ursitti, Donato, *Si può fare l'amore vestiti* [2012]

Verdone, Carlo, *Io, loro e Lara* [Me, Them, and Lara, 2009]

Verdone, Carlo, *Manuale d'amore 2* [Manual of Love 2, 2007]

Verdone, Carlo, *Un sacco bello* [Fun Is Beautiful, 1980]
Vicino, Matteo, *Outing: Fidanzati per sbaglio* [2013]
Virzì, Paolo, *Tutti i santi giorni* [Every Blessed Day, 2012]
Walsh, Aisling, *Song for a Raggy Boy* [2003]
Zeffirelli, Franco, *Brother Son, Sister Moon* [1976]
Zuccon, Ivan, *L'altrove* [The Darkness Beyond, 2000]

Index